The Indians of the Southwest

THE CIVILIZATION OF THE AMERICAN INDIAN SERIES

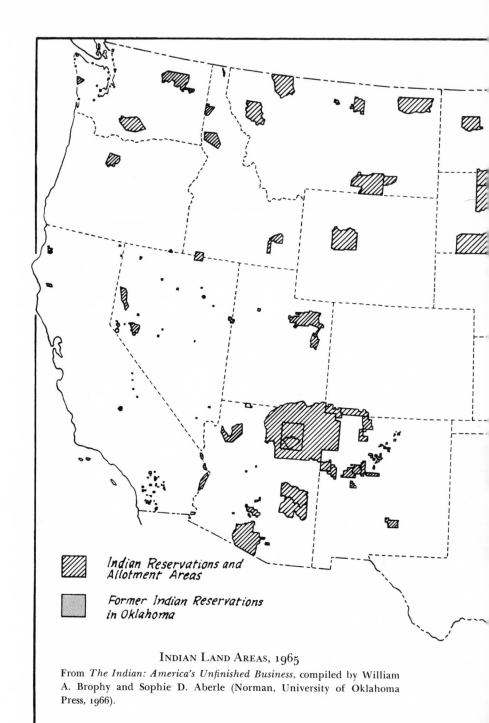

INDIAN LAND AREAS, 1965

From *The Indian: America's Unfinished Business*, compiled by William A. Brophy and Sophie D. Aberle (Norman, University of Oklahoma Press, 1966).

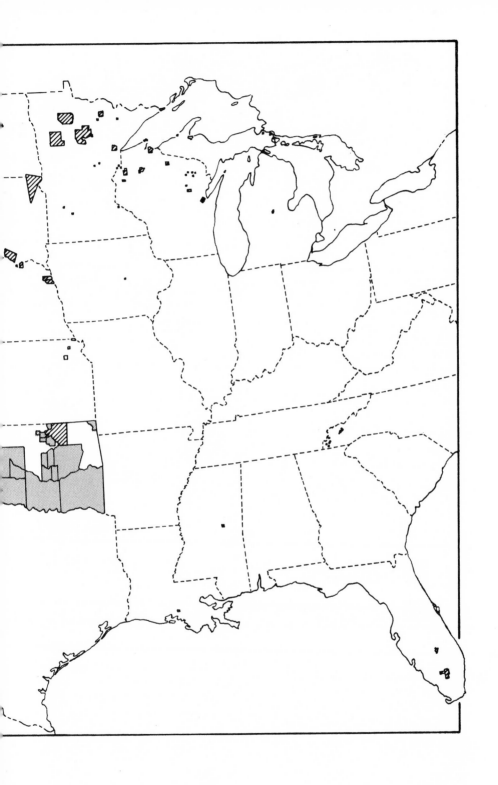

THE INDIANS OF THE SOUTHWEST

A Century of Development under the United States

by

Edward Everett Dale

UNIVERSITY OF OKLAHOMA PRESS

Norman

BY EDWARD EVERETT DALE

Territorial Acquisitions of the United States (Privately printed, 1912)

Tales of the Tepee (Boston, 1919)

(With J. S. Buchanan) *A History of Oklahoma* (Chicago, 1924)

Letters of Lafayette (Oklahoma City, 1925)

(With Meriam and others) *The Problem of Indian Administration* (Baltimore, 1928)

The Prairie Schooner and Other Poems (Guthrie, 1929)

(With M. L. Wardell) *Outline and References for Oklahoma History* (Privately printed, 1929)

(With J. L. Rader) *Readings in Oklahoma History* (Chicago, 1930)

The Range Cattle Industry (Norman, 1930)

Frontier Trails (ed.) (Boston, 1930) (Norman, 1966)

Grant Foreman: A Brief Biography (Norman, 1933)

A Rider of the Cherokee Strip (ed.) (Boston, 1936)

(With Gaston Litton) *Cherokee Cavaliers* (Norman, 1939)

Cow Country (Norman, 1942)

(With Dwight L. Dumond and Edgar B. Wesley) *History of United States* (Boston, 1948)

(With M. L. Wardell) *History of Oklahoma* (New York, 1948)

Oklahoma: The Story of a State (Evanston, 1949)

The Indians of the Southwest (Norman, 1949)

INTERNATIONAL STANDARD BOOK NUMBER: 0–8061–0195–4

DEDICATED TO

MY SON

Preface to the Third Printing

IT IS COMFORTING to know that my study, originally published in 1949, retains its validity and importance to the extent that it is being reprinted again. I feel, however, that a few additional introductory words are in order at this time.

The book surveys a century of federal relations with the Indians living in the territory acquired from Mexico in 1848 and 1853. "It recounts," as a reviewer in the *American Sociological Review* points out, "the slow and painful steps by which the Indians who thus came under American sovereignty have been guided by the federal government in their pursuit of education and civilization. It is a story of neglect, treaty violation, corruption, graft, and incompetence, but also of patient effort to improve the condition of the Indians, look after their health, advance their health, advance their education, and protect them."

The method, as another reviewer, in the *Deseret News*, observed is "to look into the situation calmly and dispassionately from an historical viewpoint, in order to get a complete picture and thus know how to proceed intelligently—know what measures to sustain and what to urge upon congressmen."

Having been a member of the Meriam Commission in 1926–27, having done the leg-work and research for my own study, having read subsequent reports, and having the benefit of a longer personal perspective than most observers, I wish I could report that all is now well. Unfortunately, I cannot. The characters have changed, another generation contends with problems, and several government administrations have come and gone, but the story is the same. Policies come and go in cycles like those for women's clothes: suppression or encouragement of native culture, education at or away from home, employment at home or relocation, retention or abolishment of reservations, and so on. There has been progress, of course, but how slow and minor it seems.

It is said that those who forget history will be forgotten by it. Here is a history of a century, a record, such as it was, of accomplishment. I still hope that we can learn from the past how to improve the future—or at least avoid the mistakes of the past.

EDWARD EVERETT DALE

Norman, Oklahoma
October, 1970

Preface

THIS BOOK gives briefly the story of a hundred years of federal relations with the Indians of the territory acquired from Mexico in 1848, to which a small addition was made in 1853. The region is two-thirds as large as all that part of the United States lying east of the Mississippi, or larger than the combined areas of Great Britain, France, Germany, and Italy. In 1848 the total white population was only a few thousand, but scattered widely over its broad stretches of plains, desert, and mountains were many tribes of Indians varying widely in culture and degree of civilization. The total number of these aboriginal inhabitants has been estimated at from 125,000 to 200,000.

Early in 1944 the Henry E. Huntington Library offered me a fellowship to do this study of federal relations with the Indians of the Southwest. I welcomed the opportunity to do further work on peoples that had been one of my chief interests since childhood and to whose affairs I had already given considerable time and effort. My first book dealing with Indians was published in 1919, while in 1926–27 it was my privilege to serve as a member of the so-called Meriam Commission of the Institute for Government Research. This group spent about eight months in travel among the Indians, during which time we visited every important reservation in the Southwest. I spent four months in Washington working in the files of the Indian Office and assisting in preparing the report. The latter was published in 1928 by the Johns Hopkins University Press under the title, *The Problem of Indian Administration*.

Work on the present volume was begun in the Henry E. Huntington Library in the summer of 1944 and was continued there during the summers of 1945 and 1946. Research was also done in the library materials of the Southwest Museum in Los Angeles and at various other places. From 1945 until the completion of the manuscript much work was done each academic year in the Frank Phillips Collection of the University of Oklahoma, which contains valuable Indian material. The opportunity was also taken in 1946 and 1947 to visit three or four of the more important reservations in the Southwest, including the reservation of the Navajo. These visits revealed that, while considerable progress has been made since the time of the Meriam Survey, the problems of both the Indians and the Indian Service in the Southwest were essentially the same in 1947 as they had been twenty years earlier.

Obviously it has not been possible to present in a single volume a detailed account of the highly complex relations of our national government with many tribes for an entire century. All that has been attempted is a broad general survey of the more important aspects of one hundred years of Indian administration in the Southwest, with special emphasis on those activities which have proved of permanent value.

The chief purpose of this volume is to give to the general reader a better knowledge and understanding of the Southwestern tribes as they are today by tracing briefly the story of the events which have helped to create present conditions. It is also hoped that the volume may be of value to scholars interested in the Southwest by furnishing a body of information which will serve as a background for the preparation of more detailed studies on special subjects touching the Indians of this area.

To all those who have furnished counsel and assistance, I wish to express my sincere appreciation. I am especially grateful to the Rockefeller Foundation for its generosity in granting funds to the Henry E. Huntington Library and Art Gallery for the purpose of promoting research on various topics connected with the development of the Southwest, and to the trustees of the latter institution for a substantial grant from such funds for the preparation of this study. My thanks and deep appreciation go also to many officials of the Henry E. Huntington Library who have given valuable advice and aid. Among those who should receive special mention are the librarian, Mr. Leslie Bliss, Mr. Dixon Wecter, Mr. Robert O. Schad, Mr. Carey Bliss, and Miss Mary Isabel Fry. There are many others, also, whose courteous and helpful attitude at all times made the research work done in that library pleasant and profitable. My special indebtedness is hereby acknowledged to Dr. Louis B. Wright and, above all others, to Dr. Robert G. Cleland who originally suggested that the study be made, and whose sympathetic interest and encouragement have been invaluable; and to Mrs. Marion Tinling of the Huntington Library staff, whose aid to me in the final preparation of the manuscript was generous and highly effective. To Dr. Frederick Webb Hodge of the Southwest Museum and the members of his staff, I am deeply grateful for many courtesies. To Mr. Frank Phillips of Bartlesville, Oklahoma, whose generosity in establishing the Frank Phillips Collection of Western History at the University of Oklahoma has made available for the use of scholars a wealth of material on the American Indian, my debt of gratitude is particularly great. Finally, I wish to express my appreciation and thanks to my secretary, Mrs. Josephine Nicholson Bond, and to my wife, Mrs. Rosalie Gilkey Dale, both of whom have worked diligently in typing the manuscript, checking references, and reading proof. Without their aid and encouragement, the book could hardly have been written.

EDWARD EVERETT DALE

Norman, Oklahoma

Contents

Illustrations and Maps

The Indians of the Southwest

I

The Problem and Its Background

THE TREATY OF GUADALUPE HIDALGO, signed February 2, 1848, and bringing the war with Mexico to a formal conclusion, rounded out the boundaries of the United States and gave the country jurisdiction over the vast territory commonly known as the "Mexican Cession." The United States thus became responsible for the many tribes of Indians who roamed the plains and deserts of the great region or lived in long-established villages along its streams and in its fertile valleys. Except for a thin line of settlements established by Spain and Mexico along the Río Grande River and in California, and the newly planted Mormon colony in Utah, the Indians were virtually the only inhabitants of the huge area.

The stroke of a pen gave the victorious nation full responsibility for governing these widely scattered aboriginal peoples and for promoting their welfare. Henceforth the United States government must not only protect them against the aggression of unscrupulous whites but must also curb the predatory and warlike tendencies of the wilder tribes and prevent their preying upon their more peaceful neighbors, red or white. It must also, so far as possible, feed the hungry, care for the sick and helpless, educate the children, and make every effort to turn the Indian's feet away from the time-worn path of his fathers into the unfamiliar road of the white man.

Obviously this was an enormous task, which would require generations for its completion. It was a project, moreover, that would demand vision, energy, patience, and perseverance, especially from those officials who had the direct responsibility for it and who knew that it could not be finished within the limits of a single lifetime.

The purpose of this book is to trace briefly the story of this great federal undertaking with reference to the Indians of southern and central California, Nevada, Utah, Arizona, and the western half of

New Mexico. Even in this comparatively narrow geographical field the subject is still so broad that it has been necessary to impose certain more or less arbitrary limitations on it. Since Texas claimed that part of New Mexico lying east of the Río Grande River, the Pueblo Indians living in the valley of that stream have been considered only in connection with the tribes farther west, such as the Navajo and Apache, who at times attacked the peaceful pueblo dwellers unless restrained by the strong hand of the federal government.

At the time of the acquisition of this new territory, the United States had been a nation for more than sixty years, and, during that period, it had created certain governmental instrumentalities for dealing with the Indians and had developed, through a number of precedents, well-defined policies respecting Indian affairs. These policies were utilized in the federal government's relations with the tribes newly brought under its jurisdiction by the Mexican Cession, and from time to time new instrumentalities were created, or new policies established, to meet changing needs.

During the colonial period of American history, England had at first left control of Indian affairs in the hands of the colonial governors. After the Peace of Paris in 1763, however, the royal government drew a line at the crest of the Appalachian Mountains and forbade all settlement beyond it, apparently with the intention of creating a great Indian territory in the West. It also provided for the appointment by the crown of two Indian agents, one in the North and one in the South.

Perhaps with this action as a precedent, the Articles of Confederation gave Congress the exclusive right and power to manage Indian affairs, and that body established, in 1786, two large Indian districts not unlike those created earlier by the British government. The Constitution also reserved to Congress exclusive control of Indian affairs, and when the War Department was created in 1789, it was given the management of relations with the Indians. This department's control continued for sixty years, or until 1849, when the act of Congress establishing the Department of the Interior provided for the transfer of Indian affairs to the new department.

During the sixty-year period of the War Department's administration of Indian affairs, a reasonably effective machinery for carrying on the work was developed. In 1793, Congress authorized the President to appoint temporary agents "to reside among the Indians." In 1796, Congress, at the request of President Washington, authorized the establishment of trading posts under the President's immediate

4

direction. Two years later the office of superintendent of Indian trade was created, and government trading houses were set up later to carry on commerce with the Indians. These trading houses were not able to compete with the establishments of private traders, however, even under the able administration of Thomas S. McKenny, superintendent of Indian trade, for many years. In 1822 the trading-house system was discontinued, and by an order issued March 11, 1824, Secretary of War Calhoun organized the Bureau of Indian Affairs, placing McKenny at its head.

For several years there were complaints of inefficiency and mismanagement against the Indian Bureau, which may have been partly responsible for the act of Congress of July 9, 1832, authorizing the President "to appoint, by and with the advice and consent of the Senate, a Commissioner of Indian Affairs who under the direction of the Secretary of War and agreeably to such regulations as the President may, from time to time, prescribe, have the direction and management of all Indian Affairs and of all matters arising out of Indian relations."[1]

Two years after the creation of the office of commissioner of Indian affairs, Congress passed a bill (approved June 30, 1834) which is usually regarded as the organic act of the Indian Service. This law, commonly known as the "Indian Intercourse Act," did not introduce any new principle of organization but made definite provisions for a field force of twelve agents, whose salaries were fixed at $1,500 annually. The posts of these agents were specified, although the President was given power to transfer any agency to another place or tribe. The act did not alter the powers of the secretary of war or the commissioner of Indian affairs since it merely established an organization in the field and regulated trade and commerce with the Indians.[2] The governors of territories had formerly been made ex officio superintendents of Indian affairs, and this practice was continued, with some exceptions, not by any positive declaration but by the failure to repeal the earlier act assigning such duties to them. The new act also abolished some of the older agencies and superintendencies which, because of changed conditions, were no longer properly located. The superintendency of St. Louis, which had been created by an act of Congress approved May 6, 1822, "with powers over all Indians frequenting that place," was given jurisdiction over Indian affairs in "all the Indian country not within the bounds of any state

[1] 4 *Stats.*, 564.
[2] *Ibid.*, 735.

or territory, west of the Mississippi River."[3] Since no specific reference was made to Indian agents within the states, they were apparently under the direct supervision of the commissioner.

The importance of this act can hardly be exaggerated. It remained the keystone of the entire Indian Service for more than half a century, and under its provisions, with necessary changes and modifications, all federal relations with the Indians were transacted, not only in the territory ceded to the United States by Mexico, but throughout the country.

The Indian Intercourse Act of 1834 was passed when the War Department was in the midst of the difficult task of removing most of the Indians from the region east of the Mississippi to new lands that had been assigned them west of that stream.[4] During the next fifteen years, which was the period left for that department to administer Indian affairs, most of these removals were completed, and the various tribes, located in their new homes in the West, had become more or less adjusted to the change of environment.

The transfer of the Bureau of Indian Affairs in 1849 to the newly created Department of the Interior was bitterly resented by many officials of the War Department. They did not hesitate to point out the accomplishment of their own department during the sixty years that it had administered Indian affairs. It had established and developed the Indian Service, regulated trade, sought to keep peace, and, in case of war, had pushed the conflict to a quick and successful conclusion. It had, moreover, removed a number of powerful tribes to new lands west of the Mississippi and protected these newcomers against the wilder tribes that sought to attack them. It had made some beginning in the civilization and education of the Indians. Its officials were familiar with Indian problems and experienced in solving them.

The officials of the War Department further asserted that the acquisition of the great territory included in the Mexican Cession, the discovery of gold in California, and the rush to Oregon and other parts of the West, were certain to create new problems of a grave nature. White encroachments upon Indian hunting grounds would inevitably result in war, and the Department of the Interior would be forced to call upon the army to put down every Indian outbreak, however minor. The ultimate result would be divided authority and responsibility. While the administration of Indian affairs by the War Department was not perfect, there was some validity in the objections

[3] 3 *Stats.*, 683.
[4] For story of Indian removals, see 23 Cong. 1 sess., *Sen. Ex. Doc.* 512.

to the change. Officials of the Department of the Interior replied, with considerable heat, that the Indian could never be civilized and educated by officials who recognized no argument save force, and that the conduct of the military in dealing with the Indians had often been neither humane nor reasonable.[5]

Later, the outbreak of destructive Indian wars on the plains and certain scandals in the administration of Indian affairs caused insistent demands that Congress transfer the Indian Bureau back to the War Department. For many years every discussion in Congress relative to Indian administration was likely to provoke debate on whether or not a change of control was desirable. Proponents of army control accused civil officials of the Indian Service of graft and inefficiency, and members of the opposition asserted that the army had been ruthless, cruel, and unduly arbitrary in dealing with Indians. This controversy, and the mutual ill will which it created, had a bad effect on relations of the federal government with the Indians. Often it resulted in unseemly bickerings and petty squabbles between army officers and civilian agents at remote posts or agencies. Mutual jealousy and suspicion on the part of the civil and military officials in charge could have resulted in most serious consequences in a critical situation, for instance, if a band of Indians threatened to leave the reservation and go on the warpath.

This lack of co-operation between the two departments continued as long as intermittent warfare with the western Indians was common and it was necessary to keep garrisons at frontier posts to preserve order. When Indian wars had been suppressed and only the administration of the affairs of peaceful tribesmen was necessary, the demands for a change of control of the Indian Bureau lessened, and the Department of the Interior was able to carry on a policy directed towards the education of the Indian without being forced to call periodically upon the army to restore order.

Perhaps the transfer of Indian control could have been made at a more opportune time than 1849, when the United States had just acquired the vast region in the Southwest with its large population of aboriginal inhabitants. Certainly the transfer was in the nature of "swapping horses in the middle of the stream." There is no evidence, however, that federal relations with the Indians of the new territory were greatly affected by the change of control, or that they would have been essentially different had the Indian Bureau remained under

5 See various *Annual Reports of Commissioner of Indian Affairs*, especially from 1860 to 1880, for this viewpoint.

the direction of the War Department. Interdepartmental jealousies and bickerings apparently had no grave consequences until after the close of the Civil War.

The foregoing brief survey of the origins and development of the Indian Service is necessary to an understanding of the topic, because federal policies and regulations concerning the Indians as a whole governed relations with the tribes of the Southwest. These policies were formulated in Washington, and from that city instructions were issued in accordance with well-established precedents and regulations. Yet the administration of the affairs of any particular tribe was inevitably affected to a great degree by local conditions.

The agent in charge of a jurisdiction in the remote deserts of Arizona, Utah, or Nevada often found himself obliged to decide some important problem immediately. To communicate with his superior officers in the national capital and receive instructions would require many months, and in the meantime, the opportunity for action would have passed or new problems would have arisen. Under such circumstances he must use his own judgment and make his own decision, based upon his authority under the laws of Congress and the regulations of the Indian Bureau, and hope that his acts would be approved. The agent's responsibility was great, for his decisions often determined whether there would be peace or a war.

When the Indians were gradually brought under control by the aid of the army and became more peaceful, the duties and responsibilities of the civil officials in charge of their affairs were changed rather than lessened. The agent must establish schools and hospitals, issue rations, provide adult education in agriculture, stock raising, sanitation, health, homemaking, and the care of children. He must preserve order on the reservation, protect his charges against trespass or exploitation by whites, issue licenses to traders, lease Indian lands for grazing, make contracts for the sale of timber, and do all in his power to render the people committed to his charge self-supporting, to raise their standard of living, and to advance them toward the ways of white civilization.

Throughout the Southwest, and indeed throughout the country as a whole, the duties and responsibilities of Indian agents varied widely because of the great differences in the tribes to which they were assigned. These tribes were unlike in manners, customs, and degree of civilization, the geographical conditions under which they lived always being an important factor. Yet back of every field official of the Indian Service was the more or less powerful Bureau of Indian Af-

Hopi village, Second Mesa

Courtesy Milton Snow, Navajo Service

Navajo summer hogan

fairs, directing his work and his movements under the authority of acts of Congress and the executive orders and decrees of the Department of the Interior. In consequence, there was always a certain degree of unity in the work of officials in the field, although, as has been said, those remote from the capital must frequently form, within limitations, their own policies and carry them out as best they could.

The task of tracing the story of federal relations with the Indians of the Southwest throughout a period of a hundred years is clearly of such magnitude as to make intensive treatment of any phase of the problem impossible. Both conditions and policies changed radically with the passing years. All that can be done in a single volume is to present a brief survey of the subject.

Such a survey will give the reader a wider knowledge and better understanding of the Indians of the Southwest and of the slow and painful steps by which they have been guided in their pursuit of education and civilization by the federal government. For the technical scholar interested in this field of history, more detailed and comprehensive accounts are available on a few phases of the subject. On many other phases, little has been done, but it is hoped that this study will serve as a basis, or foundation, upon which may be built more detailed accounts of specific periods or aspects of the general subject.

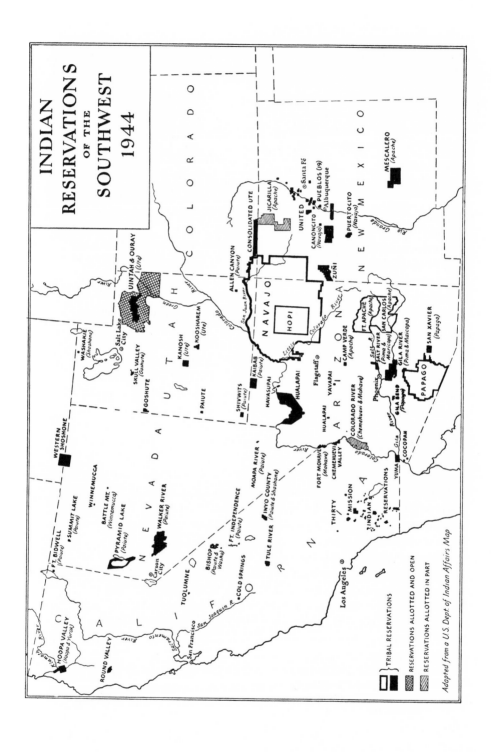

INDIAN
RESERVATIONS
OF THE
SOUTHWEST
1944

Adapted from a U.S. Dept. of Indian Affairs Map

TRIBAL RESERVATIONS

RESERVATIONS ALLOTTED AND OPEN

RESERVATIONS ALLOTTED IN PART

II

The Indians of the Southwest

THE TERRITORY CEDED TO THE UNITED STATES by Mexico in 1848 is not only "a land of magnificent distances" but also one of wide variations in topography and climate. It includes broad stretches of level plains and sandy deserts, with flat-topped mesas or curious rock formations occasionally appearing to break the monotony of the landscape. There are long ranges of lofty mountains, and high in these mountains are forests of majestic pines, alpine valleys, and perpendicular walled canyons down which tumble the clear, cold waters of narrow streams. Along the Pacific Coast and in some of the valleys are extensive tracts of fertile lands which have become garden spots of the world, supporting in comfort, and often in luxury, millions of people.

While a large part of this territory is a high plateau, there is one small area which is below sea level. The characteristic feature of the greater part of the region is lack of rainfall; consequently, there are large areas of true desert, and on most of the land irrigation is necessary for successful agriculture. These geographical features have not only greatly affected the settlement and development of the Southwest by the whites, but they also profoundly influenced the mode of life and degree of civilization of its aboriginal inhabitants.

No one can say with any degree of certainty just how many Indians resided in the territory ceded by Mexico to the United States in 1848. Figures given by contemporary writers, either for the total population or for the number in each tribe, vary so much as to suggest that, generally, they were only the wildest of guesses. Moreover, those tribes living along the international boundary, where it is only an imaginary line, moved freely back and forth across it, so that it was not always possible to determine on which side they considered their homes to be. Except in certain areas—such as California, where, because of the influx of gold miners, the Indians decreased in numbers very rapidly in the decade following 1848—it would probably be more nearly correct to estimate the number of Indians in each tribe at the earlier date from figures given later by government officials.

The census of 1850 gave the total Indian population of the United States as 400,764, while H. R. Schoolcraft, who was engaged in gathering material for his monumental work on Indians, estimated the number as 388,229.[1] The Commissioner of Indian Affairs in his *Annual Report* for 1944 gave the number of Indians in the United States under the jurisdiction of the Indian Office as 387,970,[2] approximately the same as Schoolcraft's estimate. Obviously, the number of Indians in the United States declined very rapidly after 1848— in fact, to such an extent as to give rise to the idea that the Indian belonged to a "vanishing race." About the turn of the century, however, the number of Indians in the United States as a whole began to increase, and by 1944 there were approximately as many as there had been one hundred years before.

There is some evidence that the Indians of the Southwest followed the same pattern in increasing their population. In 1944 the number of Indians under the jurisdiction of the Indian Office in California, Arizona, New Mexico, Nevada, Utah, and southwestern Colorado was 128,102.[3] Probably this is not far from the number occupying the same area in 1848. Although the California Indians declined sharply in numbers during the period of the gold rush and the years immediately following, and though the Apache Wars from 1870 to 1884 were additionally destructive to that tribe, the losses were largely restored by the extraordinary increase of the Navajo after 1900.

Broadly speaking, the Indians who inhabited the Southwest in 1848 may be divided into two great classes. One class comprised the peaceful, sedentary Indians: the pueblo dwellers of New Mexico and Arizona, including the Hopi and Zuñi, the Mission Indians of California, and such agricultural tribes as the Pima, Papago, and Maricopa, largely living in the valley of the Gila River in Arizona. The other group was composed of the wilder and more warlike tribes of the deserts and mountains. These included the various Apache groups —the Jicarilla, Mescalero, Hualapai (Walapai), Mogollon, Mimbreño, Chiricahua, and some others—their kinsmen the Navajo, and

[1] H R. Schoolcraft, *History, Condition, and Prospects of the Indian Tribes of the United States*, I, 524.

[2] *Statistical Supplement to Annual Report of Commissioner of Indian Affairs, 1944*, 4.

[3] *Ibid.*, 4–9.

the Ute, Shoshone, and occasional roving bands of Comanche. Many of these tribes were subdivided into groups or bands, sometimes considered separate tribes. In addition, there were tribes difficult to place definitely in either of the above classifications, including the Yuma, Washo, Paiute, Miwok, and Havasupai.[4] Since most tribes depended to some extent upon crop growing for subsistence, arbitrary classifications such as "sedentary" and "nomadic" would never be more than approximately correct. The smaller tribes and bands were relatively unimportant, so far as difficulties with the federal government went, but the larger tribes presented many perplexing problems.

Among the important groups were the village dwellers of New Mexico commonly called the Pueblo. A great number of them lived east of the Río Grande on lands early claimed by Texas; and, in consequence, it has seemed best to consider them only briefly in this study. Their later relations were so involved as to require an extensive monograph for any adequate treatment. During the early years when the Indian Bureau was organizing its work in the Southwest, frequent raids on the Pueblo by the Navajo and Apache complicated its problem.

There is good evidence that the Pueblo were far more numerous centuries ago than in recent times and that they extended over a large territory in the Southwest. In 1848, however, they probably numbered ten thousand or less.[5] They occupied some twenty villages, mostly scattered along the valley of the Río Grande from Isleta, a few miles south of Albuquerque, to Taos, near the foot of the mountains not far from the northern border of New Mexico. Nearly fifty miles west of the river is the important pueblo of Laguna, and some thirty-five miles southwest of it is Ácoma, built on the flat top of a gigantic rock rising hundreds of feet above the level of the plain. Far to the west near the present boundary between New Mexico and Arizona is Zuñi, estimated to have had some 1,800 inhabitants in 1848 and slightly over 2,400 in 1944.[6] Laguna, with 2,700 people, is the largest pueblo to the east today and doubtless was in 1848. Others that in 1944 had a

4 It is impossible to list all tribes of the Southwest since they are so broken up into groups as to make it difficult at times to determine what constitutes a distinct tribe.

5 Calhoun to Medill, October 4, 1849, in A. H. Abel (ed.), *Correspondence of James S. Calhoun*, 39. A census ordered by the legislative assembly of New Mexico convened in December, 1847, gave the total number of Pueblo Indians five years of age and upwards as 6,524. *Ibid.*, 39–40.

6 *Statistical Supplement to Annual Report of Commissioner of Indian Affairs*, *1944*, 9.

population in excess of 1,000 are Ácoma, Santo Domingo, and Taos, while the rest varied from upwards of 700 to little more than 100—or even less in one nearly extinct pueblo. The population of these pueblos has probably not changed greatly in the past one hundred years; however, ruins and remains in the soil indicate that a numerous population of sedentary agricultural Indians once lived in the region.[7]

The first Europeans to visit the Pueblo of New Mexico were Fray Marcos of Niza and Coronado in the years 1539–42. The Spaniards had little further contact with them until 1598 when Juan de Oñate led a colonizing expedition northward from Mexico and established a settlement a short distance above the confluence of the Chama and the Río Grande rivers near San Juan. Some ten or twelve years later, Santa Fé was founded, and, during the next three-quarters of a century, other Spanish settlements and mission stations were established along the Río Grande and its tributaries.

The Spaniards brought to the Indians cattle, sheep, goats, horses, and burros, as well as many of the fruits and plants of the Iberian Peninsula. Many Indians embraced the Roman Catholic faith, at least nominally, and partially adopted the manners and customs of the Spanish. In 1680, however, under the leadership of the able chieftain, Popé, the Pueblo revolted. Most of the Spaniards were either killed or driven out of the country, and for ten years they lost control of New Mexico. Then, in 1692 the reconquest by Diego de Vargas re-established the domination of Spain in that region, which continued until Mexico won its independence about 1821. The substitution of Mexican for Spanish rule made little change in the government of New Mexico or in the relations of the Indians with their conquerors, since the authority of the viceroy and the Spanish imperial government was merely replaced by that of the Republic of Mexico and its president.

Both Spain and Mexico had granted to each separate pueblo a large measure of self-government. Each village chose annually an official called the governor who, together with his council, nominally administered the local affairs of the community, although, actually, much power was retained by the local tribal leaders known as "caciques."

In 1848 the Pueblo were a kindly, hospitable people living in

---

[7] Pueblo tribes in 1944 were Ácoma, Cochití, Jémez, Laguna, Nambé, Picuris, Sandia, San Felipe, San Ildefonso, San Juan, Santa Ana, Santa Clara, Santo Domingo, Taos, Tesuque, Zía, and Zuñi. In addition was the nearly extinct pueblo of Pojoaque with only twenty-six people. *Ibid.,* 9.

permanent villages, some of which had been in existence for centuries. The houses, built of stone or adobe, were often grouped about the village square or plaza. Some of them were very large and several stories high, so that one such structure might furnish living quarters for many families. They were the first real apartment houses on the North American continent, since they very likely antedated the communal dwellings of the Iroquois of the Long House. Near the center of the village was the "round house" or kiva, partially underground, which had some attributes of a temple, a lodge room, a club, and a hostelry. Here were hung the masks, robes, and other regalia used in the dances. Here were held important tribal ceremonials and councils, and here young men sometimes slept or elders talked over matters affecting the common welfare.

In addition to the domestic animals and plants which the Pueblo had received from Spain, they had also acquired, during the two and one-half centuries of rule by Spain and Mexico, a veneer of Spanish culture. Similar as were the peoples of the different pueblos in manners and customs, they belonged to at least three linguistic groups, but in general Spanish became their international language. Nominally Roman Catholic, they clung closely to their old superstitions and retained much of their ancient religion.[8] Each pueblo held its land in common ownership by virtue of a grant from the Spanish crown, confirmed by Mexico, after the latter had become independent, and by the United States after 1848. Agriculture was the chief vocation. Diversion dams made of brush and stones were built to raise the water of the near-by stream sufficiently that it could be brought by ditches to the little fields lying about the villages. They grew bounteous crops of corn, beans, pumpkins, squashes, peppers, and other vegetables, as well as peaches, plums, grapes, apricots, pears, and melons. Herders pastured small flocks of sheep and goats near by, and brought them into corrals each evening. Burros and horses were used as beasts of burden. The Pueblo also made baskets and pottery, did spinning and weaving, hunted and fished, and gathered such native products as piñon nuts, and berries.

The Pueblo were a clean, industrious, and thrifty people and would have been quite prosperous except for periodical raids made upon them by the Navajo and Apache and some other wild tribes. Even when such attacks were infrequent, the threat of them hung

8 Ferdinand Andrews, "The Indians of Arizona and New Mexico," II, 31–43. Manuscript found in the Huntington Library. N. d., but apparently written about 1868. Hereafter referred to as Andrews MS.

over every village, and the necessity for watchfulness and prepared-ness seriously interfered with economic progress. Santa Fé traders, reaching out from Missouri to engage in commerce with the capital of New Mexico as early as 1821, soon established some contacts with the Pueblo, and the "mountain men" who engaged in the fur trade often gathered at Taos. On the whole, the Pueblo were probably better known to the Anglo-Americans when the Mexican War started than was any other important tribe of Indians in this portion of the Southwest.[9]

Far to the northwest of the upper Río Grande Valley there lived, deep in the heart of the Enchanted Desert of northern Arizona, an-other important group of pueblo dwellers known as the Hopi, former-ly called the Moqui. Extending out from the great Kaibab Plateau are three long ridges like the fingers of a giant hand pointing south into the desert. These gigantic fingers are broken off near their tips to form three high, flat-topped mesas; and on the top of each of these, commonly called First, Second, and Third Mesas, there were in 1848 two or three Hopi towns. Contemporary writers gave the number of towns at that time as seven, with a total population of 6,720 persons. But this figure is evidently too large, for John Ward, who visited the towns in 1861, gave 2,500 as the total population of the seven Hopi towns. In 1944 the *Annual Report* of the commissioner of Indian af-fairs gave the population of the Hopi reservation as 3,538.

The Hopi are a short, olive-skinned people of oriental appear-ance whose homes and manner of life are not unlike those of the Pueblo of the Río Grande Valley; but by 1848 they had been far less touched than the Pueblo by European civilization. Apparently they had been visited by one of Coronado's officers in 1540 and by another Spanish explorer in 1583. When Oñate led his expedition into New Mexico, he also paid a visit to the Hopi late in 1598, and returned for a brief stay in 1604. Some time later, a Franciscan priest came to establish himself among these Indians and other priests followed; so that at the time of the Pueblo revolt in 1680, four Franciscans were living and working in the Hopi towns. They were promptly killed by the Indians when the general revolt broke out. When de Vargas reconquered New Mexico, in 1692, for Spain,[10] the Hopi Indians sub-mitted readily, but the Spanish sent no more missionaries to them.

[9] *Ibid.* See Charles Lummis, *Mesa, Canyon, and Pueblo,* for some discussion of Pueblo life.

[10] Thomas Donaldson, *Moqui Pueblo Indians of Arizona and Pueblo Indians of New Mexico,* Extra Census Bulletin, 11th Census, 35.

A Papago home

Second Mesa woman shelling corn

Although there may have been occasional visits made to them, and the matter of converting them to Christianity was frequently discussed, the Hopi had little further contact with Spanish-American civilization until the acquisition of New Mexico by the United States. They did, however, have domestic animals and European fruits and vegetables, which had been brought to them by the Franciscan priests before the Pueblo revolt. Therefore, the Hopi, unlike the Pueblo, had virtually no veneer of Spanish culture. In 1848 theirs was purely an Indian civilization. They spoke their own language exclusively and knew nothing of Christianity, but worshipped as their ancestors had for many centuries. Also, unlike the Pueblo, they did not practice irrigation to any great extent, but depended largely upon the scanty rainfall for the production of crops of corn, beans, and squash. Near the foot of each mesa lay their little fields and orchards, so situated as to receive the maximum drainage from the side of the mesa. Life was precarious at best and could be maintained only by hard work and the utmost care and thrift. If the rains were insufficient, or were too long delayed, the Hopi were threatened with starvation. The snake dance was held annually to appease the rain gods, and every crop of corn harvested was divided into three parts—one for seed, another for use as food, and the third for use in cases of emergency when lack of rain or storms or enemies destroyed the crops.

Work and prayer were the chief ends of Hopi existence. The ground must be prepared for seeding, crops planted and cultivated with great care, and every effort made to protect them from damage by insects or animals. Sheep and goats were herded by day on the desert lying about the mesa and brought into sheepfolds near its foot at night to avoid loss from wolves or from raids of the Navajo. Water must be carried from springs at the base of the mesa in large jars balanced on the heads of women. Timbers for construction, or wood for fuel, had to be cut from canyons sometimes miles away and borne on the backs of burros or human beings to the mesa and up the steep, winding trail to the village. Homes must be kept clean and in good repair and corn pounded in a mortar to make the "piki bread" which was a staple article of diet. Peaches and pumpkins, the latter peeled and cut into long strips, were dried in the sun and stored away for winter use. Wool was spun and woven into fabrics for clothing and bedding, pottery was made and fired, and tools, weapons, and utensils were made of wood or stone. For men and women alike, life must have been a continuous round of unremitting toil.

There was always time, however, for prayer and religious observances. While the annual snake dance was the most important ceremonial, it was only one of many. Religion was, moreover, practiced every day and almost every hour. When water was brought from the springs, a tiny stick with a few blades of grass bound to it, or a feather to which was attached a bit of yarn was left near by as the symbol that a prayer had been delivered, asking that the spring be not allowed to become dry or rain withheld from the heavens. Young eagles were taken from their nests and carefully nurtured until they were able to fly; then they were killed by strangulation so that no blood was shed and, as the eagle died, a prayer for rain was uttered in the belief that the soul of the eagle would carry it upward to the god of rain. Despite the endless round of work and prayer, the Hopi were a gay, kindly, hospitable people who seemed at all times cheerful, happy, and contented. Life flowed on, generation after generation, for centuries with little change. They were a peaceful people, however, and dread of the Navajo, whose attacks had driven them to these natural fortifications, always hung like a shadow over the sun-drenched mesas.[11]

In southern Arizona, largely in the drainage basin of the Gila River, are other important tribes of sedentary Indians—the Pima, Maricopa, and Papago. All of these Indians had been visited quite early by Spanish friars from Mexico. In 1687 the Jesuit Father Eusebio Francisco Kino entered this region and worked among the Indians of northern Sonora and southern Arizona until his death in 1711.[12] As a result of his work and that of others who followed him, many of the sedentary Indians became Roman Catholic nominally and acquired some degree of Spanish culture.

The Pima occupied a large area of the valley of the Gila nearly 150 miles above its confluence with the Colorado River, and for centuries prior to 1848 they had apparently undergone very little change.[13] They probably numbered in 1848 some 5,000 to 6,000 people, including a few hundred Maricopa who spoke a different language but had by this time become almost completely merged with the larger tribe; the habits and mode of life of the two were almost identical. They lived in villages, but, unlike the Pueblo and Hopi, their homes were built of cacti or the wood of other desert

[11] *Ibid.* See also Leo Crane, *Indians of the Enchanted Desert,* for interesting account of Hopi life.

[12] H. E. Bolton (ed.), *Historical Memoirs of Pimería Alta.* See also *Los Misiones de Sonora y Arizona* for account of Kino's work.

[13] Andrews MS, 21–29.

plants and shrubs, rather than of stone or adobe. They practiced irrigation, bringing water to the little fields lying about their village by means of diversion dams and ditches constructed by communal labor. Their crops were corn, wheat, vegetables of various kinds, tobacco, and fruit. They had domestic animals and poultry, and they were clever craftsmen, making excellent pottery and baskets. A peaceful, agricultural people, these Indians often suffered from raids made on their villages by the Apache; although not aggressive, they were brave fighters in defense of their homes and possessions.[14]

South of the Gila, and largely in the territory secured not by the Treaty of Guadalupe Hidalgo but by the Gadsden Purchase five years later, lived the Papago. They were in some respects similar to the Pima. They had in 1848 some twenty villages scattered over a wide area, reaching across into Mexico, with a total population of perhaps 6,000. The Papago did not practice irrigation to any great extent but planted their crops in little fields at the bases of hills, erecting a low wall of earth on every side of the field, except the one next to the hill, in order to retain the drainage from the hillside. After the first spring rain, corn and other crops were planted in the muddy ground where they matured with little rainfall. The Papago built small artificial lakes or *charcas* in order to provide water for their domestic animals and for household use, and sometimes brought water thence to gardens or fields. They had sheep, goats, cattle, and horses obtained at an earlier date from the Spaniards. Like the Pima, they made beautiful baskets and pottery.[15]

On the whole they seem to have absorbed more of the Spanish customs and way of life than had the Pima. Most of them were able to speak Spanish and were nominally Catholic, although they still retained many of their old superstitions and much of their earlier religion. In many respects, however, they resembled the Mexican population of rural areas farther south, since they usually wore the same type of dress and practiced many of the Mexican customs.[16]

West of the Pima and Papago in the valley of the Colorado lived several other tribes or groups of Indians who depended in part upon crop growing for their subsistence. These included the Yuma, said to number from 2,000 to 3,000 people in 1848. They were a tall, powerful people more warlike than the Pima and Papago, and apparently had less Spanish culture than these tribes. They grew small crops

[14] *Ibid.*
[15] *Ibid.*, 65–71.
[16] *Ibid.*

planted in the mud of overflow lands and were essentially a riparian people who looked to the river to supply many of their needs.[17] Apparently they declined in numbers and in nearly every other way after a few years of contact with the whites.

Some two hundred miles above the mouth of the Colorado begins a broad valley nearly forty miles long and several miles wide, occupied by a Yuman tribe called the Mojave, often confused with the Apache because they were sometimes associated with the latter tribe. They may have numbered over 1,000 in 1848, although no accurate figures are available. These Indians were farmers, subsisting largely on their crops and on such native products as mesquite beans. They occupied fairly good flat-topped houses made of earth. They were an intelligent people, usually friendly.[18] Near the Arizona–New Mexico border lived the Zuñi, a group of pueblo dwellers not unlike those of the Río Grande Valley.

The total number of Indians in California in 1848 cannot be determined with any degree of accuracy. Estimates range all the way from 40,000 to between 200,000 and 300,000.[19] Obviously the last two figures are absurd, but it is possible that the first may be too low. Between 1769 and 1823, twenty-one missions had been established by Franciscans under the leadership of Fray Junípero Serra and his successors. They taught the California Indians agriculture, stock raising, and various arts and crafts while they Christianized them. Commodious and attractive buildings were erected, fields cleared, plowed, and planted, and orchards and vineyards established. Large herds of cattle, sheep, goats, and horses were developed, and the Indians were rapidly advancing in civilization when secularization came, in accordance with the policy of the Mexican government.[20]

With mission control removed, some Indians remained on lands which they had formerly tilled under the supervision of the Franciscans, while other groups joined wilder tribes in the interior of the country, or retired to remote mountain valleys where they lived as squatters on land to which they had no other right. The mission herds were slaughtered, the orchards and vineyards died, and the manufacture of flour, lumber, leather, wine, and other commodities was given up. The lands were sold or granted in large tracts to rancheros,

[17] *Ibid.,* 77–89.

[18] *Ibid.,* 95–101.

[19] See Alban Hoopes, *Indian Affairs and Their Administration with Special Reference to the Far West,* 56, for discussion of the Indian population of California.

[20] Theodore H. Hittell, *History of California,* I, 741–42.

who generally showed little interest in the welfare of the Indians. Yet, at the time the United States acquired this region, the Indians were still a sedentary, agricultural people, with considerable Spanish civilization. They not only grew crops, but also owned some livestock and made beautiful baskets. Almost all of them spoke Spanish, and some of them had secured at least the rudiments of an education.[21]

Turning to the wilder and more warlike tribes, the most important of these were the Navajo and the various Apache groups. The Navajo occupied an enormous territory in northern Arizona, and northwestern New Mexico, and extended into southwestern Colorado and southeastern Utah. Their precise number is unknown, but it was probably between twelve and fifteen thousand. They had had little contact with white civilization, but by raids on the Pueblo and the Spanish settlements in the Río Grande Valley they had acquired large herds of sheep and goats, a great many horses, and possibly a few cattle. The Navajo were divided into numerous bands that moved about over their wide territory seeking pasturage for their herds. Their central stronghold was Canyon de Chelly, where they cultivated many small fields, growing crops of corn, melons, and vegetables; in some cases they planted orchards of apple, pear, peach, and plum trees. Their only government consisted of the chiefs of various bands who sometimes decided, in council, matters of importance to the Navajo people as a whole. Their homes were timber-framed hogans or round beehive-shaped structures made largely of earth. The Navajo were skillful workers in silver but made no pottery, although they wove attractive blankets from the wool of their sheep. They subsisted in part from hunting and gathering native products, especially piñon nuts, which formed an important source of their food supply. Predatory, warlike, and restless, they were a perpetual source of trouble to Spanish or Mexican settlers farther south and to the peaceful pueblo dwellers.

Raiding, however, was not all on one side. Expeditions were formed in the Mexican settlements and among the Pueblo to invade the Navajo country in order to obtain cattle, sheep, and horses, or to take captives—usually children—to be used as slaves. In fact, it was estimated that in 1848 many hundreds of Navajo slaves were held by the Mexicans and Pueblos.[22] Generation after generation these forays

21 The volume of materials on the Mission Indians is enormous. See George Wharton James, *In and Out of the Old Missions of California*, or I. M. Richman, *California Under Spain and Mexico*, for good popular accounts.

22 Andrews MS, 72–73.

were carried on in a fashion not unlike those along the Scottish border that served to enliven a long period of English history.

Next to the Navajo, by far the most important of the wilder tribes of the Southwest was the Apache. They belong to the same linguistic stock as the Navajo, but the two tribes differ greatly in manners, customs, and way of life. The Apache were broken up into a number of tribes, widely scattered over New Mexico and Arizona. Moreover, the tribes were themselves subdivided into groups, so that any attempt at classification of the Apache is very difficult. Apparently, however, there were three or four major divisions of the Apache peoples. These include the Querecho with such tribes as the Mescalero, Jicarilla, Faraon, Llanero, and possibly the Lipan; the Coyotero that include the White Mountain and Pimal divisions; the Arivaipa; and the Gila Apache which include the Mimbreño, Mogollon, Gileño, and Tonto.

The total number of Apache may have been twelve thousand or more in 1848, although any estimate of the numbers of a people so widely scattered and of such a roving nature can only be a rough approximation. They roamed over a region extending from the Pecos to the Colorado rivers and from southern Colorado or Utah south to the Mexican border and far beyond. For generations, they carried on unrelenting warfare against the Mexicans in New Mexico and Arizona and even in settlements far south of the border.

The Apache early learned something of farming from the sedentary tribes of this region but, as a rule, did not grow crops to any great extent nor did they have flocks and herds like the Navajo. They subsisted largely upon such native products as piñon nuts, mesquite beans, and the fruit of the cactus, and upon game, which was quite abundant in the mountain valleys. Much of their living, moreover, came from the spoils of war or sudden raids made on their peaceful neighbors. In such raids they would drive off sheep, cattle, and horses, or seize quantities of corn, beans, and other foodstuffs.

The Apache lived, as a rule, in crude shelters built of brush or in rough tepees made of grass. They were not skillful craftsmen, as were the Navajo, but made attractive baskets, covering some of them with a coat of gum so that they could be used for carrying or storing water. The most northern branch of the tribe, the Jicarilla, were said to have intermarried extensively with the neighboring Utes. Because of the nature of the land and climate and their own restless and warlike spirits, the Apache were most difficult to control, and for a generation after the acquisition of this territory by the United States, they proved a most troublesome and expensive problem for the government.[23] It has been said that the Apache was the original bad man of the Southwest. Low in the scale of civilization when judged by the white man's standard, he was cruel and warlike, and had great strength and endurance; terror and desolation could be spread throughout a wide area by a very few Apache warriors.

In Utah, which in 1848 included most of Nevada and parts of Colorado and Wyoming, there were perhaps 11,000 to 12,000 Indians. The most important tribe was the Ute, a wandering, warlike people living mostly by hunting. Other tribes were the Shoshone, Washo, and Shivwits. The Utes were divided into three important groups: the Uinta, White River, and Uncompahgre. Most of these Indians were low in the scale of civilization. They wandered over the deserts, subsisting largely upon small animals and roots and berries. Their homes were small, temporary structures made of brush or grass and their occupants were as poor and degraded as any Indians of the Southwest.[24]

Farther west in central and northern California were the Miwok, a numerous tribe made up of various little bands who wandered widely and lived upon such native products as they could find. They, too, were poor and low in the scale of civilization. Along the coast were several small tribes or groups that were eventually to be given such reservations as Round Valley and Hoopa Valley. Other Indians lived in the territory of the Mexican Cession, but few were important. They include the Hualapai living in northwestern Arizona, near the Grand Canyon, the Havasupai, who had found refuge in a deep canyon which opens into that of the Colorado, and the Cocopa. Comanche war parties at times raided in this region, but it is doubtful whether bands from their tribe often penetrated the region beyond the Río Grande.[25]

The United States was clearly faced with a very serious problem when suddenly called upon to assume jurisdiction over these numerous and widely scattered Indian peoples of such great diversity in civilization and culture. The topography and climate of the region, and the remoteness of many tribes from the sea or any navigable river further complicated the problem. To reach the Indians along the California coast, it was necessary to make either the arduous

23 *Ibid.,* 111–17.
24 *Ibid.,* 61–64. Also *Annual Report of Commissioner of Indian Affairs, 1859,* 362–69.
25 *Ibid.* See also Alban W. Hoopes, *op. cit.,* for some account of other Indians of the Southwest.

journey westward across the treeless plains, rugged mountain ranges, and barren deserts, or the even longer and often perilous voyage around the Horn, or via Panama, where sometimes a ship to California could be secured only after days of waiting. The New Mexico Pueblo could be reached by traveling down the Santa Fé Trail, extending from Westport Landing, Missouri, to the New Mexican capital, but the journey required many weeks and involved hardship. Once at Santa Fé, the government official sent out to assume control of the Navajo, Hopi, Apache, Pima, or Papago was still a long way from his destination and to reach it must traverse a dangerous stretch of wide, waterless plains and deserts.

When he had reached his station, he dealt with a people who spoke no English and of whose customs and way of life he was totally ignorant. The earliest agents had to set up living quarters and begin to carry out their duties under conditions of great hardship and at times real danger. The number of Indian agents and their subordinates who met violent death at the hands of their charges indicates only too clearly the hazards to which a government employee at the more remote posts was often exposed. His burdens, moreover, were frequently increased by instructions issued by his superior officers in Washington, who had all too little knowledge of conditions, or by demands for information which could be secured only through infinite labor. Under such circumstances it would seem that only a man imbued with a strong missionary spirit or with an eager desire for adventure would accept the appointment of Indian agent in these far-off posts, unless he were profoundly ignorant of the situation he must face, particularly since the annual salary of an agent was only $1,500 and that of a subagent $750.[26]

The commissioner of Indian affairs and other important officials of the Indian Bureau probably had little conception of the magnitude of the task of the Indian agent. The region covered by the Mexican Cession was so far away and so little known that these men had only the vaguest of ideas about its Indian peoples, their degree of civilization, and their needs and about how these situations were to be met.

[26] Salaries of agents were fixed by the Indian Intercourse Act of 1834, 4 *Stats.*, 735.

III

Relations with the Indians of California, 1848–68

CALIFORNIA WAS REGARDED as by far the most important portion of the Mexican Cession. For many years prior to the outbreak of the war with Mexico, this great territory lying along the Pacific Coast had been a land of mystery and romance to many Americans. The beauty and fertility of the region, with its towering mountains, extensive valleys, giant trees, and strange plant and animal life, had aroused the keenest interest and stimulated the imagination of every early explorer and visitor. Many of these travelers returned home with glowing accounts of the wonderful country and of the appearance, customs, and way of life of its native inhabitants.

It is impossible to state with any degree of accuracy even the approximate number of Indians in California at the time of its acquisition by the United States. John C. Frémont estimated 40,000 in 1850, while O. M. Wozencraft a year later suggested that there might be 200,000 to 300,000.[1] The latter figures are doubtless far too large, and even the estimate of 75,000 to 100,000 given by Superintendent E. F. Beale in 1852 is probably excessive.[2] Most of the early explorers overestimated the number of Indians in a region since the routes followed in exploration usually lay along water courses, where the villages were commonly established. Government agents likely exaggerated the numbers of the people under their jurisdiction in order to magnify the importance of their work.[3] However, the native

---

[1] 33 Cong., spec. sess., *Sen. Ex. Doc. 4*, 62–63. Hereafter referred to as *Sen. Doc. 4*.

[2] *Ibid.*, 379. Superintendent Thomas J. Henley estimated the number as 61,600 in 1856. The official census of 1862 gave it as 17,562 outside of San Diego County. Superintendent Charles Maltby in 1866 gave the number as 24,548, while Special Commissioner Robert J. Stevens estimated the Indian population of California to be 21,000 in 1867. See *Annual Report of Commissioner of Indian Affairs, 1867*, 132.

[3] The author is deeply indebted to Alban W. Hoopes, *Indian Affairs, 1849–60*,

population in California did, apparently, outnumber that in all the rest of the territory in the Mexican Cession.

The first official contacts of the United States with the Indians of this region were made by General S. W. Kearny, who, upon the outbreak of war with Mexico, led an army for the invasion of New Mexico and California. Kearny marched from Missouri to Santa Fé and entered that city without opposition on August 18, 1846. He served as military governor of New Mexico for a time, but on September 25 set out with a strong force for California, which he reached in December. After some minor battles, the conquest was completed early in 1847, and in April, Kearny, by virtue of his military authority, appointed John A. Sutter Indian subagent for those tribes and bands living on or near the Sacramento and San Joaquin rivers and M. G. Vallejo subagent in charge of the Indians north of San Francisco Bay.[4] On August 1, J. D. Hunter was informed that he had been appointed subagent at San Luis Rey.[5]

Both Governor Kearny and his successor, Governor Mason, showed a very real interest in the Indians of California and earnestly sought to promote their welfare. Kearny recommended that presents be given the Indians to cultivate their good will, and Mason urged that efforts be made to reclaim those neophytes of the missions who had gone to the mountains and deserts to join their wilder tribesmen.[6] In spite of the confused conditions of government in California in the period between Kearny's conquest and the gold rush, relations with the Indians were fairly peaceful. There were occasional raids on the herds of the ranchmen and some retaliation by the whites, but the white population was still so small that there was little cause for friction.

The basic law governing Indian relations at that time was the Indian Intercourse Act of 1834. It limited the number of agents to twelve, which, after the annexation of Texas, the acquisition of Oregon, and the Mexican Cession, was far too few. Congress, however, did not take any immediate action to increase the number, and the Indian Bureau had to do the best it could with the field force that was available or could be recruited under existing laws and appropriations. Fortunately, there was no limit to the number of subagents

---

for much information. Any errors of fact or interpretation, however, must be charged to the author and not to Mr. Hoopes.

[4] 31 Cong., 1 sess., *House Ex. Doc. 17*, 294–97. Quoted in Hoopes, *op. cit.*, 36.
[5] *Ibid.*, 344–45.
[6] *Ibid.*, 344–45; Hoopes, *op. cit.*, 37.

who might be appointed; also, under the terms of this fundamental law, agencies might be transferred from one location to another.

In 1849, when the control of Indian affairs was transferred from the War Department to the Department of the Interior, there were five superintendents in the Indian Service. Two of these were also agents, and two—the governors of Oregon and Minnesota territories —were superintendents ex officio. This left only one man—the superintendent of St. Louis—who could devote full time to administering his superintendency.[7] The discovery of gold in California created great excitement, and by the spring of 1849 the gold rush had begun and promised to grow to enormous proportions. Officials in Washington recognized that this great outpouring of people to the Far West obliged the federal government to strengthen its authority and control in that part of the country. Therefore, on April 3, 1849, the Department of State appointed Thomas Butler King special agent to investigate general conditions in California. While not charged specifically with the task of reporting upon Indian affairs, he nevertheless suggested that it would be well to concentrate the various tribes upon reservations, where they could be more easily controlled and protected.

The Department of the Interior transferred the location of one of its agencies to "Salt Lake City, California," and, on April 7, appointed John Wilson Indian agent there. But when the eastern boundary of the state was drawn in 1850, Salt Lake City was far beyond it, and Wilson never had any connection with Indian affairs in California.

On the day of Wilson's appointment, Adam Johnston was made subagent with jurisdiction over the Indians in the valleys of the San Joaquin and Sacramento rivers. He was given explicit instructions concerning his duties and methods of procedure. He was to go to St. Louis, where he could take advantage of the military escort going west to California and where he would receive his first year's salary of $750, together with funds for carrying on his work. He was given $400 for interpreters and an additional $1,200, from which he was authorized to purchase two horses, the remainder of the money to be used for travel, fuel, house rent, stationery, presents for the Indians, the collection of statistics, and incidentals. His chief duty was to collect information and make quarterly reports to the Bureau of Indian Affairs. He was to try to secure the release of any captives held by the

[7] In 1849 the superintendencies were Minnesota, Oregon, Southwestern, Michigan, and St. Louis. Hoopes, op. cit., 19.

California Indians; but he must avoid, if possible, paying any compensation for their surrender, lest he encourage a practice of taking prisoners and holding them for ransom. Since the total sum allotted him for all purposes, including salary, was only $2,350, the caution that he should practice the greatest economy seems a trifle superfluous, especially when prices prevailing in California in 1849 and 1850 are considered. Obviously the newly fledged Department of the Interior was determined that any criticism which it might incur should not be for extravagance.[8]

Johnston reached his station in California early in November. His first report, made late in January, 1850, was on the Mission Indians. He intimated that they had been unlawfully deprived of their lands and suggested that a commission be appointed to investigate and settle land titles affecting these tribes.[9]

In the meantime, the Secretary of the Interior had apparently decided that Johnston's jurisdiction was too large for one man, and in November, 1849, had offered John A. Sutter an appointment as subagent for the Indians along the Sacramento River, leaving to Johnston jurisdiction only over those along the San Joaquin.[10] Sutter declined this post, declaring that Adam Johnston was fully competent to discharge the duties of subagent in both the Sacramento and San Joaquin districts, and urging that he receive a salary "in keeping with the business and prices of the country." Sutter further recommended that provision be made for more interpreters and that a much larger sum be allotted for contingent expenses.[11] Johnston seems to have carried on his duties with energy and skill, although he must have been faced with many perplexing problems.

By 1850 the eyes of the entire world were fixed upon California; no other area on the globe was the subject of so much inquiry and discussion. People were pouring in by land and sea, attracted by tales of fabulous wealth to be found in its hills and streams. It was plain that there would inevitably be clashes between this heterogeneous, turbulent population of gold seekers and the native people of the country, unless the federal government intervened with a strong hand.

In spite of the urgent need for action, the Office of Indian Affairs

[8] For these instructions, see Medill to Johnston, April 14, 1849, *Sen. Doc. 4,* 3–4.

[9] Johnston to Brown, January 31, 1850, *ibid.,* 34–36.

[10] Brown to Sutter, November 24, 1849, *ibid.,* 3–5.

[11] Letter of J. A. Sutter, May 23, 1850, *ibid.,* 37.

was handicapped by the failure of Congress to enact legislation authorizing the appointment of additional agents and providing necessary funds. At last, on September 28, 1850, Congress authorized the appointment of three agents for California.[12] Two days later it also authorized the appointment of commissioners to make treaties with the Indians of California and appropriated $25,000 for that purpose.[13] Redick McKee of Virginia, George W. Barbour of Kentucky, and Oliver M. Wozencraft of Louisiana were appointed agents; but when it was discovered that no appropriation had been made for salaries for the agents, they were reappointed commissioners under the second act. Soon thereafter Congress enacted legislation providing that treaties should be made by regular agents of the Indian Office, who were to receive no additional compensation for such service.[14] This anomalous condition was eventually cleared up by again appointing these three men agents, and a deficiency act passed by Congress appropriated $6,750 to pay their salaries as agents from October 1, 1850, to June 30, 1851.[15] The confusion attending the early establishment of federal relations with the Indians of California was to characterize all such relations for two decades and to some extent for very much longer.

The three commissioners, with McKee as the disbursing officer, purchased presents for the Indians and proceeded to San Francisco, where they held a meeting on January 13, 1851, and chose John McKee, son of Redick McKee, secretary. [16]

The commissioners soon realized that they faced a difficult if not impossible assignment. As the Indians were scattered over almost the entire state, reaching them was an extremely arduous task. They were, moreover, broken up into many scores of small tribes that were in turn subdivided into bands. Tribal organization was loose and chieftains had little control of their people. Throughout the entire area there was no single large tribe which could be dealt with as a unit.

The tribes differed greatly in economic conditions, language, manners, customs, and degree of civilization. In the northern and central portions of the state, most of the Indians were peaceful. Many wandered over the territory, living on acorns, grass seeds, roots, insects, birds, and small animals; and along the coast and the rivers, fish

---

[12] 9 *Stats.*, 519.
[13] *Ibid.*, 558.
[14] *Ibid.*, 586.
[15] 9 *Stats.*, 572.
[16] McKee to Lea, January 13, 1851, *Sen. Doc. 4*, 53–54.

was a staple food. Their homes were temporary structures made of grass, brush, or the branches of trees, and they wore little clothing.[17]

Farther south, near the coast, were the bands of so-called Mission Indians, some of whom had been greatly influenced by contact with Spanish culture. East of these, among the mountains and extending into the desert as far as the Colorado River, were wilder tribes and bands, some of which had been joined by neophytes from the missions. Like most mountain Indians, the ones in this region were dangerous; they were, moreover, sufficiently numerous to form a real menace to the ranchmen, who were spread thinly over a large area in the south, with livestock that was especially vulnerable in case of Indian attack.[18]

To add to the difficulties of the commissioners, conditions among the white population were almost as chaotic as among the Indians. The military government had recently come to an end, and the state civil government was functioning; but its authority could hardly reach the remote mining camps widely scattered throughout the mountainous areas. There was little government of any kind in these places except such local rules and regulations as were made by common consent. Here laws were enacted by stern necessity and administered in rough-and-ready fashion by self-constituted tribunals who were at once judge, jury, and executioner. Still deeper in the mountains were individual prospectors, moving about from place to place; and in large areas there was practically no law, either state or local.

While the mining population was made up primarily of honest men with restless and adventurous spirits, it also included a significant number of brutal and lawless individuals seeking "easy money." Among these were gamblers, saloonkeepers, thieves, and opportunists of every type. Not many men, even of the better type, had any particular regard for the natives. Some feared and others despised the Indians, and few felt that they had any rights which a white man was bound to respect.

These were the conditions under which the commissioners began their work. They were to make treaties protecting the Indians, safeguarding their rights, providing necessities, and setting aside for their use large areas of land. It is probable that even the wisest of men would have failed in so enormous a task, but these three showed an ineptitude and even a lack of common sense which had tragic results for the future of the Indians of California.

[17] See Johnston to Brown, July 6, 1850, *ibid.*, 38–42, or Barbour to Lea, undated, *ibid.*, 249–64, for descriptions of California Indians.
[18] Wozencraft to Lea, October 14, 1851, *ibid.*, 203–11.

Nevertheless, they began their task with enthusiasm and ostentation. They first visited the capital at San José and called on Governor McDougal and the legislature. Indian hostilities had broken out and the belligerent Governor had ordered out state troops to chastise the Indians of the Mariposa district. He offered the commissioners an escort from the state militia, which was refused since General P. F. Smith of the United States Army had already agreed to place at their disposal a force of more than one hundred men under the command of Captain E. D. King.[19]

The commissioners traveled up the San Joaquin River by steamer to Stockton, and from there set out for the Mariposa region with their military escort, three covered wagons, each drawn by six mules, and 150 pack mules loaded with their baggage and supplies and goods for the Indians. Captain Carson, a brother of Kit Carson, had been employed to act as interpreter. War had driven most of the Indians into the mountains, and the situation was considered bad but not hopeless. Evidently the commission believed they had made a good start. At any rate, an expedition of this size must have been impressive to Indians and whites alike. Hostilities soon came to an end, and on March 19, 1851, the commissioners made a treaty with six tribes or bands of the "Mountain and Mercede Indians" granting them "all the land they demanded since this land was not of a character to be useful to the whites."[20] On April 19 another treaty was signed with sixteen tribes or bands.[21] In order to get the Indians together, Indian runners were sent into the mountains to invite representatives of various tribes and bands to come to the camp of the agents. Those who came were fed and given presents, with the result that it was not long until many Indians had assembled.

The commissioners decided to divide the state into three districts, with one commissioner dealing with the Indians of a single district. Accordingly, lots were cast on May 1, 1851; the northern district fell to McKee, the middle to Wozencraft, and the southern to Barbour,[22] and each assumed jurisdiction over the territory allotted him.

Barbour proceeded to the south, and by the latter part of July had made a number of treaties and secured the removal of most of

---

[19] McKee to Lea, February 11, 1851, *ibid.*, 54–56. Also Commissioners to Lea, February 17, 1851, *ibid.*, 57–59.

[20] McKee to Lea, March 24, 1851, *ibid.*, 67–69.

[21] *Journal of U. S. Indian Commissioners for California,* April 29, *ibid.*, 96–97. Also Commissioners to Lea, May 1, 1851, *ibid.*, 74–76.

[22] *Journal of the U. S. Indian Commissioners for California,* May 1, 1851, *ibid.*, 97–98.

the whites from the reservations set aside for the Indians.[23] He had made contracts earlier with John C. Frémont for supplying, at fifteen cents a pound, the beef promised under the terms of the treaties.[24] In his letter of July 28, to the Commissioner of Indian Affairs, Barbour had asked permission to visit his family in Kentucky. Receiving no reply, he evidently decided to take silence for consent and in the late autumn of 1851 returned to his home, where he received a severe reprimand from Commissioner Luke Lea for leaving his post without permission, and for drawing upon the Secretary of the Interior for large sums of money.[25] Barbour apparently became discouraged with his task and resigned his position on February 2, 1852.[26] He prepared an excellent report on the work of the agents, describing conditions among the Indians, and stating that he had drawn a draft on the Secretary of the Interior for $183,825 to pay for beef furnished by J. C. Frémont.[27]

In the meantime, Wozencraft, in charge of the middle district, was busily engaged in making treaties and pledging large sums of money for carrying out their terms. He wrote voluminous and frequent letters to the Indian Office describing his work and the difficulties which he had encountered. Adam Johnston, who had been in California for more than a year when the commissioners arrived, gave them much information and, as long as they worked together as a commission, accompanied them. When the territory was divided, his jurisdiction fell within Wozencraft's portion. Johnston worked hard to place the Indians on the reservations assigned to them but apparently resented receiving communications from the Indian Office through Wozencraft, and complained that he was not under the latter's authority. Nevertheless, he remained until early in 1852, when he was notified of his dismissal from the Indian Service.[28] On the whole, Johnston seems to have been able and efficient.

In addition to arousing the resentment of Johnston, Wozencraft also became involved in controversies with McKee.[29] Apparently Wozencraft was ambitious; for, upon hearing rumors that a superintendent of Indian affairs for California and Oregon was to be ap-

23 Barbour to Lea, July 28, 1851, *ibid.*, 122–27.
24 Frémont to Barbour, May 19, 1851, and Barbour to Frémont, May 28, 1851, *ibid.*, 267–68.
25 Lea to Barbour, December 23, 1851, *ibid.*, 23–24.
26 Barbour to President Filmore, February 2, 1852, *ibid.*, 268.
27 Undated report, Barbour to Lea, *ibid.*, 249–64.
28 Lea to Johnston, January 9, 1852, *ibid.*, 24.
29 Wozencraft to Lea, August 7, 1851, *ibid.*, 131–34.

The Navajo silversmith

Courtesy Milton Snow, Navajo Service

Navajo spinning and weaving

pointed, he promptly applied for the position.[30] By this time his superior officers in Washington must have begun to feel that he was not only lacking in any understanding of business matters but deficient in common sense. During the period of his treaty negotiations extending from May 28 to September 10, 1851, he had directed the delivery to the Indians of beef worth $60,060 at twenty cents a pound, and he estimated that an additional $346,135 would be required during the next two years to carry out the terms of the treaties he had made.[31] The price of the beef was grossly excessive. Wozencraft declared later that he could have purchased it for eight cents a pound for cash, and that the high price was demanded because the contractor must wait a year for the payment of drafts drawn on the United States government.[32]

While this may have been true, there seems to have been no possible excuse for the practices employed by Wozencraft in connection with beef deliveries. There was no supervision, and only the word of the trader, who was in some cases also the contractor, guaranteed that the beef had been delivered according to contract. The cattle were not weighed but were estimated by someone on the ground. Contracts were merely verbal at times, and large numbers of cattle were promised to Indian tribes by treaty without any knowledge of how many persons the tribe might include.[33] It is not surprising that such methods of carrying on the business of the federal government should have brought Agent Wozencraft into the bad graces of the Department of the Interior. Apparently his explanations were not well received, and on September 4, 1852, he was notified that his connection with the Indian Service was at an end.[34]

While Wozencraft was busy making treaties and carrying out their provisions and the provisions of the treaties made by Barbour (who upon his departure from California had left his jurisdiction in Wozencraft's charge), McKee was engaged in the same type of work in the northern district. As disbursing officer for the commission, however, he was obliged to return to San Francisco to await funds or to try to secure them; and his expedition into northern California was delayed until early in August. On the eleventh, he left Sonoma with

30 Wozencraft to Lea, October 10, 1851, *ibid.*, 203.

31 Statement and estimate of Wozencraft, *ibid.*, 189–90.

32 Wozencraft to Lea, June 23, 1852, *ibid.*, 336–40. This letter also reveals the bad feeling between McKee and Wozencraft.

33 Memorandum of communication with O. M. Wozencraft, September 14, 1852, *ibid.*, 368–69.

34 Lea to Wozencraft, September 4, 1852, *ibid.*, 29.

an escort of thirty-six dragoons from the United States Army under the command of Major W. W. Wessells. He employed men to take charge of his train of pack mules loaded with provisions, baggage, and Indian goods, and also arranged with a beef contractor to drive some cattle with the expedition in order to feed the Indians who met in council. The contractor seems also to have expected to supply some beef to mining camps along the route of travel. The expedition did not return to San Francisco until December 29, 1851.[35]

McKee made several treaties but unfortunately became involved in controversies with General E. A. Hitchcock, commander of the Pacific Division, who had furnished the military escort, and with Governor John Bigler and, to some extent, with various whites residing on lands which he had set aside for Indian reservations. General Hitchcock complained of irregularities in the expedition, including the charging of exorbitant prices for beef furnished the escort of soldiers and the Indians. It was alleged that McKee's son, John, was a partner of the beef contractor, General Estelle, and shared in the profits of the enterprise.[36] McKee defended his own actions and his son's, declaring that the latter had merely kept the accounts of the beef sold and that no formal contract had been made for beef. The controversy, however, attracted considerable attention.

McKee's difficulties with Governor Bigler concerned Indian depredations and the reserving of lands by treaty. McKee placed a large share of the blame for Indian troubles in general upon lawless whites, while Governor Bigler blamed the Indians alone. McKee defended the necessity for treaties setting aside reservations, but Bigler declared that the California legislature opposed the treaties and that the entire state delegation in Congress was pledged to oppose their ratification.[37] Actually, the controversies with a few whites occupying a small part of the lands designated by the new treaties as Indian reservations were not serious. Most of the men threatened with removal from lands merely set forth their grievances and asked for adequate compensation; occasionally they asked to be allowed to remain in order to develop a mine. McKee also received a number of claims for damages from Indian depredations, some of them listing fantastic prices for property destroyed.[38]

[35] For general account of this expedition, see minutes kept by John McKee, secretary, and continued by Redick McKee, *ibid.*, 134–80.

[36] Hitchcock to McKee, March 23, 1852, *ibid.*, 301–302.

[37] See correspondence between McKee and Bigler, April 5 to 16, 1852, *ibid.*, 310–24.

[38] For requests for compensation for improvements or payment for property

With the completion of McKee's expedition into northern California, the work of the three commissioners in treaty-making was complete. They had made a total of eighteen treaties with nearly 140 tribes or bands of Indians and had set aside as reservations 11,700 square miles or 7,488,000 acres.[39] The treaties sent to Washington for ratification by the Senate were much alike: the Indians recognized the United States as sole sovereign of the land ceded by Mexico, and acknowledged themselves to be under its protection; they gave up all claim to any land except that set aside for reservations, which was to be theirs forever; they were to have annuities in goods and clothing; and farmers, teachers, and blacksmiths were to be provided for them at federal expense for five years.[40]

By the early part of 1852, the enthusiasm at first manifested by the Indian Office toward its three commissioners in California was beginning to cool. Criticism had reached the office from various sources. The drafts drawn by Barbour on the Secretary of the Interior had reached Washington. Although a total of only $50,000 for use in California had been appropriated by Congress, the commission had spent or contracted to spend $716,394.79.[41] Of this amount, John C. Frémont's and Samuel J. Hensley's claims for beef cattle in the amounts of $183,825 and $96,375, respectively, were allowed, and a claim of Wozencraft's for $7,000 was paid, but all other claims were rejected.[42]

The embarrassment caused the Indian Office by these large drafts and the criticisms of the agents' activities, together with the influence exerted by the senators and representatives from California—who reflected the objections of the people of California to having state lands set aside for Indian reservations—stirred Congress to enact new laws. On March 3, 1852, an act of Congress established an independent

destroyed, see *Sen. Ex. Doc. 4*, 269–82. In one such claim flour, pork, beans, salt, sugar, coffee, and rice are all listed at a value of one dollar a pound while one large washtub is given a value of eighty dollars. Schedule of property lost by Ford, Penny, and Holman for goods lost on or about June 17, 1851, *ibid.*, 275–76.

Claims were also made in other districts for property destroyed, the largest being that of J. J. Warner in Southern California on account of the attack on his ranch on November 23, 1851. This was for a total of $58,745, and while prices seem high—$160 for 1,000 feet of sawed boards, for example—flour was valued at only $12.50 a hundred pounds. *Ibid.*, 290–91.

39 Wm. H. Ellison, "The Federal Indian Policy in California," *Mississippi Valley Historical Review*, Vol. IX, No. 1, 57.

40 Hoopes, *op. cit.*, 44–45.

41 32 Cong., 1 sess., *Sen. Ex. Doc. 61*, IX, 1–2. Quoted in Hoopes, *op. cit.*, 46.

42 Ellison, *loc. cit.*, 58–59.

superintendency for California,[43] and the following day Edward F. Beale was appointed superintendent. As Congress had not reached the Indian appropriation bill and the treaties had not been acted upon by the Senate, Beale delayed his departure to California until August. In reply to an inquiry by the Commissioner of Indian Affairs, he expressed his approval of the treaties and said that the line of policy pursued by the commissioners and agents in their negotiations was proper.[44] However, the treaties submitted to the Senate on July 1, 1852, were rejected on July 8.[45] Evidently the voice of the people of California had been weighty: Representative McCorkle of that state had asserted that the reservations set aside comprised some of the most valuable agricultural and mineral lands in the state.[46]

Beale estimated that $42,500 would be required annually for operation of the California superintendency.[47] With Congressional action on the appropriation still delayed, funds were advanced by the Indian Office, and Beale started for California in August, reporting his arrival there and the beginning of his work on September 16. Benjamin D. Wilson had been appointed agent for the Indians of southern California to replace Wozencraft, and Samuel Shelden had been appointed for the Indians of northern California.[48] In the meantime, the Indian Appropriation Act of August 30, 1852, had provided $14,000 for the salary of Beale and his clerk, together with contingent expenses, and $100,000 to preserve peace with the Indians.[49]

When Beale received the accounts of Agents McKee and Wozencraft, he complained bitterly of gross mismanagement and neglect in the matter of contracts. He urged a rigid investigation in order to do justice to the innocent and punish the guilty.[50] Later he stated that he had received little exact information from these agents, since neither of them had been in the Indian country for some six months. Consequently, delivery of beef cattle was unsupervised, and there was evidence that large sums of money had been squandered. The agents claimed that no funds were available for travel; but, since they had involved the government to a large amount to furnish supplies, they

---

[43] 10 *Stats.*, 2–3.
[44] Hoopes, *op. cit.*, 45.
[45] *Ibid.* The treaties were held secret after their rejection until January 18, 1905. Hoopes, *op. cit.*, 44 n.
[46] *Congressional Globe*, 32 Cong., 1 sess., 890.
[47] Beale to Lea, July 14, 1852, *Sen. Doc. 4*, 344.
[48] Lea to Beale, September 4, 1852, *ibid.*, 28–29.
[49] 10 *Stats.*, 55–56.
[50] Beale to Lea, September 16, 1852, *Sen. Doc. 4*, 361.

would have been wise, perhaps, to create another small liability in order to supervise their issue. Their drafts on the government had been protested, and the whole matter of Indian affairs in California was in almost hopeless confusion.[51]

Nevertheless, Beale attacked the problem with vigor and ability. McKee was assigned to the middle district of California as agent; but eventually he became involved in a controversy with Beale, claiming that he was not subject to the authority of the latter, and as a result he was suspended by Beale on November 30.[52] McKee left the service soon thereafter, and the story of the three commissioners was ended, although the results of their work appeared again and again to embarrass the government.

The great influx of white population which promised to occupy "every habitable foot of ground in the entire state to the exclusion of the original inhabitants" prompted Beale to propose a series of military posts or reservations to which the Indians would be invited to come and live under the jurisdiction of an agent. These were to be regarded as military reserves and each should have a garrison of suitable size, the expense of maintaining the troops to be borne by the surplus produce of the Indian labor.[53]

The treaties setting aside Indian reservations had been rejected, but Beale apparently hoped to provide lands which would serve as refuges for Indians by the establishment of these military posts. His plan, which is faintly reminiscent of the old mission system, may have been the best that could be devised under the circumstances; but the placing of Indians in proximity to soldiers of a military post has usually engendered many evils.

Beale was enthusiastic about his plan and urged an appropriation of $500,000 to carry it out, asserting that Indian labor had been productive under the mission system and could be made so again. He was horrified at the abuse and mistreatment the Indians suffered at the hands of the whites. He declared that the appropriation of $100,-000 was entirely inadequate for all the Indians of California and that he proposed to use it only for the southern portion of the state, because the tribes there were warlike and an outbreak would prove disastrous. It was from that region, too, that the entire beef supply for the northern settlements came. Humanity must give way to necessity, Beale said, and ignoring the wretched condition of the Indians in

52 Beale to McKee, November 30, 1852, *ibid.*, 389.
53 Beale to Lea, October 29, 1852, *ibid.*, 373–74.
54 Beale to Lea, November 22, 1852, *ibid.*, 377–80.

the northern and central portions of the state because they were harmless, he spent all available funds in the south.[54]

Here Superintendent Beale frankly advocated, on the grounds of necessity, a policy which was more or less consistently pursued by the federal government for three-quarters of a century in its dealings with Indians. Always the aggressive and warlike received consideration because they were dangerous, while the peaceful and inoffensive were neglected and furnished scant protection against lawless or unscrupulous whites. Few government officials, however, have been willing to admit this as candidly as Beale did.

General E. A. Hitchcock, in command of the Pacific Coast Division of the army, had approved Beale's plan, and the latter was eager to secure its approval by Congress. He went to Washington in the spring of 1853 in order to urge the acceptance of his ideas by Congress and the Indian Office. Evidently he was successful, for the Indian Appropriation Act of March 3, 1853, authorized the President to establish five military reservations in California (or Utah and New Mexico) of not over 25,000 acres each and not on lands inhabited by citizens of California. The sum of $250,000 was appropriated to subsist the Indians of California and to remove them to the reservations for protection.[55]

Encouraged, no doubt, by the action of Congress, Beale set out in April for California, traveling overland, and reached Los Angeles late in August, 1853.[56] Deciding to establish the first reservation in the Tejon Pass region, he visited that area and held council with various tribes of Indians. He urged them to settle on the new reservation, promising that the government would supply seeds for planting and would also provide for them until they could support themselves from products of their own labor.[57] Many were very reluctant to leave the mountains and woodlands which had been their homes for so long, but by the late autumn of 1853, the Tejon, or San Sebastian, Reservation was definitely established. By the close of the year, a square mile of land had been plowed and put in cultivation and thirty to forty plows and harrows were being used by Indians. By February, 1854, Beale reported 2,000 acres in wheat, 500 in barley, and 150 in corn. He was much pleased by the docility and industry of the Indians on the reservation, who by this time numbered about

51 Beale to Lea, September 30, 1852, *ibid.*, 366–67.
55 10 *Stats.*, 238.
56 Hoopes, *op. cit.*, 53.
57 *Ibid.*

2,500.[58] By June 20, the first year's crop of 42,000 bushels of wheat and 10,000 bushels of barley had been harvested.[59]

Benjamin D. Wilson, agent for this southern district, was of great assistance to Beale, and a warm friendship developed between the two. Beale asked Wilson, who was a man of wealth and a long-time resident of California, for information about the southern Indians and advice about the best policy of dealing with them. Wilson gave him a lengthy description of the Indians of Santa Barbara, Tulare, San Diego, and Los Angeles counties. He said that there were few whites in southern California except within sixty to seventy miles of the coast and proposed the establishment of a great Indian reservation east of this populated area, extending as far as the Colorado River, to which all of these southern California Indians should be brought.[60]

Beale was honest and able, but, being a Democrat, he had to face bitter opposition from the Whig politicians of California. In fact, any man who sought to do anything for the Indians was at that time certain to meet criticism from political leaders of the state. The pressure of other duties had caused Beale to neglect his accounts, and they were now alleged to be $250,000 in arrears. Therefore, on June 2, 1854, Commissioner Manypenny notified Beale of his removal from office.[61]

On the same day, Thomas J. Henley of Indiana was notified of his appointment as Beale's successor. The Indian Appropriation Act, approved July 31, 1854, provided for three reservations in California, but only the one at Tejon was in operation. Each reservation was to contain from 5,000 to 10,000 acres and each was to be under the immediate jurisdiction of a subagent. The sum of $200,000 was appropriated for the Indian Service in California, with not over $20,000 to be drawn by the superintendent or in his hands unexpended at any one time; and $25,000 might be spent in clearing defective titles and rights to these reserved lands.[62]

Henley left San Francisco for Tejon on July 27, 1854, and for some two months he traveled extensively among the Indians of the state in order to learn their problems by personal observation. He approved of Beale's general policy, and in September, 1854, he estab-

58 *Ibid.*, 54–55.
59 *Ibid.*
60 Wilson's reply to Beale was printed in the *Los Angeles Star* beginning July 18, 1868, and extending through ten issues. Photostatic copies are in the collections of the Huntington Library.
61 Hoopes, *op. cit.*, 56. Beale was later fully proved guiltless of all charges.
62 10 *Stats.*, 332.

lished the Nome Lackee Reservation by setting aside a tract of 25,000 acres in the foothills of the Coast Range, overlooking the Sacramento Valley. H. L. Ford was made subagent of this reservation and given very detailed instructions concerning methods of procedure. Before the close of the year 1854, it was estimated that there were 800 Indians at Nome Lackee.[63] Henley urged that three more reservations be created, one east of the mountains and outside the limits of the state, to which all California Indians might eventually be removed in order to "rid the state of this class of population."[64] This suggests that Henley was eager to win the favor of local political leaders.

The Appropriation Act of March 3, 1855, provided for the creation of two reservations in addition to the three already authorized. A total of $275,000 was granted for Indian affairs in California, of which $15,000 was for setting up the new reserves and subsisting the Indians on them, and $125,000 was for subsisting the Indians on the reserves already in existence.[65]

Henley pushed his program vigorously and by September, 1856, reservations had been established in Mendocino and Klamath.[66] In addition, some farms or small, temporary reserves had been created. Klamath Reservation extended along the river of that name from the ocean for twenty miles, and Mendocino, located by Major H. P. Heintzelman, acting under orders of Henley, late in 1855, lay between the Pacific Ocean and the first range of mountains to the east and between the Noyo River and Hale Creek.[67]

Rumors of inefficiency and mismanagement had reached the Indian Office in Washington, and on May 1, 1857, James Ross Browne was appointed to investigate the condition of Indian affairs in Washington, Oregon, and California. Nearly a year passed before Browne was able to give his attention to California, but a visit to Mendocino in April, 1858, convinced him that conditions were very bad and that Henley and his associates had been guilty of gross irregularities, involving the diversion to their own use of funds appropriated for the Indians. Henley was charged with misappropriation of public funds and was dismissed. James McDuffie was notified that he had been appointed superintendent of Indian affairs in California on April 4, 1859.[68]

[63] Hoopes, *op. cit.*, 58.
[64] *Ibid.*, 59.
[65] 10 *Stats.*, 698–99.
[66] Ellison, *loc. cit.*
[67] Hoopes, *op. cit.*, 61.
[68] *Ibid.*, 65.

Fort Yuma, California, on the Colorado River
opposite mouth of the Gila River

From William Rich Hutton, California in 1847–53

Mission of San Luis Rey, 1848

McDuffie was instructed to visit the different reservations and to make an inventory of all public property. At his request Henley named five reservations, to some of which farms were attached: Fresno, Mendocino, Nome Lackee, Tejon, and Klamath. In September, 1859, however, when McDuffie made a detailed report listing all reserves in California, he included these five and three others—Nome Cult, Tule River, and Kings River. These latter reserves had apparently been considered "farms" by Henley. Conditions at Klamath were reported good, with some 2,000 Indians engaged chiefly in farming.[69]

It seems likely that Congress was disgusted with the way in which Indian affairs in California had been administered; for the Indian Appropriation Act of February 28, 1859, provided only $7,500 for general expenses, such as travel and subsistence of officials in California, and an additional $50,000 for the Indians. The commissioner, with the advice and consent of the Secretary of the Interior, was authorized to increase the number of reservations in California, provided the total area of all such reservations did not exceed 125,000 acres.[70]

The next Indian Appropriation Bill, June 19, 1860, authorized the division of California into two districts, each to be under a superintending agent. Each of these agents might appoint a supervisor in his district, at a salary of $1,800 a year, and four laborers at $50 a month to teach the Indians to farm. The appropriation was $57,000—the same as the year before.[71] John A. Dreibelbis was appointed superintendent of the northern district and McDuffie remained as superintendent of the southern district.[72]

The Civil War did not affect Indian affairs in California nearly so much as in some other parts of the country. Yet there were minor outbreaks in 1862, 1863, and 1866. In fact, not a year passed without some Indian hostilities or a threat of an uprising.

Neither McDuffie nor Dreibelbis remained in office long. By 1862, George M. Hanson was supervising agent of the northern district and John P. H. Wentworth of the southern district. Both had their offices at San Francisco, and the Commissioner of Indian Affairs urged that the two districts be abolished.[73]

An act of Congress, approved April 8, 1864, placed the state once more under a single superintendent, and crystallized the reservation

---

[69] See *ibid.*, 66–77, for more detailed report.
[70] 11 *Stats.*, 400.
[71] 12 *Stats.*, 57.
[72] Hoopes, *op. cit.*, 68.
[73] *Annual Report of Commissioner of Indian Affairs, 1862*, 8–9.

system. By this act the President was authorized to establish reservations in California, not to exceed four, which might or might not include some of the present reservations, at the discretion of the President. If any existing reservations were included, the boundaries might be extended if necessary. No limit was placed on the size of the reservations, but they were to be as far from white settlements as practicable and at least one reservation must be in the former northern district. For each reservation the President was to appoint an agent, who must reside there and who was not to visit Washington except at the request of the commissioner of Indian affairs. The agents were to receive an annual salary of $1,800 each, for four year terms, and the superintendent was to receive an annual salary of $3,600.[74]

Austin Wiley became superintendent, but on May 5, 1865, he was superseded by Charles Maltby. Commissioner of Indian Affairs D. N. Cooley stated that Wiley had left office with an outstanding indebtedness of over $35,000, most of which could not be paid for lack of funds and that there was a very large additional indebtedness, some of it extending back for fifteen years.[75] Cooley further declared that ever since the federal government had taken over the Indians of California, the management of their affairs had been unsatisfactory. Every superintendent except the present one had spent far more money than had been appropriated, and the heavy indebtedness thus incurred had brought the credit of the department into disrepute.[76] Robert J. Stevens was appointed special commissioner to investigate Indian affairs in California and make a complete report on conditions and needs.

After a long investigation, including extensive travel, Stevens made his report on January 1, 1867. He estimated the number of Indians in California at 21,000—evidently an enormous decrease in twenty years.[77] He described in some detail the various reservations on which approximately 3,000 Indians lived, but he was indefinite about which reservations should be retained and which abandoned. The remaining 18,000 Indians were still scattered over the state.

There were at this time four authorized reservations in California: Hoopa Valley, in the northwest about twenty miles northeast of Eureka; Round Valley, some sixty miles south and slightly east of Hoopa Valley; Smith's River, near the Oregon line on Smith River,

74 13 *Stats.*, 39–41.
75 *Annual Report of Commissioner of Indian Affairs, 1866*, 115–16.
76 *Ibid.*
77 *Ibid.*, 132.

three miles above the point where the river meets the ocean; and Tule River, in the south, some thirty miles north and slightly east of Bakersfield.[78] Round Valley was first selected by Superintendent Henley in 1856, and in 1863 it was surveyed and set apart as a reservation by order of the Secretary of the Interior. Hoopa Valley was selected in 1864, and the following year an appropriation of $65,000 was made, to pay white settlers within its limits for their improvements. Smith's River consisted of lands leased from whites for the use of the Indians and some forest lands set aside by the Secretary of the Interior. Superintendent B. C. Whiting recommended that it be abandoned and the Indians removed to Round Valley and Hoopa Valley. Tule River included two townships of government land set aside for use of the Indians and 1,280 acres of very productive irrigated lands leased from Thomas P. Madden. It was established in 1863, and the Indians of Tejon Reserve were removed to it when General Edward F. Beale received a patent for the lands included in Tejon, which he had purchased from the original grantees. The Indian Office urged that the Madden tract be purchased and Tule River developed as a permanent reservation.[79]

Charles Maltby's service as superintendent of California was brief. Early in 1867 he was succeeded by B. C. Whiting, who remained in office until 1869. The Indian Appropriation Act of July 27, 1868, provided for a superintendent and four agents in California. It gave $40,000 for the subsistence and civilization of the Indians, in addition to providing for physicians, blacksmiths, and farmers. It also abolished the Smith's River Reservation, transferring the Indians to Hoopa Valley, and provided for restoring the Mendocino Reserve to the public domain.[80] In accordance with the terms of this act, Superintendent Whiting removed the government property and Indians from Smith's River, though not without some difficulty. A few fled, but a great number of them were brought back and taken to Hoopa.[81]

The years 1867–68 had been a troublous period for the Indian Service. War had flamed out all over the Plains region and both the army and the Indian Bureau had worked hard, each in its own way, to restore peace. Military campaigns and treaty negotiation had alternated in rapid succession. The Peace Commission, composed of four distinguished civilians and three army officers not lower in rank

[78] *Ibid.*, 116.
[79] *Annual Report of Commissioner of Indian Affairs, 1867*, 8.
[80] 15 *Stats.*, 221.
[81] *Annual Report of Commissioner of Indian Affairs, 1869*, 197–98.

than brigadier general, had been appointed.[82] It held the great council of Medicine Lodge and made treaties in the summer of 1867, but the following year brought new Indian wars and Custer's destruction of Black Kettle's camp in the Battle of the Washita. Investigations and reports were made by Congress, and Indian affairs were widely discussed in the newspapers, with important effects upon federal relations with the California Indians.

When General Grant became president on March 4, 1869, the United States, through the Department of the Interior, had administered Indian affairs in California for twenty years. Its achievement during that period was far from impressive, and the results were meager. In the first ten years, $1,737,493 had been expended, and nearly $925,000 in additional funds had been appropriated by Congress to reimburse the state for expenses it had incurred in Indian wars. The first figure, moreover, covers civil administration alone and does not include the funds required by the army in waging war against hostile Indians or while engaged in garrison duty.[83] The treaties made by the three agents, which would have granted the Indians some 7,500,000 acres of land, had been rejected by the Senate, and, except for three small reservations occupied by some 3,000 people, the Indians were homeless. Many lived as squatters on lands clearly belonging to whites; others had a vague claim to the lands they occupied; but the greater part of them were landless, wandering from place to place, sometimes over wide territory, sometimes within comparatively narrow limits. All of the Indians were extremely poor and had no civil rights. For many years Indians were prohibited from giving evidence in favor of or against white persons in criminal cases or in civil cases in which a white person was a party.[84] Indians found guilty of loitering or vagrancy could be arrested and their services sold to the highest bidder for any length of term up to four months.[85] Young Indian children were often kidnapped and sold for servants.[86] Contemporary records are filled with accounts of the abuse and cruelty heaped by brutal whites upon the helpless Indians. Disease took a

[82] 15 *Stats.*, 17. The commission was composed of Commissioner of Indian Affairs N. G. Taylor, chairman, and Senators J. B. Henderson, John B. Sanborn, and S. F. Tappan, and Generals W. T. Sherman, Alfred H. Terry, William S. Harney, and C. C. Augur.

[83] Ellison, *loc. cit.*

[84] Chauncey S. Goodrich, "Legal Status of California Indian," *California Law Review*, January and March, 1926.

[85] *Ibid.*, 11. See also *Calif. Stats.*, *1850*, 408–409.

[86] *Annual Report of Commissioner of Indian Affairs, 1862*, 315.

heavy toll in many tribes. In these two decades the Indian population had declined between 50 and 80 per cent.

The ineffective handling of Indian affairs during this period by the federal government must be blamed on the inherent difficulties of the task rather than on a lack of good intentions on the part of the officials of the Indian Bureau. The problem of administration was greatly complicated by the remoteness of California from Washington. The vast influx of a heterogeneous mining population following the discovery of gold, the confusion of land titles because of early Spanish or Mexican grants, racial prejudices—fostered, perhaps, by the presence of a large Spanish-speaking population and some Asiatics —the uncertain legal status of the Indian, and the reluctance of the Indian to change his manner of living, all complicated the task.

There were tragic mistakes made in the choice of officials. A few, such as Beale, were both able and honest; but others were inefficient, and some were unquestionably venal and corrupt. The failure to recognize the Indians' usufructuary right to the soil was perhaps the greatest mistake, judged by its results, for the native population. It was assumed that the land, having been purchased from Mexico by the United States, became part of the public domain, and that the Indian had no land rights to be extinguished. However, there is every evidence that Mexico had regarded the Indians as citizens, and, if that were the case, they became citizens of the United States by the terms of the Treaty of Guadalupe Hidalgo. In practice, this was denied and the Indian was left without either the advantage of citizenship or the right of occupancy of the land.

The election of Grant to the presidency ushered in a new era in the administration of Indian affairs as a whole by the federal government. New policies were established, which naturally had far-reaching effects upon federal relations with the Indians of California. That story will be told in a later chapter.

IV

Indian Affairs in New Mexico and Arizona, 1848–68

MOST OF THE NEW MEXICO AND ARIZONA INDIANS were very different from those of California. While the Pueblo, Hopi, Pima, and Papago peoples were peaceful and much more advanced in civilization than any of the California tribes, the Navajo, occupying the deserts and mountains of northern Arizona and New Mexico, and the Apache, widely scattered throughout this whole region, were as fierce and warlike as any tribes on the North American continent.

When James S. Calhoun was appointed the first Indian agent for New Mexico, on April 7, 1849, he was informed by the commissioner that very little was known about the Indians in the region. His first duty would be to make a survey and report on their numbers, the territory each tribe occupied, their manners and habits, their feelings toward Mexico and the United States, their languages, and what regulations and laws would be necessary for their government.[1]

A brief and turbulent period of military relations with the Indians of New Mexico had preceded the creation of the Department of the Interior. When General S. W. Kearny closed his term as military governor of New Mexico on September 22, 1846, and departed with his army for California, he left Charles Bent in New Mexico as civil governor. The fact that the United States now held New Mexico meant little to the Navajo, who for generations had been accustomed to raid the settlements of Mexicans and peaceful Pueblo Indians. On October 2, 1846, General Kearny sent orders to Colonel A. W. Doniphan to march into the Navajo country and compel the Indians there to give up prisoners and property taken in raids and instructed him to obtain security for their future good conduct "by taking hostages or otherwise."[2]

---

[1] Abel (ed.), *op. cit.*, 3. This is the most important source of information on Indian affairs in New Mexico in the period from 1849 to 1852.
[2] William E. Connelley, *Doniphan's Expedition*, 266.

Doniphan accordingly sent an expedition which marched in three separate columns, meeting at Ojo Oso (Bear Spring). Here Doniphan himself joined them with a small guard of soldiers, and on November 22, 1846, signed a treaty with the chiefs and headmen of the Navajo. The Indians signed with reluctance, asserting that they had been at war for many years with the Pueblo and Mexicans and that this was their own war, with which the United States should not concern itself. Moreover, they could not understand why the United States wanted them to give up prisoners and property taken from the New Mexicans. Doniphan explained that peace had been made and that all the people of New Mexico must now stop any war-like activity. It is doubtful, however, if the Navajo were able to grasp his meaning, even though they agreed to what he asked. Doniphan arranged a treaty between the Navajo and the Zuñi before departing with his army for El Paso and the invasion of Mexico.[3]

Quiet had been restored but it was not to last long. On January 19, 1847, Governor Bent and several other Americans were killed at Taos by a party of rebellious Mexicans and Indians. The insurgents then marched south toward Santa Fé, but were met and defeated by troops under the command of Colonel Sterling Price, including some New Mexico volunteers led by Ceran St. Vrain.[4]

With the death of Bent, Secretary Donociano Vigil became acting governor, and in December he was appointed governor. Various military men were in command in New Mexico for the next two or three years and in October, 1849, one of these, Lieutenant Colonel John Munroe, assumed both military and civil authority, which he held until New Mexico was made a territory in 1851.[5]

During the early years of the pre-territorial period, the chief objective relating to the Indians was to preserve peace and check raids by the Navajo and Apache. It was not until more than a year after the signing of the Treaty of Guadalupe Hidalgo that the Indian Bureau took formal steps to establish relations with the Indians of New Mexico. On March 29, 1849, the President directed that the Indian Agency at Council Bluffs be transferred to Santa Fé, New Mexico.[6] The Secretary of Interior early in April authorized the Indian Office to pay the Indian agents at "Salt Lake, California" and Santa Fé, New Mexico, a year's salary in advance, to allow them the

[3] *Ibid.*, 305, 311.
[4] See R. E. Twitchell, *Leading Facts of New Mexican History*, II, 229–62; or Helen Haines, *History of New Mexico*, 186–94, for account of this uprising.
[5] Haines, *op. cit.*, 197–98.
[6] Abel (ed.), *op. cit.*, 2.

necessary interpreters at an annual salary of $300 each, and $1,000 each for contingencies, presents, etc., as well as a reasonable sum for procuring statistical information. In addition, the agent at Santa Fé was allowed $300 for seeking and obtaining the release of a Mexican boy alleged to be held captive by the Indians and in whose release the government of Mexico had expressed an interest.[7] James S. Calhoun was accordingly appointed Indian agent for New Mexico at a salary of $1,500 a year; an additional sum of $2,300 was placed in his hands for the purposes indicated by the Secretary of the Interior. Calhoun was furnished a copy of the Treaty of Guadalupe Hidalgo, together with reports about the nature of the region and the Indians made by Governor Bent, Frémont, Emory, Abert, and Cooke.[8]

Calhoun reached Santa Fé on July 22, and on July 29, he made a lengthy report to the Indian Office in which he asserted that the Pueblo Indians were entitled to the early and especial consideration of the United States. The New Mexico legislature had, in 1847, enacted a law that constituted each Indian Pueblo a body politic and corporate, under which the people and their successors should have perpetual possession of the lands. Calhoun said that the Pueblo desired the establishment of schools and the receipt of agricultural information. They were preyed upon, however, by wild tribes who had never cultivated the soil but depended upon depredations for a livelihood. These predatory Indians, he asserted, could not be destroyed, and yet no earthly power could stop their raids until their hunger, both physical and mental, was relieved.[9]

Calhoun, a soldier, was one of the ablest Indian agents ever to serve the United States. He was no sentimentalist but faced his problems realistically, with vision and common sense. The Navajo had been very troublesome in the summer of 1849, as they had been, in fact, almost every summer. Plunder, to the Navajo, and to the Apache also, was a business. They did not destroy the settlements of Mexicans or Pueblo Indians, however, or wantonly ravage their fields and herds. They wanted these peaceful communities to exist and produce livestock, grain, and other commodities which could be seized, along with a few captives to be used as slaves. The Mexican settlers and Pueblo Indians would not infrequently retaliate by making expeditions into the Navajo country to capture sheep and horses, as well as children to be enslaved. Such reprisals had been allowed and perhaps

[7] *Ibid.*
[8] *Ibid.*, 3–9.
[9] *Ibid.*, 17–20.

Fort Sumner, New Mexico
Company quarters in course of erection

Kit Carson's home, Taos, New Mexico

even encouraged under Spanish and Mexican rule; but they were forbidden by the American government, with the result that what had formerly been an eternal war had become a one-sided affair. The Navajo, relieved of the fear of retaliation, became increasingly bold and active in their raids, and Calhoun urged that the settlers be allowed to defend themselves, unless the federal government expected to pay from the United States Treasury all losses due to Indian depredations.[10]

Within a month after reaching his post, Calhoun started a military campaign against the tribe. Under the command of Colonel J. M. Washington, the expedition penetrated deep into the Navajo country. In a minor skirmish one Navajo chief was killed. Washington then entered Canyon de Chelly, the stronghold of the tribe, and effected a treaty which was signed on September 9, 1849. It provided that the Navajo acknowledge themselves to be under the jurisdiction and protection of the United States, that they remain at peace, and that they deliver within thirty days all captives and property taken from Mexicans, Americans, or other peoples at peace with the United States. The United States agreed to protect the Navajo against aggression by others, establish trading houses and military posts in their country, survey and adjust their boundaries, grant to them presents and donations, and adopt toward them liberal and humane measures.[11] Some captives, livestock, and other property were surrendered by the Navajo, but it was not long until new raids were made. Calhoun's numerous letters to the Indian Office are filled with accounts of Indian outrages. He urged a new and strong policy, saying that unless the Indians could be subdued and brought under control within the next twelve months, it would not be possible to do it for many years.

For the peaceful Pueblo he had great respect and recommended that their twenty or more villages be divided into six or seven districts and that an agent be placed in each. He urged that they be given firearms, powder, and lead, so that they could defend themselves and supplement the United States forces when needed. He suggested that blacksmiths be sent to them, and that fifteen or twenty of the Pueblo chiefs be brought to Washington for a visit, in order that they might gain some conception of American strength. Later he urged that a subagent be located at every pueblo.[12]

10 Calhoun to Brown, November 7, 1849, *ibid.*, 73–74.
11 9 *Stats.* 974. Also, Abel (ed.), *op. cit.*, 21–25.
12 Abel (ed.), *op. cit.*, 37–41.

Calhoun met the Utes at Abiquiu on December 30, 1849, and signed a treaty with them. When they showed a reluctance to sign, expressing "their *utter aversion to labor*" and asking how they were to sustain life, Calhoun promised that the government would take care of them.[13]

New Mexico became a territory of the United States by an act of Congress approved September 9, 1850.[14] It included Arizona, which was not given a separate status until 1863.[15] January 7, 1851, the Senate confirmed the President's appointment of Calhoun as governor of New Mexico, and he was inaugurated at Santa Fé on March 3.[16] His appointment as territorial governor made him ex officio superintendent of Indian affairs. Congress recognized the need for more Indian agents and on February 27, 1851, appointed four agents for the new territory, at an annual salary of $1,500 each.[17]

Colonel E. V. Sumner, commander of the Ninth Military Department, led an expedition into the Navajo country in 1851; but he accomplished little except the establishment of Fort Defiance. Depredations were continued, and at last a company of volunteers composed of citizens of Santa Fé was formed, with the avowed intention of waging war on the Navajo. They asked Calhoun to procure arms for them from Colonel Sumner, and the latter agreed to furnish seventy-five flintlock muskets on condition that they be returned immediately upon the demand of the commander of the district and not be used for any raid on Indian country unless by consent of the regular army. The volunteers refused to accept the arms on these terms, and Calhoun and Sumner engaged in a bitter controversy over the question of sending volunteer companies to attack the Navajo. Calhoun believed that the "best defense is attack," but Sumner protested against private expeditions on the grounds that they interfered with his own duties and violated orders of the War Department.[18]

In May, 1852, Calhoun departed for the States and late in June he died.[19]

---

[13] 9 *Stats.*, 984. Abel (ed.), *op. cit.*, 97.

[14] 9 *Stats.*, 446–52.

[15] 12 *Stats.*, 664.

[16] Abel (ed.), *op. cit.*, 296.

[17] 9 *Stats.*, 587. This act also extended the Indian Intercourse laws over New Mexico and Utah. The agents, Richard H. Wrightman, A. R. Wooley, John Greiner, and Edward H. Wingfield, reached Santa Fé in July, 1851.

[18] Abel (ed.), *op. cit.*, 445–56.

[19] *Ibid.*, 535–42, for documents relative to Calhoun's departure from New Mexico.

Colonel Sumner took over the duties of chief executive of New Mexico, but John Greiner remained acting superintendent of Indian affairs during the summer and early autumn of 1852, in spite of conflicts with Sumner over authority. July 1, 1852, Sumner and Greiner made a treaty with the Mescalero Apache, who agreed to refrain from raids in Mexico. But Mangas Coloradas, the chief of the Gila Apache who met the officials of the government at Ácoma, refused to agree to such a treaty, asserting that his own people were attacked by Mexicans and that they must have the privilege of protecting themselves.[20] Nevertheless, the Apache and nearly all other Indians of New Mexico remained reasonably quiet until the latter part of 1853.

Greiner was succeeded as superintendent of Indian affairs by William Carr Lane, the newly-appointed governor of New Mexico, who reached Santa Fé in September, 1852. An idealist, almost a visionary, Lane issued rules and regulations to his subordinates that made good reading but were impracticable. He wished to remove the Indians from the area east of the Río Grande and south of the Arkansas to the territory west of the Río Grande, declaring that all the Utahs and more than half of the Jicarilla Apache were already west of that stream and that the others should be forced to join them. His plan was to put them in permanent camps and teach them farming. This plan was not approved by the Indian Office, however, possibly because Congress had in 1853 granted only $10,000 for the general expenses of Indian administration in New Mexico,[21] a sum wholly inadequate for any such scheme.

Lane was succeeded as governor of New Mexico by David Meriwether, who took the oath of office in May, 1853, and reached Santa Fé on August 8.[22] Soon after his arrival, the Mescalero Apache again became troublesome. Meriwether declared that the Indians would either have to be fed and clothed by the federal government or chastised in thoroughgoing fashion. He complained that his predecessor's expenditures had caused the Indians to expect continued assistance, but that the amount of money remaining made this impossible.[23] While Meriwether was absent from the territory in March, 1854, the starving Jicarilla and Mescalero Apache began an uprising which lasted, in more or less serious degree, until the summer of 1855. Meriwether hastened back to his post and sought to try a policy of force.

[20] Hoopes, *op. cit.*, 168.
[21] 10 *Stats.*, 226.
[22] Hoopes, *op. cit.*, 171.
[23] *Ibid.*, 172.

After a destructive war, the Indians were at last brought under temporary control.

The need for action being once again brought to the attention of Congress, it granted $30,000 in 1854 for making treaties with the Apache, Ute, and Navajo, and $25,000 for general expenses of the Indian service in New Mexico.[24] Meriwether was given authority to negotiate treaties, and, during the summer of 1855, he signed treaties with a number of tribes, none of which was ever ratified by the Senate.[25]

The Indian Appropriation acts of 1856 and 1857 indicated the desirability of establishing reservations in New Mexico. More important, perhaps, the latter act provided for the separation of the offices of governor and superintendent of Indian affairs in New Mexico.[26] James L. Collins was named superintendent of Indian affairs, and in January, 1858, he outlined to the Commissioner his plans for concentrating the Indians upon reservations. He proposed to place the Utes on the San Juan River and all the Apache on reservations along the Gila, thus removing both groups long distances from white settlements of any size. Military posts were to be established near the Indians to check any tendency toward an outbreak of hostilities.[27] Late in February, 1859, Congress authorized the creation of a reserve for the Pima and Maricopa on or near the Gila River,[28] the first Indian reservation in the New Mexico–Arizona area. Another was approved by the Indian Office in May, 1860, for the Apache, but this was later returned to the public domain. Before this reservation was authorized, however, the temporary peace which had been established by the treaties made in the summer of 1855 had been rudely shattered by the outbreak of war.

The Navajo war was precipitated on July 12, 1858, when a young Indian killed a Negro slave owned by Major Brooks, post commander at Fort Defiance. Hostilities began when Brooks' demand for the surrender of the murderer was refused. Early in September Colonel D. S. Miles invaded the Navajo country with a force of over 300 men. Little was accomplished, and a second expedition, under the command of Major Electus Backus, was sent out. This incursion again gained little except the destruction of the Indians' crops and sheep or

24 10 *Stats.*, 330.
25 Hoopes, *op. cit.*, 175.
26 11 *Stats.*, 185.
27 Hoopes, *op. cit.*, 176–77.
28 11 *Stats.*, 401. This was the first permanent reservation created in the Southwest. It is still occupied by these tribes (in 1949).

other livestock. The purpose, theoretically, was to teach the Navajo a lesson; but the destruction of their means of subsistence made raids on their part absolutely necessary if they were not to starve. Although peace was made by Superintendent Collins and Colonel Bonneville at Fort Defiance on December 25, 1858,[29] it was of short duration. Faced by starvation, the Navajo began to raid settlements again and became increasingly active with the coming of spring and summer. Colonel Fauntleroy, who succeeded Bonneville as department commander in October, 1859, called in the military expedition which was out against the Indians. He did not believe in war to force the Navajo to keep the treaty, but Superintendent Collins did not concur in this policy.[30] Fauntleroy also opposed independent companies' taking the field against the Indians and refused to sanction them or furnish arms and ammunition.

At last the Secretary of War ordered that an expedition be sent out, and Fauntleroy sent Lieutenant Colonel E. R. S. Canby to invade the Navajo country in the winter of 1860–61. Private expeditions were also out that winter, including one under Miguel E. Pierro, while Albert H. Pfeiffer, subagent at Abiquiu, led a party of Mexicans and Utes into the Navajo country and seized livestock and prisoners. In 1861 an armistice was made.[31] It is possible that the outbreak of war between the states may have been an influence in patching up a temporary peace with the Navajo.

The conflict between North and South had other important effects upon Indian affairs in New Mexico. General Henry H. Sibley, of the Confederate Army, invaded New Mexico with a force of Texans and seized Albuquerque, and eventually the Confederates gained possession of the southern portion of the present state and the greater part of Arizona. The Apache promptly began to raid the mining camps and the settlements along the rivers. In most cases the settlers fled, abandoning their homes and crops, while mining operations also came to a standstill. The Navajo were also causing trouble again.[32]

The people of Arizona became very much alarmed, the press asserting that "nineteen-twentieths of the entire territory of Arizona is under the undisputed control of the Apache."[33] Since it was

29 See Frank D. Reeve, "Federal Indian Policy in New Mexico," *New Mexico Historical Review*, Vol. XII, No. 3 (July, 1937).
30 *Ibid.*, 238–39.   31 *Ibid.*, 244.
32 *Annual Report of Commissioner of Indian Affairs, 1861*, 122–27.
33 *Mesilla Times*, October 3, 1861. Quoted in *Annual Report of Commissioner of Indian Affairs, 1861*, 123.

necessary to expel the Confederates in order to regain control of the Indians, General Canby, with a small army of regulars and New Mexico volunteers, began this task. He defeated Sibley's force in two or three minor engagements. When troops from California, under the command of General James H. Carleton, marched into Arizona, the Texans were driven from the territory and the Gila Apache brought under control.

On September 18, 1862, Carleton succeeded Canby as commander of the Department of New Mexico. With the aid of Colonel Kit Carson the Mescalero were subdued by January 1, 1863, and the entire tribe was subsequently removed to a reservation lying near Fort Sumner on the Pecos River known as Bosque Redondo.[34]

During the autumn of 1862, while Carleton was busy with the Mescalero, the governor and many people of New Mexico were much concerned about the Navajo. H. S. Johnson requested Acting Governor Arny to authorize the invasion of the Navajo country by Juan Padilla with a force of two hundred men who would furnish their own arms, ammunition, and subsistence, and receive their compensation from any spoils they might take from the Indians. The governor refused, declaring that private expeditions did not discriminate between friendly and unfriendly Indians. He also said that the military and Superintendent Collins had under their protection some fifteen hundred friendly Navajo and that measures were now being adopted to reach and punish the unfriendly ones.[35]

In the spring of 1863, Carleton built Fort Wingate. The Navajo were told that Bosque Redondo was to be their permanent home, and those who refused to go willingly would be conquered and forced to go.[36] By the late summer of 1863, the war was well under way. Kit Carson started in August to invade the Navajo country with an expedition composed mostly of New Mexico volunteers.[37] General Carleton's orders to Carson were specific. He was to push the campaign vigorously and kill all Navajo men who were hostile. Prisoners were to be sent to Bosque Redondo. Prize money of twenty dollars for each horse or

[34] Reeve, "Federal Indian Policy in New Mexico," *New Mexico Historical Review*, Vol. XII, No. 3 (July, 1937), 248–49.

[35] *Annual Report of Commissioner of Indian Affairs, 1862*, 251–52.

[36] Reeve, "Federal Indian Policy in New Mexico," *New Mexico Historical Review*, Vol. XII, No. 2 (July, 1937), 248–49.

[37] MS. "Kit Carson's Expedition Against the Navajo." This manuscript written by an officer of Company B, First New Mexico Volunteers, is a valuable contemporary record although the officer does not give his name. The document is in the manuscript collections of the Huntington Library.

mule and one dollar for every sheep captured was to be paid the soldiers. The Indian Office objected to this, but Carleton insisted that it would help the campaign. Captive children, even if taken by scouts, could not be sold into slavery but must be sent to Bosque Redondo.[38]

Carson, a humane man who had established Fort Canby, now notified the peaceful Navajo that they would have until July 20 to surrender and go to the new home provided for them. A few Indians went to Bosque Redondo in September, more of them in November, and the following spring some Navajo captives were sent there. By 1865 there were probably more than 8,500 Navajo on the reservation at Bosque Redondo.[39] Scouts, interviewers, and friendly emissaries from among the Indians were all used to induce the hostiles to come in and surrender. While some fled to remote refuges deep in the mountains and were able to elude the troops, the power of the Navajo nation was at last broken. Their fields and orchards had been destroyed and their livestock seized. A proud people who for two centuries had carried on intermittent warfare with the inhabitants of New Mexico were conquered and confined to a comparatively small reservation under the supervision and control of the United States Army.

Union control of Arizona had not been re-established until 1863. In that year Arizona was made a separate territory by the organic act approved February 24, 1863.[40] It was also made a separate superintendency and Charles D. Poston was named as the first superintendent. Before setting out for his post, he wrote the Commissioner of Indian Affairs giving a list of tribes that would come under his jurisdiction and estimating the total Indian population of the territory at 58,100.[41] He urged the setting aside of a reservation for the Papago which would include lands lying about the mission of San Xavier del Bac.[42] Commissioner W. P. Dole agreed that the reservation should be established, and authorized Poston to select lands for this and for other reservations on the Gila and Colorado.[43]

In New Mexico, Michael Steck, who had formerly been so successful in dealing with the Apache, replaced Collins on May 23, 1863. With the Mescalero and Navajo under control and his jurisdiction reduced to New Mexico, Steck's only concern was with the Jicarilla Apache and Mohuache Ute now under the agency at Cimarron, the

38 Reeve, "Federal Indian Policy in New Mexico," *New Mexico Historical Review*, Vol. XII, No. 3 (July, 1937), 250-51.
39 *Ibid.*, 255.
40 12 Stats., 664-65.
41 *Annual Report of Commissioner of Indian Affairs, 1863*, 383-90.
42 *Ibid.*   43 *Ibid.*, 390-91.

Capote Ute at Abiquiu Agency, the Gila Apache at Mesilla, and, of course, the peaceful Pueblo.[44] Of these tribes only the bands of Apache along the Gila were troublesome.

Changes in officials followed one another with bewildering rapidity. Felipe Delgado followed Steck, but Delgado resigned in 1866 and A. B. Norton became superintendent. In Arizona, George W. Leihy was made superintendent, but was replaced late in 1866 by G. W. Dent, brother-in-law of General U. S. Grant. Dent reached his post on December 19, 1866, to discover that Leihy and his clerk, had been killed by Apache. Additional troops had been placed in the field but the Apache were elusive, and Dent asserted that unless an aggressive campaign with overwhelming forces was carried on persistently the Apache war would be interminable.[45] The Pima and Maricopa were living peacefully upon their reservation, but the Papago had not as yet been placed upon a reservation. One had been selected on the Colorado River, however, for the tribes dwelling along that stream, and the superintendent for Arizona had high hopes of assembling all the Colorado River tribes on this reservation.

Although most of the Navajo had by 1866 been brought to Bosque Redondo, the Navajo problem was by no means ended. Bosque Redondo was a reserve forty miles square with Fort Sumner near its center. It had been established by an executive order of the President issued on January 15, 1864. The Mescalero sent there were given lands to cultivate, but when more and more Navajo were brought in captive, the Mescalero were forced to surrender these lands to the Navajo and accept others on a different part of the reservation. The site they got was dry, with little fertile land, insufficient wood, and bad water. When Michael Steck became superintendent of Indian affairs in New Mexico, he refused to send an agent to Bosque Redondo, despite the request of the military. Steck said that the Indians were prisoners of war, and therefore the military must care for them. He himself had no funds for that purpose. He also objected to the site of the reservation and thought the Navajo should be placed on a reserve located somewhere along the Little Colorado River.[46] On November 3, 1865, the Mescalero left the reservation in a body and returned to their old haunts, where they began depredations once more. Superintendent Norton recommended that a new reservation

---

[44] *Ibid.*, 116. When Kit Carson at Taos resigned as Indian agent, the agency was removed to Cimarron and W. F. Arny became agent.

[45] *Annual Report of Commissioner of Indian Affairs, 1867*, 155–56.

[46] Reeve, "Federal Indian Policy in New Mexico," *New Mexico Historical Review*, Vol. XII, No. 3 (July, 1937), 256–57.

be established for them and a military post erected on or near it to keep them in order.[47]

Since the superintendent of Indian affairs had disclaimed responsibility for the Navajo, their administration remained exclusively with the post commander at Fort Sumner. An irrigation ditch was constructed and some 3,800 acres of land placed under cultivation. Of this area, 2,800 acres were included in a government farm, while the remaining thousand acres were farmed in small tracts by the Navajo themselves. The labor was done by Indians under the direction of soldiers who, in many cases, knew little of farming. The results were disappointing. In 1865 the total production of foodstuff, mostly corn but with some wheat, beans, and pumpkins, was around half a million pounds, which is a pitifully poor return for the acreage planted. The yield supplied only a small fraction of the food required by the seven thousand to nine thousand people on the reservation. The remainder must be furnished by the War Department. From January 11, 1865, to December 5, 1865, the total cost of subsistence for the Navajo was $748,308.87.[48] More surprising, in view of the fact that the Navajo had such large herds of sheep in their old homeland, the number of their sheep at Bosque Redondo was estimated as 1,100, which, with about the same number of horses and mules and 450 goats, constituted their entire holdings of livestock.[49] In addition to subsistence, blankets and clothing were issued to the Navajo, making the entire cost of maintaining them upon the reservation approximately $1,500,000 annually, if the expense of laborers and of the necessary military establishment were added to that of feeding and clothing them.[50] Eventually bitter criticism of Bosque Redondo began to be heard and the question of keeping the Navajo there permanently became an issue in New Mexico politics, resulting in the formation of Bosque and anti-Bosque political factions.[51]

The New Mexico situation seemed so deeply involved that J. K. Graves was appointed September 12, 1865, a special agent to visit that territory and make a complete report on conditions, together with recommendations concerning the future policy of the Indian Office with respect to this region. His report, made in 1866 after long and detailed study, had considerable influence upon the policies of the Office of Indian Affairs.[52]

47 *Annual Report of Commissioner of Indian Affairs, 1866,* 145.
48 *Ibid., 1866,* 149–50.   49 *Ibid.*
50 *Ibid.,* 146.   51 *Ibid.,* 130–31.
52 A large part of Graves report may be found in *ibid.,* 131–42.

Graves estimated that the number of Indians in New Mexico was slightly fewer than 20,000 and that there had been approximately twice that many in 1846. He praised the work of General Carleton and urged that the Navajo be kept permanently at Bosque Redondo. Pasturage there, he declared, was abundant and there were plenty of mesquite roots for fuel at present, moreover young cottonwood trees which had been planted and were growing rapidly would eventually supply fire wood. Other wood was available at a distance of twenty-five miles and could be floated down the river. Water, he naïvely asserted, was "good though somewhat brackish." He admitted that the cost of maintaining the Indians there had been great in the past, but he believed that in the future it could be done for $675,000 annually.

Further recommendations were that the Utes of New Mexico be concentrated on the reservation in Colorado, which had been given the Tabeguache band of that tribe in 1863.[53] It was also recommended that all the Apache be placed on a large reservation on the Gila River. The New Mexico legislature reported that since 1846 some 123 citizens had been killed, a number wounded or taken captive, and property, mostly livestock, to the value of $1,377,329.60 had been lost by Indian depredations.[54] According to Graves, no compensation had been made by the United States, but he urged that all claims be carefully audited before they were paid. Liberal appropriations for the Indian Service in New Mexico were recommended. Money thus granted, he pointed out, might be spent wisely by purchasing sheep for the Navajo and permitting them to weave blankets instead of purchasing them in the East.[55]

Graves insisted that the government do everything possible to stop the enslavement, or peonage, of Indians. Territorial law sanctioned volunteer expeditions against the Indians, and participants kept plunder and also kept captives as slaves. The latter were worth from $75 to $400 each.[56] Finally, Graves asked that appropriations be

[53] 13 Stats., 673.

[54] For this memorial of the New Mexico legislature addressed to Congress, see Annual Report of Commissioner of Indian Affairs, 1866, 152–53.

[55] Gross extravagance and inefficiency characterized the maintenance of the Navajo at Bosque Redondo, and it is difficult to believe that there was not graft and corruption as well. Blankets were purchased at twenty-one dollars a pair when better ones were bought for the army at a little over one-third that price. Food prices were high also. The amount of money expended should have provided generously for these Indians, but they were apparently nearly always hungry and badly clothed.

[56] The use of slave, or peon, labor was almost universal in New Mexico and had been for generations. Graves asserted that there were 400 such slaves in Santa

made to help the peaceful Pueblo by providing them with schools as well as mills, farming implements, fruit trees, and seeds for planting.

Despite Steck's refusal to accept any responsibility for the Navajo at Bosque Redondo, the Office of Indian Affairs had no intention of leaving this tribe permanently under the sole jurisdiction of the military. The Appropriation Act of March 3, 1865, granted $100,000 to the Indian Bureau for use in caring for the Navajo and when Special Agent Graves reached New Mexico, he purchased a considerable supply of goods for their use. Theodore H. Dodd was appointed agent for them and reached the reservation June 28, 1866, with 160 head of cattle and 17 large wagons loaded with goods and farming implements for the Navajo. He reported 6,915 Indians on the reservation although a year earlier there had been 8,491. This decrease during the year Dodd could account for only by deaths or desertions. He asked that the tribe be furnished with sheep and that ten good practical farmers and an assistant for each be employed to teach the Indians to farm.[57]

No doubt the War Department was eager to be rid of the responsibility of the Navajo, but not until November 1, 1867, was the transfer actually made to Agent Dodd by Major Charles J. Whiting. Superintendent A. B. Norton assumed this new responsibility reluctantly, for appropriations made for the care of the large number of Indians were meager. In spite of the request for $600,000 for the Navajo made by the Department of the Interior, the Indian Appropriation Act of March 3, 1867, granted only $100,000 for subsistence, sheep, seeds, and breaking ground, and an additional $100,000 for their relief, with the proviso that no rations or supplies were to be furnished by the Department of War after July 1, 1867, except in case of great need.[58] From January 1 to July 31, 1866, the military had expended $407,669.04 for sustaining the Navajo at Bosque Redondo; yet the Department of the Interior was expected to maintain them for an entire year for less than half that sum!

As a matter of fact, by 1867 it had become apparent to most people familiar with Indian affairs in New Mexico that the "noble experiment" of General Carleton's at Bosque Redondo was a tragic mistake. Contrary to Graves's report, there was little wood, the land

Fé alone and that nearly every federal official, including the superintendent of Indian affairs, held persons in service. The number in the whole of New Mexico was estimated at 2,000. Peonage was abolished by the act of Congress of March 2, 1867 (14 *Stats.*, 546).

[57] *Annual Report of Commissioner of Indian Affairs, 1866*, 148–50.
[58] 14 *Stats.*, 514.

was poor, the water bad, and the Comanche Indians were near enough the reservation to make frequent attacks on the nearly helpless Navajo. Superintendent Norton earnestly urged that the reservation be given up and the Indians be allowed to remove to new lands where they would have wood, water, and fertile soil for crop growing. Many other government officials, including members of Congress, urged the abandonment of the experiment, which it was asserted had already cost the Government $10,000,000.[59]

The appointment in 1867 of the Peace Commission referred to in the preceding chapter was of great importance to the administration of Indian affairs in New Mexico.[60] This commission met August 13 at Fort Leavenworth and held councils with the Plains tribes at Medicine Lodge and Fort Laramie. It bitterly criticised many things in the administration of Indian affairs, particularly the activities of volunteer expeditions and state troops against the Indians. It declared the Chivington massacre at Sand Creek, Colorado, had been responsible for an Indian war costing the federal government thirty million dollars and many lives.[61] It recommended a complete revision of intercourse laws with Indian tribes and asked Congress to enact a law fixing a date not later than February 1, 1869, at which time the positions of all agents and special agents should be vacated. The Indian Bureau could then reappoint men who had proved themselves worthy and replace others with abler and more competent officials.

The commission asserted that the Indian Service should be under civil rather than military authority, but recommended that the Indian Bureau be made an independent department with its head either a member of the Cabinet or an independent bureau chief. It further declared that making territorial governors ex officio superintendents of Indian affairs was a bad practice and urged that no governor or legislature of a state or territory be permitted to call out troops to wage war against the Indians. It asked for stringent regulations governing the Indian trade and traders and for new provisions directing the military to remove intruders from Indian lands. Two great Indian territories were recommended, one in the south and the other in the north. Finally, it asked that a treaty be made with the Navajo removing them from Bosque Redondo and that, with their consent, they be placed in the southern territory suggested.[62]

[59] *Annual Report of Commissioner of Indian Affairs, 1867,* 190.
[60] See 15 *Stats.,* 17, for act establishing this commission.
[61] 40 Cong., 2 sess., *House Ex. Doc. 97,* 8–9.
[62] *Ibid.,* 1–22.

The commission, having made treaties with the Plains tribes, was very eager to negotiate similar ones with the Indians of New Mexico. Accordingly, representatives of the Ute bands were brought to Washington and a treaty negotiated with them on March 2, 1868. This was signed by N. G. Taylor, commissioner of Indian affairs, A. C. Hunt, and Kit Carson for the United States, and by ten chiefs of various Ute bands. It provided that these bands should join the Tabeguache Ute on their reservation, the boundaries of which were extended and defined. Inducements were offered to individual Indians to choose lands and begin farming, and provisions were made for schools and for the civilization of the Indians. Farmers, blacksmiths, carpenters, and millers were to be furnished the Indians, and a sum not to exceed $60,000 annually for thirty years was to be appropriated to supply their actual needs for food, clothing, blankets, and other goods.[63]

General W. T. Sherman and Colonel S. F. Tappan were the members of the commission designated to go to New Mexico and negotiate a treaty with the Navajo. Tappan, after some days at Fort Sumner, declared bitterly that keeping the Navajo at Bosque Redondo was a crime, an opinion undoubtedly shared by Superintendent Norton and Agent Dodd. Accordingly on June 1, 1868, a treaty was signed by the two commissioners and the Navajo leaders. It provided the Navajo with a large reservation in their old home lands. The Indians agreed to give up all territory outside the limits of the reservation but were permitted to hunt upon contiguous lands as long as large game was to be found there. The federal government was to establish an agency on their lands. A school and chapel, and blacksmith and carpenter shops were also to be erected near the agency. A school was to be provided for every group of thirty children, and the Indians agreed to send children between the ages of six and sixteen to school. Implements and seeds were to be given to every head of a family who selected 160 acres of land as a home and began farming. $150,000 was appropriated to remove the Indians to the reservation. Fifteen thousand sheep and goats were to be purchased for them at a cost of not over $30,000. For their subsistence the first year, 500 beef cattle and one million pounds of corn were to be purchased, and the remainder of the $150,000, if any were left, was to be used for the benefit of the Indians in the manner their agent thought best. The United States government was pledged to deliver to the agency each year for ten years goods not to exceed $5.00 in value for every Indian.[64]

[63] 15 *Stats.*, 619–22.
[64] 15 *Stats.*, 667–71.

The Navajo were eager to see the last of Bosque Redondo and to be back once more among the mesas and canyons they loved. They had been brought to Bosque Redondo by the military; now they were to return home in charge of the military, for Major Whiting had been placed in charge of removal. They had come reluctantly, prisoners of war; but they returned gladly, with a great sense of freedom. The start was made on July 1, just thirty days after the treaty was signed. In a procession ten miles long, they moved westward to Albuquerque by way of San Jose and the Tijeras Canyon, and seven days later had crossed the Río Grande. At last they reached New Fort Wingate on July 22, twenty-two days after leaving Fort Sumner.[65] Here Agent Dodd took charge of them, and they soon began to spread out over the hills and mesas of their native land. The agency was placed at Fort Defiance and Dodd remained their agent until his death on July 16, 1869.[66]

Although the treaty of 1868 was better than most Indian treaties, some of its provisions were based upon assumptions that were fundamentally unsound. One of these was that the Navajo might choose allotments and speedily become farmers. Both the nature of the Indians and of the lands they occupied made this highly improbable if not impossible. It was also assumed that the Navajo would become selfsupporting within a year, and in consequence no provision was made for their subsistence after the expiration of that period of time. This was far too much to expect of a people that had been held for four years as prisoners and subsisted by the federal government, especially in view of the fact that their livestock, orchards, and hogans had been destroyed and their fields had been left untilled for years. Crop failures and the slowness of the federal government in providing aid brought them close to starvation at times during the next few years, but the Navajo had learned their lesson well and there were few depredations upon the whites. The menace which for nearly two centuries had so disturbed the peaceful Pueblo and the settlers of New Mexico was gone forever.

There continued to be some trouble with the Jicarilla and Ute, as well as with the Mescalero Apache, after the latter had abandoned Bosque Redondo. The greatest difficulty, however, was in Arizona, where the Apache continued in 1867 to 1868 a reign of terror. The small military garrisons were too weak to do more than chase the

[65] Reeve, "Federal Indian Policy in New Mexico," *New Mexico Historical Review*, Vol. XIII, No. 1 (January, 1938).
[66] *Ibid.*

marauding bands about from place to place, a game in which the Indians had every advantage. It was not until later, with the appearance of the greatest of all Indian fighters, General George F. Crook, that the Apache were humbled and brought under control through a series of bloody and strenuous campaigns.

When General U. S. Grant became president of the United States, a new era in the relations of the government with the Indians was begun. A change of policy affected Indian affairs in New Mexico and Arizona as much as in other parts of the country. The period of pioneering was over. The federal government had at last definite objectives concerning the future of these Indian peoples for whom it was responsible. Peace with all tribes was not to be attained for nearly two decades. Some things had been learned, but many perplexing problems remained to be solved.

The federal officials administering Indian affairs in New Mexico and Arizona from 1849 to 1869 had been far abler than federal officials in California, with the result that a more successful administration prevailed for the Indians in the former states. Except for Edward F. Beale, it is doubtful if California had a single man who could compare with Calhoun or some of his successors. By far the most conspicuous failure in the administration of Indian affairs in New Mexico was the tragic experiment at Bosque Redondo, which was most costly both in money and in human values. For this, however, the military rather than the civil government must bear a large share of responsibility.

The reservation system had been definitely established, and three reservations—the Pima, Colorado, and Navajo—had been set aside and were in more or less successful operation.[67] In addition, there were the small reservations containing some twenty villages of the Pueblo Indians whose lands, granted them by Spain, had been confirmed by Mexico, and the Ute reservation in Colorado occupied by Indians formerly in New Mexico.

67 The Colorado River Reservation had been formally established by an act of Congress approved March 3, 1865 (13 *Stats.*, 559).

V

Federal Indian Administration in Utah and Nevada, 1848–68

In the Utah-Nevada area the bitter feeling between the Mormon and non-Mormon elements in the white population seriously interfered with Indian administration. But there were other factors which made the work of the Indian Service officials in this area especially difficult. Not the least of these was the character of the land itself. While vision and diligent labor had made some areas in the Great Basin veritable gardens of beauty, the region was, one the whole, an inhospitable land of barren deserts with few resources in either plant or animal life. There was game in abundance in the mountains, and to the east and northeast on the plains were buffalo herds, a potential source of food, clothing, and shelter for the Plains Indians.

Apparently none of the tribes of Utah and Nevada hunted the buffalo except the Shoshone, in the northeastern part of Utah, and the Utes. Back in the deserts were the Washo and other tribes, miserable wanderers, undernourished, eating, as Agent James S. Calhoun said, "anything which runs, flies, creeps, or crawls," as poor and low in the scale of civilization as any people on the North American continent. These less aggressive Indians were driven into the inhospitable deserts of the Great Basin by wilder and fiercer tribes, and once there, the scanty resources caused them to degenerate still further. The Ute, however, a tall, well-formed race, were warriors who traded with the Navajo and who sometimes attacked white settlements. One band, the Mohuache, lived with the Jicarilla Apache, with whom they intermarried. Their history belongs more nearly to that of the Indians of New Mexico.

Before the Mormon migration, the Indians of this area were visited by the trappers and mountain men under such leaders as William H. Ashley, Jedediah Smith, and James Bridger, who had been accustomed to hold an annual rendezvous near Great Salt Lake.

In 1843 Bridger built the fort which carries his name, in the southwest corner of Wyoming, near the boundary of the present state of Utah. Some trade was carried on with the Shoshone and some of the Utes, in spite of the fact that the two tribes were often at war, but the Washo and other desert dwellers never had anything of importance to trade.

When the Mormons moved from Illinois to Utah in 1847, they won the friendship of the Indians there for a while by their kindly overtures,[1] but when other immigrants came, settling on the best land and killing the game, the Indians grew suspicious.

On April 7, 1849, John Wilson was appointed Indian agent "at Salt Lake, California," at the regular salary of $1,500.[2] Arriving there in the late summer, he reported on August 22, that the Mormons had greatly reduced the supply of fish in that region and that the rush for California had driven away most of the game.[3] Since the resources of the land under normal conditions were barely sufficient to supply the absolute needs of the Indians, it seemed certain that anything which served to reduce these resources was sure to bring real want if not starvation. On September 4, Wilson wrote again, making definite proposals about his charges. He said that it was the duty of the government to extinguish by treaty the claim of the Indians to the Salt Lake Valley and to negotiate for a highway to this valley. He also recommended the establishment of a military post at Fort Bridger, anticipating the emigration to California and Oregon which would pass that place. He urged that in return the northern section of Utah be set aside for the Indians. This region, he pointed out, was not suitable for white settlement but was well adapted for Indians! He thought the Indians should be taught farming in order to tie them "to a local spot" and thus assist in their civilization.[4]

Wilson's plans (never put into operation) are typical of the paradoxical attitude long held by so many Indian agents, congressmen, and citizens. They insisted that the Indian must be civilized according to the white man's ways, but they were constantly trying to push him to some spot remote from white settlement. They declared that the Indian's future lay in agriculture, but the reservations allotted him were lands so exceedingly arid that farming was impossible. Most people seemed to believe that Indians *preferred* to live in the

1 Brigham Young was always generous in his dealings with Indians and earnestly urged that they be well treated at all times.
2 31 Cong., 1 sess., *House Ex. Doc. 17*, Vol. V, 182–84.
3 *Ibid.*, 184–87.
4 *Ibid.*, 104–12. Quoted in Hoopes, *op. cit.*, 132–33.

most unfruitful and desolate regions of the country, although the greater part of the native population was found originally in the river valleys or in other productive areas.[5]

Wilson did not remain long in charge of the Indians of this area. On December 30, 1849, James S. Calhoun made the first treaty between the United States and the Utes. The Utes acknowledged themselves to be under the jurisdiction of the United States and promised to remain at peace and to deliver all captives and stolen property to an authorized official of the federal government. They further agreed to permit the free passage of whites through their country. The federal government promised to designate and adjust the boundaries of Ute lands, to establish military posts and agencies, and to give to the Indians presents and implements. The treaty was ratified by the Senate, and an appropriation of $18,000 was made by Congress for carrying out its provisions.[6]

Utah was governed by officials of the Mormon Church until September 9, 1850, when the Organic Act creating the Territory of Utah was approved.[7] This act provided that the governor should be ex officio superintendent of Indian affairs and, as compensation for the additional work, he would have $1,000 annually added to his salary. This policy had many objectionable features. The duties of two such offices would be very heavy for one man, and those qualities desirable for a governor were not always the ones most necessary for an administrator of Indian affairs. Brigham Young, the first territorial governor, apparently took his responsibility for the Indians very seriously, and his administration of their affairs was carried on honestly and efficiently.[8]

No Indian agent was provided for the new territory, which included the present states of Utah and Nevada, until February 27, 1851. The act approved on that date extended the intercourse laws of the United States over both that territory and New Mexico.[9] Jacob H. Holeman was appointed agent and Henry R. Day and Stephen B. Rose, a Mormon, were made subagents.

Young divided the territory into three districts, the Pauvan,

---

[5] The late Will Rogers once said that Indian treaties always guaranteed them their lands "so long as grass grows and water flows" but that the lands so granted were of a type upon which grass refused to grow and water did not ever flow.

[6] 9 *Stats.*, 572.

[7] 9 *Stats.*, 453–58.

[8] 37 Cong., 2 sess., *House Ex. Doc. 29,* for report on an examination of the accounts of Brigham Young.

[9] 9 *Stats.*, 587.

Uintah, and Parowan, and assigned them to Day, Rose, and Holeman in the order named.[10]

Holeman, together with some of his Shoshone Indians, attended a great council held at Fort Laramie in September, 1851, hoping, no doubt, to share in the council and perhaps effect a treaty. They were treated courteously and given presents, but they were not invited to take part in negotiations and no treaty was made with them.[11] The Utes, who were almost constantly at war with the Shoshone, had refused to go to the council. Day finally effected an agreement with them to remain peaceful, in October, 1851.[12]

Holeman and Day, the non-Mormon agents, were as suspicious of Brigham Young and his people as the Indians were. After Day left for Washington on September 28, 1851, resigning his post the following February,[13] Holeman complained in a letter to the Commissioner of Indian Affairs that Young and Rose were concealing their movements from him, and were not consulting with him concerning Indian affairs, and, moreover, that the Mormons were hostile to the United States Government to the point of resisting its authority when it conflicted with their church or personal ideas. Undoubtedly there was much to be said on the side of the Mormons. The memory of their tragic experiences in Missouri and Illinois was still fresh. They had suffered greatly for their religion and had fled beyond the limits of the United States hoping to gather others of their own faith about them and live in peace. Scarcely had they established their settlement when a treaty signed in an obscure little Mexican town had brought them again within the limits of a nation whose government had afforded them scant protection in the past. Nevertheless, the distrust of the Mormons and non-Mormons for each other, and their lack of co-operation was fatal to constructive work, resulting in tragedy for the native population.

When the situation for the Indians grew more acute, because of the increased number of Mormons, who always appropriated the best lands for themselves, and the rapid decrease in natural resources, Holeman pleaded without success for authority to make treaties. Governor Young gave presents of food and clothing to the Indians to the limit of his governmental appropriations, but they were still hungry and miserable. Finally, in desperation, the starving Indians began to make raids on the whites.

Holeman reported that clashes between the Indians and the Cali-

10 Hoopes, *op. cit.*, 134–35.
11 *Ibid.*, 135.   12 *Ibid.*, 137.   13 *Ibid.*, 138–39.

fornia-bound emigrants were frequent and that most of them were caused by the brutality of evil white men. A greater source of danger, however, lay in the "white Indians," renegades forced to flee from California who had joined the Utah Indians and incited them to savagery.[14] In 1853 there were serious outbreaks of war, precipitated by efforts of the Mormons to stop the traffic in captive Indian women and children who were sold by the Utes to the Navajo or to Mexican traders. Often the Indians offered to sell children to the white settlers of Utah, and if the latter refused to buy, the Indians threatened that the children would be killed or sold to the Mexicans.[15] The territorial legislature of Utah enacted a law, March 7, 1852, authorizing the enforced apprenticeship of Indian children, but only for the purpose of inducing church members to purchase those who would otherwise be sold into slavery or who had been abandoned by their parents. The trouble was aggravated when the governor sought to prevent Mexican traders from selling guns and ammunition to the Utes.

Precipitated by a minor incident, which resulted in a fight between a white settler and some Indians, war broke out with Chief Walker's band of Utes. A dozen or more white settlers were killed and some $200,000 was used in defense measures, including the building of military posts. Cold weather finally put a stop to active operations, and in the spring of 1854 Walker asked for peace, which was effected in May.[16] The Gunnison massacre occurred in the same year. It was brought about by the murder of one Indian and the wounding of two others at Meadow Creek by the frightened leader of a wagon train which was passing through the territory.[17] Late in October, friends of the murdered Indian retaliated by attacking Lieutenant J. W. Gunnison, who was engaged in surveying a route for a railroad. Gunnison and seven of his party of eight men were killed, one scout escaping.

Agent Holeman, discouraged by the conditions in Utah, had left Salt Lake City, July 1, 1853, before the period of the Walker War and the Gunnison massacre, and E. A. Bedell had taken his place

---

[14] *Ibid.,* 141.

[15] A contemporary writer has related that Chief Walker, who offered to sell a captive child to a Mormon settler dashed its brains out when the latter refused to purchase. Walker then complained bitterly of the inhumanity of these white people who preferred to see a child killed rather than to part with a little money or a few goods.

[16] Hoopes, *op. cit.,* 143.

[17] *Ibid.,* 144.

temporarily; but in August, 1854, Dr. Garland Hurt was appointed agent for Utah.

When Hurt reached Salt Lake City on February 5, 1855, he found conditions unsettled and the Indians in a very "dubious state of feeling toward the whites." Chief Walker had died on January 29, and the Indians were mourning their leader. The military commander had demanded that they surrender the murderers of Lieutenant Gunnison and his party. But no hostilities occurred, and by April Hurt reported that a general feeling of quiet prevailed in Utah.[18] He was shocked by the destitution of the Indians. Appropriations by Congress were meager: in 1854 Utah received only $10,000 for incidental expenses, including presents and subsistence for the Indians.[19] In 1855 the amount was doubled and an additional $5,000 was appropriated annually to carry out that provision of the Treaty of 1849 relative to presents for the Utes.[20]

Agent Hurt planned farms for the Indians, and established three, employing a white farmer at each to supervise the work of the Indians and to teach them agriculture. The lands selected for the farms were in the valleys of Utah, Salt Creek, and Fillmore. The Indian Office tentatively approved the plan, and Hurt made a long trip to southern Utah[21] to study the farming operations and observe the progress the Indians were making. These farms were, in effect, reservations, although never confirmed by treaties. Hurt asked, as Agent Holeman had, to be permitted to make treaties with the various tribes. On July 31, 1854, Congress had appropriated $45,000 for the making of treaties with the Indians of Utah and for making presents of goods and provisions to them, but for some reason no treaties had been made.[22] In August, 1855, Hurt made a treaty of peace with the Shoshone, the most dangerous Indians in the territory, but it was never ratified.

Hurt made another trip to southern Utah in the autumn of 1855. He located some good land for a reserve on Corn Creek, laid out a reservation of 144 square miles in Sanpete County at the confluence of Sanpete and Twelve Mile creeks, and another small reserve of 640 acres on Spanish Fork.[23]

The year 1856 was peaceful, and with his Indian farms in operation Hurt was apparently hopeful for the future. In August, Congress appropriated $45,000 for the Indian Service in Utah.[24] Never-

18 *Ibid.*, 146. 19 10 *Stats.*, 226.
20 See 10 *Stats.*, 315. 21 Hoopes, *op. cit.*, 148–49.
22 10 *Stats.*, 330. 23 Hoopes, *op. cit.*, 148–49.
24 11 *Stats.*, 79.

theless, the Indian situation in Utah was far from satisfactory. Hurt shared his predecessor's suspicion of the Mormons. He wrote the Indian Office in 1855 that the Mormons were seeking to prejudice the Indians against whites who were not of that faith. There is a great deal of evidence that the converse was also true. Certainly the California emigrants from Missouri, Arkansas, and Illinois were usually very hostile to the Mormons, and the non-Mormons who settled in Utah were almost always strongly prejudiced against the ruling class. Any persons who dealt with the Indians were almost certain to try to prejudice them against peoples of other tenets or creeds in order to enhance their own relationship as the "real friends" of the Indians.

The Mormons were probably no more aggressive in displacing the native inhabitants than other frontier Americans had been, but here the natural resentment of the displaced was aggravated by the hostility of the white minority towards the ruling class.[25]

Rumors of the growing strength of Mormonism in Utah and of the arbitrary powers exercised by Governor Brigham Young had reached Washington, and in 1857 President Buchanan decided to change all officials in that territory. The act of March 3, 1857, separated the office of territorial governor and superintendent of Indian affairs in Utah, Arizona, and New Mexico, and gave the President authority to appoint a superintendent in each of these territories.[26] Accordingly, Alfred Cumming was appointed governor of Utah to succeed Brigham Young, and Jacob Forney was made superintendent of Indian affairs in lieu of Dr. Garland Hurt. The President was fearful, however, that the opposition of Young and many of his people to any change would be so great that these new appointees might meet with forcible resistance when they sought to take over their offices. It was therefore decided to send a strong military unit to Utah to protect the new officials and, if necessary, to aid in the execution of the laws. General William S. Harney was first placed in command of the troops, but before a start was made, he was replaced by General Albert Sydney Johnston.[27]

[25] In 1927 the author was holding council with the Uintah at Fort Duchesne when an old Indian rose and made a speech in which he sought to classify all peoples with whom he had ever come in contact. The Indians, he asserted, formed the highest class and were the people he liked best. Next he considered were the whites. Third, but considerably below the whites, he said, were the Negroes, and fourth, and lowest of all, he solemnly declared, were the Mormons!

[26] 11 *Stats.*, 185.

[27] There are many accounts of this expedition. Hoopes, *op. cit.*, 156, gives a brief statement of the facts.

News of the coming of this expedition reached Utah in July and created much excitement. The first detachment had begun a westward march July 18, but the main body of troops with the new governor did not start until about the middle of September. In the meantime, there had occurred in Utah the most tragic event in the entire history of the territory—the Mountain Meadows massacre.

The tragedy at Mountain Meadows belongs to the larger story of Indian affairs in Utah. However, it may be found in many historical accounts and will, therefore, be dealt with briefly here. Certainly, it had far-reaching results and increased greatly the bitter feeling against the Mormons and their religion, a feeling which was already strong throughout the nation. A party of approximately one hundred and forty emigrants from Arkansas, commonly known as the Fancher party, passed through Salt Lake City late in July en route to California. Their conduct en route aroused the resentment of Mormons and Indians alike. Encamped at Mountain Meadows, the emigrants were attacked by Indians, and, finding themselves hard pressed, sent two of their men for help. One of the two men was killed by a group of three other white men they met. The other emigrant returned to camp and reported that the Mormons of the vicinity were in league with the Indians.

The advance of Johnston's army had created great tension among the Mormons. Already they feared another army might be sent against them from California, and, faced with the probability of such an unfavorable story reaching that state, they called a council to decide the fate of the Arkansas emigrants. John D. Lee met with the council, and its decision was that the entire party, except the young children, must be killed. The emigrants were ambushed and the decision of council carried out. Sixteen or seventeen very young children were the only survivors. The news spread rapidly over the entire country, creating intense indignation against the Mormon people, although Governor Young had sent a message, received too late, that the emigrants should be protected if it required the services of every man in the county to do it. Lee fled to Arizona, but many years later (in 1877) was captured, tried, and shot at Mountain Meadows.[28]

Agent Hurt felt that his life was in danger, and fled to the mountains, where he wandered about for twenty-seven days until the troops with the new officials arrived at Camp Scott. He then set out for Washington, and on November 30, 1857, made a report on the Indian

[28] See H. H. Bancroft, *History of Utah*, 543-71, for detailed account of Mountain Meadows massacre.

farms which he had established. His report showed that the Spanish Fork Farm, with 336 acres under cultivation, had produced 11,000 bushels of wheat and 5,500 bushels of potatoes, which together with other crops had a value of over $24,000. At Corn Creek, 145 acres were cultivated and at Twelve Mile Creek, 195 acres.[29]

The new superintendent, Jacob Forney, and Governor Cumming remained at Camp Scott under the protection of the troops until April, 1858, when they went to Salt Lake and quietly took over their offices. Apparently both had expected opposition and hostility from Brigham Young and other Mormon leaders, but they met with neither. Instead they found a welcome and excellent co-operation.[30]

Forney was enthusiastic about the success of the Indian farms which Hurt had established and commended him highly. In fact, he felt that the farms were thriving enough to justify the creation of others and, accordingly, established one for the Goshute in Deep Creek Valley, 150 miles from Salt Lake City, and another for the Humboldt Shoshone in the Ruby Valley, nearly 250 miles from the Utah capital.[31]

Forney had been superintendent only a little over a year, when he was removed in September, 1859. Nevertheless, the policy of establishing more farms was carried on by Agent Frederick Dodge, who asked that the northwest part of the Truckee River Valley including Pyramid Lake be set aside as a reserve and also that the northeast part of the Walker River Valley and Walker Lake be reserved, in both cases for the Paiute. His suggestion approved, Dodge set aside these reservations, thus establishing *de facto* the two most important Indian reservations of Nevada, although legally they were not created until some years later. The act of Congress on February 28, 1859, appropriated $45,000 for the incidental expenses of the Indian Service in Utah.[32] The sum granted for 1861 was the same, with an additional appropriation of $1,200 for surveying and mapping four farms and reservations.[33]

More than a year elapsed before a successor to Superintendent Forney was appointed. The man chosen was Benjamin Davies, who reached his station on November 11, 1860. At this time Agent Dodge was in charge of Indians in the western part of the region, and A. Humphreys, who for two years had been in charge at Spanish Fork

29 Hoopes, *op. cit.*, 156–57.   30 *Ibid.*   31 *Ibid.*
32 11 *Stats.*, 400. Pyramid Lake Reservation lies about thirty miles northeast of Reno, while Walker Reservation is some forty miles southeast of Carson City and embraces most of Walker Lake.
33 12 *Stats.*, 58.

Carson Indian School (Nevada) in 1927

Hopi cattle at Buck Pasture Corral

farm, was temporarily out of the territory. Davies asserted that the Indians were very close to starvation and had lost confidence in the government and its promises.[34] This sorry state of affairs was attributed "to the natural poverty of the country, the destruction of the wild game by the whites, and the selfish policy of the Mormon people."[35]

A more important cause of the situation in Utah was the failure of the federal government to establish a definite constructive policy and to provide sufficient funds for carrying it out. The very promising experiment of collecting the Indians on reserves and assisting them to produce a living for themselves by growing crops had been abandoned by 1860. The Indians were hungry, nearly naked, and miserable. Davies gave them food and presents, which he reported saved hundreds of lives. At first sullen and suspicious, the Indians soon gave the new superintendent their confidence. Davies estimated the total number of Indians in his jurisdiction to be twenty thousand, which he admitted was only a guess.[36]

Henry Martin soon succeeded Davies. He reached his post on August 5, 1861, and reported that the Indians were in a lamentable state of destitution. Davies had used all available funds, regardless of the purpose for which they were granted, to relieve the wants of the Indians and had ordered Agent Humphreys at Spanish Fork to sell most of the livestock and farming implements from that and other reserves in order to provide more money for the same purpose. The dams and ditches were in sore need of repair. Martin found no office equipment for himself and no records except a few bundles of old papers. He asked that the appropriations be increased to at least $65,000 for the following year. He also urged, as almost every other superintendent had, that treaties be made and the Indians be given definite reservations upon their cession of all claim to the remaining lands of the territory.[37]

Agent Humphreys resigned soon after the arrival of Superintendent Martin. In a report dated September 30, 1861, he declared that the Mormons had been permitted to take possession of all the valleys from which the Indians formerly derived their chief subsistence. Like all other non-Mormon officials, he bitterly criticized Brigham Young, questioned his loyalty to the United States, and

---

34 *Annual Report of Commissioner of Indian Affairs, 1861*, 129.
35 *Ibid.*
36 *Ibid.*, 130-34.
37 See Martin's report, *ibid.*, 134-38.

asserted that most of the farms except a newly-created one at Winter Valley were almost useless as Indian reserves because of the proximity of so many settlers, and that even the last named area was the goal of new Mormon emigration.[38]

The War between the States complicated Martin's problem and made it more difficult for him to secure adequate funds. On the other hand, the extent of his jurisdiction and the number of Indians under his supervision had been greatly reduced by the act of Congress of March 2, 1861, organizing the Territory of Nevada.[39] James W. Nye was appointed governor and ex officio superintendent of Indian affairs of the new territory. Agent Frederick Dodge had settled all accounts of the Indian Service up to March 31, 1861, and left Nevada before the arrival of Governor Nye, designating Warren Wasson as acting agent. The latter was an able man of much experience in dealing with Indians and proved invaluable to the new governor.[40] The two reservations in Nevada, Walker River and Pyramid Lake, were both occupied by this time by a large number of Indians, although the Washo, numbering some 500, and various other bands still had no fixed territory. All Indians in the area were very poor. Wasson estimated the total number at 7,500, while Governor Nye suggested that the number might be 10,000.[41] Both Nye and Wasson wished to have the reservations formally set aside for the benefit of the Indians and to furnish them with tools, implements, and seeds for planting. Wasson also urged that they be given cattle and sheep, and that schools be established. He said, too, that a number of white families were willing to adopt Indian children and recommended that this be authorized when practicable. He asked for an appropriation of $29,280 for 1862, and said if this were granted, $18,750 would be sufficient for 1863. He was certain that with an appropriation of five dollars per capita the first year and three dollars the second year, peace would be assured and that within five years the Indians of that agency could be made self-sustaining and prosperous. He said frankly that in the event of war, every Paiute warrior was capable of costing the government of the United States $5,000.[42]

Little heed was given to his recommendations, however, and Nevada received a total of only $7,500 for the Indian Service for

[38] *Annual Report of Commissioner of Indian Affairs, 1861*, 139–41.
[39] 12 *Stats.*, 209.
[40] It was at this time that Mark Twain came to Nevada to act as secretary to his brother, who was secretary of Nevada Territory.
[41] *Annual Report of Commissioner of Indian Affairs, 1861*, 110–12.
[42] *Ibid.*, 113–16.

1863.[43] For 1864 it was given $25,000, with a corresponding sum for Utah.[44]

Governor Nye was much troubled by whites seeking grazing contracts for leases on the reservations. He refused them, on the grounds that if such contracts were made, it would open the way to others, thus bringing whites on the lands set aside for Indians.[45] It was feared that the Indians might attack the stations of the Overland Mail, but the apprehension proved groundless. Officials in charge of these stations apparently sought to reduce the danger by feeding the hungry Indians, which Nye thought tended to pauperize them. The fear of such attacks eventually resulted in an order to Brigadier General George Wright to send a regiment of troops to protect these stations. This officer, faced with the difficulty of crossing the mountains with troops in winter, offered to transfer supplies at Fort Churchill to Governor Nye to feed the Indians. The offer was accepted and the supplies placed at stations of the Overland Mail Company to be distributed by its officials.[46]

In 1863 while Governor Nye was temporarily absent from Nevada, Orion Clemens, brother of Mark Twain, was acting governor and superintendent of Indian affairs. He reported all quiet among the Indians and commended Agent Jacob T. Lockhart, who was industriously seeking to improve the condition of his charges.[47] In Utah, the beginning of 1863 saw the Shoshone and Bannock committing outrages, and an expedition under the command of Brigadier General P. Edward Connor was sent against them. A bitter conflict was fought at Bear River late in January, 1863, and the Indians were badly defeated, one band being almost totally annihilated. Superintendent Doty—who had succeeded Martin in Utah—and General Connor then made peace with various bands. In the autumn, Doty and Nye were commissioned to make treaties with the Shoshone, and in the summer and autumn of 1863 three treaties were signed with the Shoshone bands in the northeast, west, and northwest. They granted annuities, partially defined boundaries, established peace, and authorized the President to set aside reservations for these Indians when it was deemed desirable.[48]

In 1864 Nevada became a state and Nye ceased to be ex officio superintendent of Indian affairs. After a lapse of more than a year,

43 12 *Stats.*, 629.   44 *Ibid.*, 791.

45 *Annual Report of Commissioner of Indian Affairs, 1861*, 215.

46 *Ibid.*, 216–17.   47 *Ibid., 1863*, 391–92.

48 See 13 *Stats.*, 663, and 18 *Stats.*, 685–90.

during which Superintendent T. T. Dwight had charge of Indian administration in the new state part of the time, H. G. Parker was appointed superintendent in Nevada, and he remained in that position until after the beginning of the Grant administration on March 4, 1869.[49]

In Utah, Doty was succeeded in 1864 by Superintendent O. H. Irish. On May 5, 1864, Congress provided that the four reservations of Spanish Fork, Corn Creek, Deep Creek, and Sanpete should be sold in eighty-acre tracts to the highest bidders and the money used for establishing the Indians on the one remaining reservation, Uintah. This was a large area, nearly eighty miles square, remote from white settlements and so surrounded by mountains that it was isolated for six or seven months of the year. It had been set aside by executive order of President Lincoln in 1861. Twenty-five thousand dollars was appropriated for expenses incident to removal of the Indians to that reserve.[50]

Superintendent Irish, equipped with the necessary authority and funds, negotiated a treaty with the Utes providing for the cession of all claims to land in Utah except Uintah. Annuities of $25,000 a year for ten years, $20,000 annually for the next twenty-year period, and $15,000 a year for thirty years were provided. In addition the Indians were to have $30,000 for the purchase of cattle and improvement of the reservation. Also the Indians were to have a mill erected on the reservation at a cost of not more than $15,000 and a vocational school was to be established and operated for at least ten years at a cost of not more than $10,000 a year.[51] The Senate, however, was unwilling to approve a treaty pledging funds for these Indians for a period of sixty years, and consequently the treaty was never ratified.[52]

In the spring of 1866, Irish was succeeded by F. H. Head, who remained superintendent until the Grant administration replaced nearly all important officials in the Indian Service in the Southwest with army officers. Head estimated the number of Indians in Utah at that time to be 21,250 which is probably far too high.[53]

The close of the Civil War had less effect upon the administration of Indian affairs in the area of the Great Basin than it did in

[49] The act of March 21, 1864, 13 *Stats.*, 32, provided statehood for Nevada.
[50] 13 *Stats.*, 63.
[51] *Annual Report of Commissioner of Indian Affairs, 1865,* 150–51.
[52] Superintendent Irish reported that he had received excellent co-operation from Brigham Young and officials of the Mormon Church and praised their attitude toward the Indians highly.
[53] *Annual Report of Commissioner of Indian Affairs, 1866,* 175–77.

many other parts of the country, because the war itself had not greatly affected the Indians of this region. On the plains and in the deserts farther south, the wild, warlike tribes had taken advantage of the removal of troops from the little frontier military posts. War with the Cheyenne, Sioux, Apache, Navajo, and several other tribes flamed, once the restraint of the cavalrymen at the army posts had been removed. However, except for Connor's war with the Shoshone and Bannock in 1863, and some minor Ute outbreaks, the period from 1861 to 1865 was fairly peaceful. To the Utes, the Navajo war was much more important than the remote Civil War. New Mexico complained bitterly that the Utes supplied the Navajo with arms and ammunition—allegedly obtained from the Mormons—and officials in Utah complained that runaway Navajo outlaws joined with lawless bands of Shoshone or Utes, especially with the troop led by the notorious Black Hawk, which for two or three years caused considerable trouble.

In 1869 Superintendent H. G. Parker reported conditions to be peaceful and prosperous in Nevada. By that time there were three reservations in the state with boundaries surveyed, none of which had been formally set aside by Congress: a timber reserve of about 20,000 acres, through which the Pacific Railway passed; Walker River Reservation, including Walker Lake; and the Truckee River Reserve, which included Pyramid Lake.[54] The Indian Agency for Nevada was located on Walker River Reserve and there was but one agent for the entire state, although there were at times so-called "local agents," especially at Pyramid Lake; and Indian Service farmers, or special officials, were appointed from time to time. Franklin Campbell was agent for most of the period from 1866 to 1869 and apparently did his work efficiently and well.

Parker's report for 1869 is unique, for he declared that the Indians were the best disposed people of Nevada, and that they had adequate food and clothing, since the silver mines and the Pacific Railway employed them at good wages. He insisted that the Indians would be better off for having an even greater population of whites in Nevada; and, even more surprisingly, he announced that the Indians of Nevada would no longer need the annual appropriation of $20,000. He urged that nothing be given the Indians and that the reservations be abandoned and whites encouraged to settle on them. He declared, too, that it was impossible to make farmers of the Indians but that they made good farm hands for whites.[55] In his report of the preceding

54 *Ibid.,* 116.   55 *Ibid., 1869,* 202–203.

year, Parker had declared that the Indians could not be taught to farm and that there was no reason to try to domesticate them or keep them on reservations. It would be better, he thought, to let them roam at their own will.[56]

It is interesting to contrast this report with reports of other superintendents or even with the first one made by Parker. It is also interesting to contrast this report with that of Special Agent R. N. Fenton of the United States Army, who was appointed in 1869 to make a study of the conditions of the Indians of Nevada. His report, made on October 14, 1869, a short time after that of Parker, stated that the Paiute were destitute, and that they lived on rabbits, lizards, snakes, seeds, and acorns. He asserted that four-fifths of them lived largely by pilfering from the whites and said they complained that nothing had been given them, which was largely true. Fenton said they wanted a reservation, and he had selected an area which he urged should be set aside for them. He also recommended that they be given food, clothing, and farming implements at the earliest possible moment.[57] One who studies these conflicting reports can more easily understand why the officials of Indian Affairs and members of Congress sometimes became hopelessly confused about the actual conditions in the Indian country and consequently issued orders or enacted legislation that at times seemed only to make a bad situation worse.[58]

In Utah, Superintendent Head's effort to get the Indians concentrated upon the Uintah Reservation met with indifferent success. The reservation was almost inaccessible and supplies could be sent to it only with great difficulty. It was therefore thought best to make it agriculturally self-sufficient. Superintendent Head sent Thomas Carter, an employee of the Indian Service, to Uintah in the spring of 1866 to begin a farm. Some months later D. W. Rhodes was appointed agent for this reservation. He remained a year and was followed by Pardon Dodds, who was succeeded by an army officer in 1869.

In 1868, Congress had granted a reservation in Wyoming to the Bannock and northeastern Shoshone.[59] A treaty was made with them at Fort Bridger, and soon thereafter they moved to this Wind River Reservation; thus the superintendent of Wyoming received under

[56] *Ibid., 1868,* 147–48.

[57] *Ibid., 1869,* 203–204.

[58] Parker's recommendations were not heeded. Pyramid Lake and Walker River reservations had been surveyed in 1864–65 and were formally set aside by executive order in March, 1874.

[59] 15 *Stats.,* 673.

his jurisdiction one of the most troublesome groups of Indians Utah had had. In 1868, by authority of the Ute treaty made previously, several bands of Utes were also transferred to a reservation in Colorado, known as "Consolidated Ute."

When Brevet Colonel J. E. Tourtelotte succeeded F. H. Head to the superintendency of Indian affairs of Utah in the summer of 1869, the Indian Office could point to no great accomplishment during the first twenty years of its administration of Indian affairs in that territory and Nevada. Uintah, the only reservation in Utah, was occupied by only a small number of Indians. The three reservations of Nevada were yet only *de facto* reservations; the timber reserve was later abandoned, and Pyramid Lake and Walker River were not formally established by order of the President until 1874. There was no school or mission station within the limits of the superintendency, and the Indians in both, despite Superintendent Parker's rosy picture of conditions in Nevada, were undoubtedly very poor, and in many cases absolutely destitute. Large sums of money had been spent, but the results in advancing the Indian either in civilization or economic welfare had been surprisingly small. While there was apparently better co-operation between the army and the officials of the Bureau of Indian Affairs than in some other parts of the country, suspicion and jealousy between the Mormon and non-Mormon officials and the two factions of the population as a whole prevented efficient administration. The frequent change and inefficiency of officials, especially of superintendents and agents, had interfered seriously with the formation and execution of any constructive, long-term policy. No superintendent or agent in this region was of the caliber of Edward Beale of California, or of James S. Calhoun in New Mexico. About all that can be said for the Indian Service over the twenty-year period is that an unknown region had been explored and mapped, the Indians had been brought partially under the influence and control of the government, some reservations had been established, and an effort had been made to teach the Indians farming and stock raising. A ground work had been laid for the establishment of schools and missions and for the education of children, which far-seeing officials of the Indian Office had at last begun to realize was fundamental in any program for the solution of the Indian problem.

VI

The Indians of Southern California
1868–1903

WHEN GENERAL GRANT BECAME PRESIDENT on March 4, 1869, he evidently intended to make sweeping changes in the administration of Indian affairs. A movement for reform in the Indian Service was already well under way. As early as 1864, the Indian Reorganization Act had been approved, and three years later came the report of the Peace Commission referred to in a previous chapter. One recommendation of the Commission resulted in the creation of the Board of Indian Commissioners—established by an act of Congress in 1869[1] —which consisted of not more than ten members appointed by the President. These Board members served without pay, inspecting reservations and advising and assisting the Indian Bureau. The first Board had for its chairman Felix R. Brunot of Philadelphia, and its first report was made on October 29, 1869.[2]

Another recommendation of the Peace Commission was that the offices of all superintendents and agents should be declared vacant as of a certain date and new officials appointed; those who had clearly demonstrated their fitness for such positions might be reappointed. But in his first message to Congress, President Grant announced that he had replaced all agents and superintendents with army officers, except in the Indian Territory, Kansas, and Nebraska, where he meant to appoint agents recommended by the Society of Friends.[3]

In California, Superintendent Whiting was replaced by Brevet Major General J. B. McIntosh, Lieutenant John H. Purcell succeeded Agent Charles Maltby at Tule River, and Lieutenant Augustus P.

---

[1] 16 Stats., 40.

[2] Annual Report of Commissioner of Indian Affairs, 1869, 51.

[3] Laurence Schmeckebier, The Office of Indian Affairs, 54–55. See also Grant's First Message to Congress, December 6, 1869. James D. Richardson (comp.) Messages and Papers of the Presidents, 3992–93.

Green succeeded J. Q. A. Stanley as special agent for the Mission Indians.[4]

General McIntosh, a man of energy and ability, with a keen sense of duty and a real interest in the welfare of the people under his authority, made an extended tour of the region occupied by the Mission Indians and also visited other tribes in southern California. The situation was not encouraging. In Owens Valley he found about one thousand Indians, all without lands of their own and usually working for white farmers. He estimated the number of Mission and Coahuila Indians at 3,000 to 3,500. The only reservation in southern California was the little Tule River Reserve, occupied by 200 Indians. McIntosh recommended the setting aside of two large reservations of 25,000 to 30,000 acres each, which he thought might be sufficient to furnish homes for all the Indians of this region.[5] He told the Indians plainly that they would have to work to earn a living if such reservations were set aside for their use.

The condition of the Mission Indians was pitiable. Most of them lived in small villages or rancherias, scattered over a wide area. Although the land they occupied had been tilled by them for generations, it was included in large grants made by the government of Mexico to individuals after the secularizing of the Missions. As land became more valuable, the Indians who occupied it on sufferance were forced to move. Since settlers were coming in rapidly and occupying all public lands, it was evident that there would soon be no place for the Indians except the barren deserts and rough mountains which no white man wanted. It was this situation which prompted McIntosh to urge the creation of reservations.

There were many other Indians throughout the central portion of the state who were entirely landless. Commonly known as the "Diggers," this group included the Miwok and remnants of other tribes, who when not employed as laborers for white farmers, went to the mountains where they hunted and fished. A simple, harmless people, they were usually held in low esteem by the whites, who com-

---

4 *Annual Report of Commissioner of Indian Affairs, 1870*, 90–93. Changes were also made at Round Valley and Hoopa Valley, but these reservations lie in the northern part of California and therefore are outside the limits of this study. For some twenty years after the acquisition of California by the United States, while Indian affairs there were being organized, it is almost impossible to separate Indian administration in southern and central California from that of the northern portion of the state. After 1869, however, Indian relations in the latter area seem to belong more nearly to those of Oregon and Washington and will not be considered in this and succeeding chapters.

5 *Annual Report of Commissioner of Indian Affairs, 1870*, 80–81.

plained that they were shiftless and dirty, addicted to drink, and undependable.

McIntosh did not succeed in securing the two large reservations, but in 1870 four townships of land at Pala and San Pasqual were set aside for the use of the Indians,[6] and the San Pasqual Agency was established at Temecula with Special Agent A. P. Green in charge.

The action met with violent opposition from the citizens of San Diego County, who claimed that white settlers had already occupied and improved portions of the reserved land. They insisted that the Indians were unanimously opposed to moving to these reservations, but that discoveries of gold had brought white immigrants into the region. The petitioners urged the President to rescind his executive order and restore these lands to the public domain. On February 13, 1871, Commissioner of Indian Affairs Ely S. Parker transmitted this request to Secretary of the Interior Delano, who approved and forwarded it to the President. The former order was revoked and the reservations abolished.

General McIntosh and the other army officers had little time to prove their ability in the administration of Indian affairs, since Congress in 1870 prohibited any army officer from holding a civil office either by election or appointment,[7] and Grant was therefore forced to replace army officers in the Indian Service. He decided to request the churches of the country to nominate Indian agents. Sixty-three agencies were allotted to the different religious denominations of the United States. Of these, the Society of Friends was given sixteen, Baptists five, Presbyterians nine, Christians two, Methodists fourteen, Catholics seven, Dutch Reformed five, Congregationalists three, Episcopalians eight, Unitarians two, Lutherans one, and the American Board for Foreign Missions one.[8]

The Mission Indians were assigned to the Methodist church. Former Superintendent B. C. Whiting replaced General McIntosh, while John M. Miller succeeded Lieutenant Purcell at Tule River, and J. R. Tansy replaced Green as special agent for San Pasqual. Miller was soon displaced by Charles Maltby, and when San Pasqual Agency was discontinued (April 5, 1871), the government property

[6] See *Executive Order,* January 31, 1870, in *Executive Orders Relating to Indian Reservations* from May 14, 1855, to July 1, 1912, 43. This was on recommendation of A. P. Green, approved by McIntosh.

[7] 16 *Stats.,* 319.

[8] Schmeckebier, *op. cit.,* 55 n. The policy of appointing agents nominated by churches was gradually abandoned and in a little over ten years had been entirely discontinued.

there was disposed of by the agent.[9] Whiting remained superintendent at San Francisco until 1872. In that year, acting under authority of an act of Congress of 1870, the President abolished the California super-intendency, and thereafter, Indian agents made their reports directly to the commissioner of Indian affairs.[10]

Tule River was the only agency in southern or central California until the establishment of the Mission Agency in 1877. When Tule River, a farm of 1,280 acres, was leased by the Indian Bureau from Thomas P. Madden, about two hundred Indians were living on it. In 1873 a reservation of over 45,000 acres, about forty-five miles north and slightly east of Bakersfield, was set aside by executive order; but all of this except some 250 acres consisted of mountainous and desert lands unfit for cultivation.[11] Maltby was succeeded in 1873 by J. B. Vosburgh, who remained until 1876, when he was superseded by C. G. Belknap, an appointee of the California Conference of the Methodist church. In December, 1876, the new agent removed the agency from the Madden farm to the reservation. Belknap set something of a record for tenure, since he remained in charge of Tule River for twelve years, until the jurisdiction was combined with the Mission Agency.[12] During these years the number of Indians under his supervision remained small, varying from about 160 to 250. He established a school for their children, encouraged them to farm, build better homes, and live in a cleaner and more sanitary fashion.

The revocation of the executive order, setting aside reservations at Pala and San Pasqual, created resentment on the part of the Indians and aroused the interest and sympathy of many white settlers. After the abolition of the San Pasqual Agency, the Mission Indians had no agent, although a government school teacher gave them some assistance. In 1873 John G. Ames was sent by the Indian Office as special agent to investigate conditions among them and report his findings to the Commissioner of Indian Affairs.[13] In his report Ames reviewed briefly the historical background of these Indians, described their condition, and offered detailed recommendations for resolving their problems. He said the eighth article of the Treaty of Guadalupe

9 *Annual Report of Commissioner of Indian Affairs, 1871,* 324–28.
10 16 *Stats.,* 360–61.
11 See *Executive Orders Relating to Indian Reservations, 1855–1912,* 62, for the creation of this reserve.
12 *Annual Report of Commissioner of Indian Affairs, 1876,* 17; *1877,* 41–43; *1888,* 10.
13 For his report, see 43 Cong., 1 sess., *House Ex. Doc. 91.* It also appears in *Annual Report of Commissioner of Indian Affairs, 1873,* 29–41.

Hidalgo apparently made them citizens of the United States, but that they had never been so regarded. Moreover, no treaty had ever been made with them. A committee of the United States Senate had reported that Mexico had full title to the soil, which it had passed to the United States; consequently the Indians had no rights to the land, or even to its use, that called for abrogation by treaty. He recommended the setting aside of reservations, with grazing land held in common, but each family holding in severalty a small farm. He favored a considerable number of small reservations rather than one or two large ones. He urged re-establishment of the Pala and San Pasqual reservations, even though it would be necessary to purchase the improvements of white settlers who had occupied portions of them. He estimated that $150,000 would be required for the purchase of lands and the tools and goods needed to enable the Indians to become self-supporting.

Ames' report attracted widespread attention. By that time a considerable number of citizens of southern California had become concerned about the Mission Indians. In 1873, a group of Indians living on the Temecula Ranch were forced to move from lands which they had occupied and tilled for many years,[14] and the incident caused a great deal of comment.

The next year Charles A. Wetmore was appointed special commissioner to the Mission Indians. In his report, made on January 9, 1875, Wetmore related, in greater detail than Ames had, the history of these Indians since the establishment of the Missions. He asserted that the Mission lands had been held in trust for the neophytes and intimated that the intention had been to divide the common property among the Indians as soon as they became civilized. He pointed out that this foreshadowed the reservation system adopted by the United States, although it had an advantage in the status of the lands remaining unchanged by any necessary shift in missionary personnel, while our own reservations might be abolished or restored to the public domain.[15] He described the secularization of the Missions, and the issuance of land grants by Mexico, and declared that the fatal weakness of the policy of the Missions was their failure to secure from Mexico grants in fee to be held in trust for the Indians. With bitter eloquence he deplored the wrongs which the Indians had suffered and the evil conditions which prevailed among them after the white settlers began to come into the country.

14 *Annual Report of Commissioner of Indian Affairs, 1875*, 10–11.

15 Charles A. Wetmore, *Report on the Mission Indians of California, 1875*, 1–17. (Wetmore was special commissioner of the U. S. to Mission Indians.)

The Indians have been forced by superior power to trade their patrimony and their liberties for civilized bubbles blown by the breath of political insincerity; trading by compulsion from bad to worse until they have, as the Mission Indians of California, simply the right to beg. They beg bread of their white neighbors on whose lands they are trespassers; on the roads where they are vagrants, and in the jails which are their only asylums. They have begged in vain for legal rights. Their right of petition to Congress has been ignored.[16]

He recommended that the rights of the Indians to lands on which they had settled be adjusted or determined and that small tracts be purchased for them, the title to be held in trust by the United States Government. He suggested that the Catholic Church be encouraged to re-establish mission work among them, but he did not recommend that it be given sole missionary control.

Wetmore's views were endorsed by the newspapers of southern California, country and city officials in the area, and the registrar of the United States Land Office. White citizens of this region had begun to realize the gravity of the Indian problem in southern California, with a whole population suffering from the presence of the drunken, diseased paupers which the Indians had become.

The report was effective. On December 26, 1875, President Grant set aside, by executive order, no less than nine small reservations in San Diego County for the use and benefit of the Mission Indians.[17] The following year, or on May 20, 1876, additions were made to Portrero and Agua Caliente by executive order, and six additional reserves were created, the largest consisting of three square miles, and most of them of only one square mile.[18] During the next ten or twelve years, additions were made to some of these reservations, and a number of others were established by executive order.[19] Apparently none of these orders met with serious opposition except from a few individuals who had settled on tracts of land so reserved. Minor adjustments in the grants were made as late as the twentieth century.[20] But

---

[16] *Ibid.*, 3.

[17] *Executive Orders Relating to Indian Reservations,* May, 1855 to July, 1912, 45. These nine reservations were Portrero, Coahuila, Capitan Grande, Santa Ysabel, Pala, Agua Caliente, Sycuan, Inaja, and Cosmit. They varied in size from eighty acres to some twenty-eight square miles but most of them were small.

[18] *Ibid.*, 46. The new reserves were Mission, Torres, Cabezones, and three more merely designated as villages.

[19] In 1877, 1889, 1881, 1882, 1883, 1886, 1887, and 1889. *Ibid.*, 46–50.

[20] *Ibid.*, 47–53.

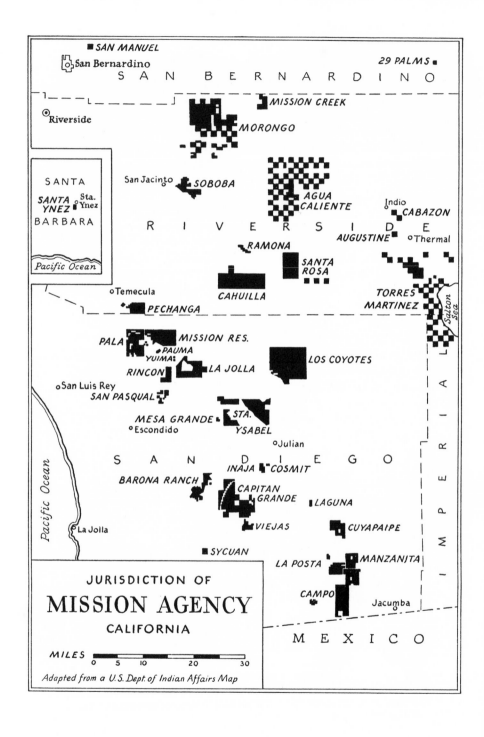

SAN MANUEL

San Bernardino   29 PALMS

S A N   B E R N A R D I N O

Riverside   MISSION CREEK

MORONGO

SANTA   San Jacinto   SOBOBA
SANTA   Sta.
YNEZ   Ynez   AGUA
BARBARA   CALIENTE   Indio
                R   I   V   E   R   S   I   D   E   CABAZON
                                                   AUGUSTINE   Thermal
Pacific Ocean   RAMONA

                                            SANTA
Temecula   ROSA
                     CAHUILLA   TORRES
PECHANGA   MARTINEZ

PALA   MISSION RES.
        PAUMA
YUIMA   LOS COYOTES
RINCON   LA JOLLA

San Luis Rey
SAN PASQUAL

MESA GRANDE   STA.
Escondido   YSABEL
                        Julian

S   A   N   D   I   E   G   O
                INAJA   COSMIT
BARONA RANCH
                     CAPITAN
                     GRANDE   LAGUNA

                VIEJAS   CUYAPAIPE
La Jolla

SYCUAN   MANZANITA
                     LA POSTA

JURISDICTION OF
MISSION AGENCY   CAMPO   Jacumba
CALIFORNIA

MILES   M E X I C O
0   5   10   20   30
Adapted from a U.S. Dept. of Indian Affairs Map

Salton Sea

Pacific Ocean

I M P E R I A L

the greater part of the lands set aside for the Indians, in this and other districts, was waterless, barren, and unproductive.

In 1877 the Mission Agency was formally created, and J. E. Colburn was appointed agent. By 1879 the work of this agency had been firmly established at San Bernardino with S. S. Lawson, a conscientious and able executive, in charge until the autumn of 1883. He reported that the Indians under his supervision were widely scattered,[21] that many were being dispossessed of the lands which they had long occupied, and that conditions in general were bad, liquor being a serious problem. He estimated the number of Mission Indians to be slightly over three thousand and said that, while the little reserves set aside for them contained about a hundred thousand acres, most of the land was valueless. Moreover, the Indians were by this time being ejected from all settlements on the Mexican land grants. The government issued wagons and plows to the Indians in 1882, which helped them in farming.[22]

In 1881 Mrs. Helen Hunt Jackson wrote *A Century of Dishonor: A Sketch of the United States Government's Dealings with Some of the Indian Tribes*. Mrs. Jackson was a highly emotional woman, and, like most reformers, she was far from realistic in her views. She saw only the wrongs committed against the Indians and their suffering; and wrote a vivid and damning story about them. She attributed these wrongs to a lack of far-sighted planning on the part of the federal government, and blamed the people of the country. "There lies but one hope of righting the wrong. It lies in appeal to the heart and the conscience of the American people. What the people demand, Congress will do."[23]

Public opinion was aroused by Mrs. Jackson and other writers, and in the next few years a number of associations in behalf of the American Indians were organized: the National Indian Association, formed in 1879; the Indian Rights Association, established in 1882; and the Mohonk Lodge Indian conferences, begun in 1883 when A. K. Smiley (then a member of the Board of Indian Commissioners) invited persons interested in Indian affairs to meet as his guests for an extended discussion of Indian problems.[24] All of these organizations became especially interested in the Mission Indians of California, and they made their protests heard in government circles.

In 1882 the President appointed Mrs. Jackson and Abbot Kinney

[21] *Annual Report of Commissioner of Indian Affairs, 1879,* 13–15; *1880,* 12–13.
[22] *Ibid., 1882,* 10–13.   [23] Page 30.
[24] Board of Indian Commissioners, *The Indian Bureau from 1824 to 1924,* 29–30.

special agents to visit the Mission Indians and make a report to the Commissioner of Indian Affairs on their welfare. The agents spent many weeks visiting the villages and settlements in southern California and made their report in July, 1883. Like Wetmore's previous report, it reviewed the history of the Indians during the mission period and after the secularization of the missions, denouncing the treatment of the Indians by whites after the acquisition of the territory by the United States, as well as the failure of the federal government to afford them protection. "That drunkenness, gambling, and other immoralities are sadly prevalent among them, cannot be denied; but the only wonder is that so many remain honest and virtuous under conditions which give them none of the incentives or motives which keep white men honest and virtuous."[25]

Ten specific recommendations were made: 1. That the reservation boundaries be surveyed and marked by honest federal surveyors and that the rights of Indians on government or railroad lands be confirmed. 2. That whites inside the reservation boundaries be removed. 3. Two possible solutions of the problem created by Indian villages within the boundaries of confirmed land grants were proposed—either to remove the Indians to other reservations or to uphold and defend their right to remain. A legal opinion was obtained in support of the latter course. 4. That all Indian lands be patented to the Indians occupying them, the federal government to hold such patents in trust for twenty-five years. "The insecurity of reservations made merely by Executive Order is apparent," as had been demonstrated in the case of the San Pasqual Reservation. 5. That more schools be established, with women teachers, and that field workers in education and religion be employed. 6. That the agent make a tour of inspection at least twice a year to supervise his charges and settle questions; and that a young, able physician be secured, to make a circuit at least four times a year through the villages. 7. That a lawyer or law firm in Los Angeles be retained as attorney for the Mission Indians. 8. That there be a judicious distribution of agricultural implements. 9. That a small appropriation be made for food and clothing for the very old and sick. "The Mission Indians . . . do not beg. They are proud-spirited and choose to earn their living. They will endure a great deal before they will ask for help." 10. Finally, the purchase of land was recommended, first the Pauma Ranch, owned by Bishop Mora of Los Angeles, and if it was necessary to move many

[25] Helen Hunt Jackson and Abbot Kinney, *Report on the Mission Indians of California, 1883,* 7.

General José Pachito and his captains at Pala, July, 1885, at meeting called by Indian Bureau to discuss matters of tribe

Colorado desert Indians cultivating the land allotted them
by the government near Indio, California

Indians from the land grants, purchase of the Santa Ysabel Ranch, of nearly 18,000 acres, offered at $95,000, was recommended.

In transmitting this report, Commissioner of Indian Affairs Hiram Price appended a statement to the effect that under the Treaty of Guadalupe Hidalgo the rights of the Indians were guaranteed. He further stated that the case of *U. S.* v. *Ritchie,* 17 Howard, 525, indicated that they were citizens. He added that Mexican laws with relation to land grants had provided that only vacant lands could be granted, and all grants by Mexico contained a clause protecting Indians in the possession of their lands.

In the tradition of earlier repercussions from investigations, this report aroused much discussion and sharp criticism of the inertia of the federal government where the Mission Indians were concerned, but it resulted in little affirmative action. The same year of the issuance of the report—October 1, 1883—Agent Lawson was succeeded by J. G. McCollum, who remained in charge of the Mission Agency until he was succeeded by John S. Ward in 1886. Meanwhile the agency was removed from San Bernardino to Colton.[26] By this time eleven schools had been established among these Indians, with a total attendance of 222 pupils.

On August 16, 1887, Ward was replaced by Joseph W. Preston. The veteran agent at the little Tule River Agency, C. G. Belknap, had recommended earlier that his jurisdiction be abolished and the agency consolidated with that for the Mission Indians, leaving only an Indian Service farmer at Tule River. This was done, and by 1888 Preston had supervision over the Consolidated Mission Agency which included not only Tule River, but also the Yuma Reservation, formerly attached to the Colorado River Agency in Arizona. The Indians belonging to the last-named jurisdiction, located on the Colorado River about two hundred miles southeast of Colton, numbered over 900. Preston reported that he had a total of 4,293 Indians under his supervision. The number of day schools had been reduced to seven, but, in addition, the Yuma Indians had an inadequate boarding school; and a boarding school for Indians had been established at San Diego by the Catholic Church. A contract was made by the Indian Service with this school, which had about sixty-five students.[27]

The Indian Rights Association took a particular interest in the Mission Indians, and its representative, C. C. Painter, paid them at least three visits. Following his third visit, he published an eighteen-

26 *Annual Report of Commissioner of Indian Affairs, 1886,* 43.
27 *Ibid., 1888,* 10.

page pamphlet in 1887, entitled *The Present Condition of the Mission Indians of California*. In this brochure he complained that the government had appointed an attorney to defend the rights of these Indians but had made no provision for his salary which was therefore being paid by the Indian Rights Association.[28] A case filed to eject a group of Indians from lands included within the limits of a Mexican grant was decided against the Indians, but an appeal had been taken; whereupon holders of other grants, especially those of Warner's Ranch, had notified the Indians residing on their claims to move. Painter cited specific cases of the unjust removals of Indians from homes they had long occupied and, like the former investigators appointed by the federal government, he insisted that the Mission Indians had a legal title to the lands they held and cultivated at the time any grant embracing their holdings had been made.[29]

The question of the legal rights of the Indians of California to lands which they had long been permitted to occupy, by both Mexico and the United States, is highly involved. In 1851 Congress enacted a law which required all claimants to land in California to present their claims within a given time to a board of land commissioners.[30] The Mission Indians, of course, failed to comply, and when the holders of Spanish or Mexican grants began to force them to move, they brought various cases to trial in the California courts. All of these were decided against the Indians, and when the cases were appealed to the Supreme Court of the United States, the Indians fared no better.[31] This court held that under the act of 1851, all claims whether to title or occupancy were void if they had not been presented to the board of land commissioners and confirmed. This caused the state courts of California to overrule a former decision stating that if a grant specifically reserved to the Indians the right of occupancy of lands upon which they lived, such right still prevailed even though another person's claim had been presented and confirmed as provided in the law of 1851.[32] With their claims denied by both the state and the United States courts, the Indians living on land grants had no recourse.[33] In spite of the efforts of the Indian Bureau and others, the central question of the Indians' land rights was never upheld.

Joseph W. Preston served only two years as agent for the Mission

28 C. C. Painter, *The Present Condition of the Mission Indians of California*, 3.

29 *Ibid.*, 6, 8–14.   30 9 *Stats.*, 631–34.

31 For the first of such cases brought before the U. S. Supreme Court, see *Botiller* v. *Dominguez* (1889), 130 U. S., 238.

32 *Byrne* v. *Alas* (1888), 74 Cal. 628, 16 Pac., 523.

Indians and was replaced by Horatio N. Rust on August 7, 1889.[34] Rust had charge of the Indians in both the Consolidated Mission, which included Yuma, and the Hoopa Valley Reservation, far to the north. A remarkable man with many unusual qualities and interests, Rust had formerly been a prominent business man in Chicago and had many friends all over the United States. He was deeply interested in archaeology and anthropology and was a collector, not only of prehistoric artifacts but of the products of modern Indian artists and craftsmen. He had long had a great interest in the welfare of the Indian which continued for many years after his services for the Mission Indians had been terminated.[35]

In 1890 Rust reported that the Yuma Indians were among the most primitive in the Southwest. He listed nineteen Mission reservations and gave the population of each, which was small in every case, the most populous having only 275 individuals.[36] Many land titles were in dispute, and Shirley C. Ward and Frank D. Lewis had been employed as attorneys for the Indians.

In 1891 a Mission Indian Commission, consisting of C. C. Painter, A. K. Smiley, and Joseph B. Moore, was appointed and charged with collecting data relative to the land rights of the Indians, selecting lands for them, adjusting boundaries, and settling controversies between Indians and whites.[37] This involved the exchange of Indian lands for others belonging to the Southern Pacific Railway Company or to private individuals, and a second act, approved July 1, 1892, authorized the purchase of lands, although the sum appropriated—five thousand dollars—was wholly inadequate.[38]

During 1892 Perris, the first government boarding school in southern California, was established about twenty miles southeast of Colton near the Santa Fé Railway. The white community donated eighty acres of land for it and two commodious buildings were con-

33 For a comprehensive account of the legal status of the California Indian see Chauncey S. Goodrich, "Legal Status of the California Indians," *California Law Review*, January and March, 1926.

34 *Annual Report of Commissioner of Indian Affairs, 1889,* 124–25.

35 Horatio N. Rust, Papers, Letters, and Scrapbooks, Manuscript collection, Huntington Library. Hereafter referred to as Rust Papers. These papers are very extensive. They reveal that Rust was a man of great versatility who was known by archaeologists all over the world. Apparently he was also a collector of autographs, for his papers contain letters written to him by scores of the most prominent men and women in America of his generation as well as many from distinguished men of other countries.

36 *Annual Report of Commissioner of Indian Affairs, 1890,* 14–20.

37 *Annual Report of Commissioner of Indian Affairs, 1891,* Part I, 47–48.

38 27 *Stats.,* 61.

structed. The school was opened in October, 1892, under the superintendency of M. H. Savage.[39]

Rust remained agent for the Mission Indians until after President Cleveland was inaugurated on March 4, 1893. Rust's early popularity waned during the latter part of his term, and he was subjected to severe criticism for neglecting the Indians and devoting his time to collecting Indian relics and craftwork. The Democratic press and some prominent citizens of southern California were especially hostile toward him and his work.[40]

His successor, Francisco Estudillo, took over the agency early in 1893 and soon thereafter began the allotment of lands in severalty on a number of reservations, including Rincon, Portrero, La Peche, La Jolla, and Pala.[41] Some homesteads were also taken by Indians under the Indian Homestead Law. A few reservations were eventually completely allotted, including Rincon and Portrero. By this time there were twenty-six Mission reservations and nine villages in addition to the Yuma and Tule River reserves. The agency now had a physician and the number of schools had been increased to eleven.[42] By 1896, the final year of Estudillo's tenure as agent, there were thirty-two reservations and five villages under his supervision. The Mission reservations were small in size, and the population, composed of landless Indians, migratory workers, or vagrants, varied from 320 at Torres to 13 at Twenty-Nine Palms.[43]

Early in 1897, Estudillo was succeeded by Lucius A. Wright. The Indian Appropriation Act of June 7 of that year provided $3,900 to locate the "Digger Indians" upon a tract of land purchased for them the preceding year by Special Agent George B. Cosby. The tract consisted of only 320 acres near Jackson on which some twenty-four Indians were placed and provided with a subagent to teach them farming.[44]

Many Mission Indians who had taken homesteads had left them in order to work for whites and therefore had not made final proof of ownership. Such homestead entries were often contested, and the agent reported that, while "equities were usually with the Indian, his ignorance of law and the land system frequently caused him to lose."[45]

[39] *Annual Report of Commissioner of Indian Affairs, 1892,* 225–26.
[40] Rust Papers, Huntington Library.
[41] *Annual Report of Commissioner of Indian Affairs, 1893,* 124–31.
[42] *Ibid., 1895,* 131–35.   [43] *Ibid., 1898,* 126–30.
[44] *Ibid., 1899,* 169. These Indians were Miwok living far to the north of the

The situation of the Indians of southern California changed little during the closing years of the nineteenth century. The Indians felt uneasy about their legal rights to the lands. Some members of the Warner's Ranch Indians, one of the largest groups threatened with eviction, were sued in the Superior Court of San Diego County in the cases of *J. Harvey Downey and the Merchants' Exchange Bank of San Francisco, plaintiffs,* v. *Alejandro Barker et al., defendants,* and by *J. Harvey Downey, plaintiff,* v. *Jesus Quevas, et al.* The plaintiffs won and the decision was affirmed by the Supreme Court of California.[46] An appeal on a writ of error was taken to the Supreme Court of the United States, which on May 13, 1901, also decided in favor of the plaintiffs, and it became clear that the Indians must move.[47]

Faced with the problem of providing lands for these dispossessed people, the Indian Bureau sent Inspector McLaughlin to southern California in December, 1901, to select lands which might be purchased for their use. He suggested that Congress be asked to appropriate the necessary funds to provide the Indians not only with lands but also with building materials, seeds, and farming implements.[48]

In 1902 Congress provided that the sum of $100,000 be appropriated for the purchase of lands for the Warner's Ranch Indians and any others that might be homeless. A sum not to exceed $30,000 of this amount, might be used for removing the Indians to these lands and for subsistence, the purchase of building materials, agricultural implements, and work animals.[49]

Three commissioners—Charles F. Lummis, Charles L. Partridge, and Russell C. Allen—were appointed to assist the Indian Bureau. On their recommendation, 3,438 acres were bought at Pala, and many of the Indians of Warner's Ranch were moved there.[50]

Agent Lucius A. Wright remained in charge of the United Mission Agency until 1903. On July 20 of that year, however, the Commissioner of Indian Affairs directed that this agency be divided into two jurisdictions, each under the control of a bonded superintendent. The southern portion, consisting of Capitan Grande, Campo, Guaypipa, Inyaha, Las Coyotes, Mesa Grande, Pala, Payuma, Portrero,

Mission country. To provide a subagent and lands at such cost for so small a group seems strange, to say the least.

45 *Ibid.,* 27.   46 *126 Calif.,* 262.

47 See *Annual Report of Commissioner of Indian Affairs, 1901,* 195–96. Also 181 U. S., 481.

48 *Annual Report of Commissioner of Indian Affairs, 1902,* 118–19.

49 32 *Stats.,* Part I, 257.

50 *Annual Report of Commissioner of Indian Affairs, 1903,* 149.

93

Rincon, Sycuan, La Posta, Manzanita, and Temecula reservations was placed under the administration of Charles F. Shell with headquarters at Pala. The northern portion, consisting of Tule River, Palm Springs, Torres, Cabezones, Morongo, San Jacinto, San Manuel, Santa Rosa, Santa Ynez, Twenty-Nine Palms, and Coahuila, remained under the jurisdiction of Wright, with headquarters continued at San Jacinto.[51]

The accomplishments of the federal government with respect to the Mission Indians during this period of thirty-five years could hardly be regarded with pride by the officials of the Indian Bureau. But by 1903 public opinion had made itself felt in numerous ways, so that, although conditions were far from ideal, they seemed to be steadily improving. No less than twenty-seven reservations had been set aside for the Mission Indians, varying in area from 280 to 38,600 acres, and in addition there was the Tule River Reserve of 45,000 acres. Since the total population of all reservations was given in 1903 as 2,552, there must have been several hundred Mission Indians living among the whites and away from any reservation.[52] Fifteen of these reservations had by this time either been patented to the Indians or allotted, while the remainder were still executive order reservations. Eleven day schools were in operation, which, together with Perris Boarding School and the Catholic Mission Boarding School at San Diego, gave reasonable facilities for education. The division of the jurisdiction into two parts indicated that the Indian Service expected to maintain closer supervision over its wards in this area in the future and to afford them a larger measure of protection. Local public opinion with respect to the Indian was rapidly changing. Frontier days and ways were passing, and the people of southern California had come to realize that if they wished to live in peace with this minority group and avoid the grave problems they created, they must co-operate with the federal government in improving their educational, economic, and moral conditions.

By the early years of the twentieth century the situation, therefore, seemed more encouraging; but the long period during which these Indians had been neglected by the federal government and exploited by a few greedy and unscrupulous whites had done its work. It required no gift of prophecy to foresee that elevating the Indians of southern California from the depths of poverty and degradation into which so many of them had sunk would require long and patient effort.

[51] *Ibid., 1904*, 169.   [52] *Ibid., 1903*, 146–47.

VII

The Army and the Apache, 1869–86

THE NUMBER OF INDIANS in New Mexico and Arizona in 1869 was estimated at slightly over fifty thousand, of which approximately thirty thousand were in Arizona and twenty thousand in New Mexico.[1] With the exception of the Navajo, Hopi, Pima, and Pueblo, comparatively few of these Indians lived upon a reservation or were more than nominally under the control of any agent. Many of them were peaceful; but the Apache, forming by far the largest group, lived mainly by plunder. During the Civil War period, their activities increased, and after the close of that struggle, it seemed almost impossible to restrain them. As a result, the settlers of Arizona not only feared these savage warriors, but had developed toward the Apache and all his works an intense hatred which caused them to inflict upon even friendly Indians shocking cruelties as barbarous as any that the red man had ever devised.

From 1869 to 1871, Apache atrocities steadily increased until southern Arizona seemed to be a land where sudden death stalked every trail and lurked behind every rock or clump of cactus. It became clear that life would be intolerable for both white settlers and peaceful Indians until the Apache were subdued. There were conflicting views about the way this could be accomplished. On the one side, force was tried. Brave and able army officers did their best to restrain or punish the marauders, but their forces were never adequate, and the vast distances to be covered, as well as the nature of the land and climate, gave the wily savages every advantage.[2] President

---

[1] *Annual Report of Commissioner of Indian Affairs, 1870,* 114–40.

[2] The study of Ralph Hedrick Ogle, *Federal Control of the Western Apaches, 1848–1886* in *New Mexico Historical Society Publications,* Vol. IX (July, 1940), has been of great value in the preparation of this chapter. Any errors of fact or interpretation, however, must be credited to me and not to Mr. Ogle. Other valuable and interesting books are: *General George Crook: His Autobiography,* edited

Grant inaugurated a peace policy by appointing agents recommended by various church groups. The Board of Indian Commissioners, keenly alive to its responsibilities, solicited Congress in 1870 for a suitable appropriation to enable it to make peace with the Apache, and $70,-000 was appropriated for this purpose.[3]

At its May meeting in 1871, the Board authorized its secretary, Vincent Colyer, to go to New Mexico and Arizona and to try to place the Apache upon suitable reservations. Clearly there was urgent need for action. The Camp Grant massacre, one of the most shocking examples of the ruthless brutality of whites toward Indians in the history of the Southwest occurred on April 30, preceding the action of the Board. A band of starving Arivaipa Apache had assembled at the military post of Camp Grant. Lieutenant Royal E. Whitman, the post commander, fed them and encouraged them to send for their friends and relatives. Many others came, and a small unofficial reservation was established. However, the white and Mexican settlers had been so incensed by continual raids that they decided to destroy this peaceful band of Indians. They attacked at dawn, when most of the visiting Indians were sleeping, and men, women, and children were slaughtered and the bodies horribly mutilated. A few wretched survivors fled to the hills, and the attacking party hastily retreated to Tucson, bearing some thirty Indian children as captives, and proudly boasting that not a man of their force had been wounded.[4]

Many citizens of Arizona felt that such treatment was justified because Apache depredations had continued to increase and the trail of the marauders led directly to the Indians encamped near Camp Grant under the nominal protection of the military force stationed at the post.[5] While the press and most of the citizens of Tucson approved the attack, although they deplored the killing of women and children, this event created a sensation in the East and resulted in a widespread demand that those guilty of such inhuman barbarity be brought to justice. President Grant notified the territorial authorities that if all who took part in the massacre were not arrested and tried in the civil courts, he would place Arizona under martial law.

by Martin F. Schmitt; Woodworth Clum, *Apache Agent: The Story of John P. Clum*; Britton Davis, *The Truth About Geronimo*; John G. Bourke, *On the Border with Crook*; Frank C. Lockwood, *The Apache Indians*; and many others.

[3] *16 Stats.*, 357.

[4] See *Third Annual Report of the Board of Indian Commissioners* for a detailed account of the Camp Grant massacre.

[5] For this view see Sidney R. DeLong, *The History of Arizona*, 31–33. For an opposite view see John P. Clum, "Es-kim-in-zin," *Arizona Historical Review*, Vol. II, No. 1, 53–57.

Fort Apache on White Mountain River, Arizona

Natchez and Geronimo at Fort Bowie, Arizona Territory
September 7, 1886

Accordingly, the leading members of the expedition were indicted and tried but were promptly acquitted by the jury, which had received a charge from the judge almost directing such a verdict.[6] But the affair resulted in the detailing of General George Crook to the command of the Department of Arizona.

Crook was a veteran of many campaigns and was doubtless the greatest Indian fighter the United States Army ever produced. He was a remarkable man. More than six feet tall, he was lean and muscular and every inch a soldier. His strength and endurance were enormous; he drove himself harder than he did the men under his command and seemed always to be ready to march or to engage in battle. Like Grant, he hated show and seldom wore a uniform except when absolutely necessary. In heat and cold he rode over rough mountains and barren deserts on his big mule "Apache." He realized the value of mules in mountain and desert campaigning and cared for his pack animals with so much solicitude that he was sometimes called the "daddy of the army mule." A strong, silent man, he listened to everyone but kept his own counsel; therefore, no one knew his plans or policies until he was ready to put them into effect.

The task confronting Crook was not easy. The citizens demanded that the Apache be exterminated. The Indian Bureau and numerous people in the East deplored the cruelty of whites toward the Indians and urged that the latter be given protection and supplied with lands. The army bitterly resented the removal of its officers from their positions as Indian agents, and this resentment was only increased by Grant's policy of church nomination of agents. To the ever-present hostility between officials of the War Department and officials of the Department of the Interior were added many personal jealousies. Finally, greedy and selfish contractors and Indian traders swindled the tribesmen at every opportunity and did not hesitate to supply them with liquor, despite the combined efforts of the army and officials of the Indian Bureau.[7]

Crook arrived to take command of the Department in June, and on July 11 he left Tucson with a considerable force and made a long march over deserts and mountains, primarily to become familiar with the country, to harden his men to campaigning, and to hold councils with various nominally peaceful groups of Apache. When he learned

[6] Frank C. Lockwood, *Pioneer Days in Arizona*, 166.

[7] A comparison of the reports of Vincent Colyer, *Third Annual Report of the Board of Indian Commissioners*, with the opinions expressed by General Crook in his autobiography, or with the account written by any other army officer, will reveal wide differences.

that Colyer was being sent to Arizona with power to make peace and to provide reservations for the Apache, he saw that this would interfere with his efforts to solve the problem by force. Nevertheless, he returned to his headquarters at Fort Whipple, countermanded all orders for active operations against the hostile Apache, and prepared to co-operate with Colyer, although he felt no faith in the success of the enterprise.[8]

Colyer reached Santa Fé in August, 1871, and, like Crook, began traveling extensively throughout New Mexico and Arizona. The people of the latter state, with even less faith in the success of his peace mission than had General Crook, did not hesitate to voice their opinions. In the columns of the local press Colyer was abused and criticised in unmeasured terms, while individuals freely threatened him with violence.

At Santa Fé, Colyer learned that the citizens of Grant County, New Mexico, inflamed by the assembling of Apache at Cañada Alamosa under Agent O. F. Piper, had threatened to massacre all Indians there and to regard as enemies anyone, whether Indian agents, army officers, or traders, who opposed their efforts to recover livestock stolen by the Apache.[9] Consequently, the Indians fled to the mountains, and Colyer found Cañada Alamosa an agency without Indians. He abandoned the idea of concentrating Indians there and designated Tularosa Valley in New Mexico as a reservation. Continuing his journey to Arizona, he set aside three reservations in that territory at Fort Apache, Camp Grant, and Camp Verde. He also designated three temporary reserves or "asylums" to which the Indians might come and receive protection and rations. These were at Camp McDowell, Beal's Spring, and Date Creek.[10]

Colyer seemed to feel that he received co-operation from Crook and the governor and other territorial officials of Arizona; nevertheless it was plain that they disagreed with his ideas and had little faith in the success of the "peace policy." On August 15, Governor A. P. K. Safford issued a proclamation directing the people to receive Colyer and his party with kindness and hospitality. He insisted that if these commissioners had come to Arizona with erroneous opinions of the Indian question and conditions in the territory, they might be convinced of their errors by kindly treatment and fair, truthful representation.[11]

[8] Crook, *Autobiography*, 163–68.
[9] *Third Annual Report of the Board of Indian Commissioners*, 69–72.
[10] *Ibid.*, 73–74.   [11] *Ibid.*, 80.

Upon Colyer's return to Washington in the autumn of 1871, the reservations he had selected, upon which he had placed large numbers of Indians, were approved by the President on the recommendation of the Secretary of the Interior. Army officers, temporarily in command of the Indians on these reservations were charged with supplying them food, clothing, and blankets and encouraging them to grow food.

However, depredations continued in Arizona, and the people insisted that many of them were committed by Indians from the reservations, who, stealing away to rob and murder, would then hurry back to the protection of the agency, thus making the reservation a "city of refuge." Moreover, Chief Cochise, with a large band of Chiricahua Apache, established himself in the remote wilds of the Dragoon Mountains near the Arizona-Sonora boundary and from this fastness continued to carry on widespread marauding.

With the departure of Colyer, Crook once more made ready to wage an active campaign. President Grant was determined to give the peace policy a thorough trial, however, and early in 1872 sent General Oliver O. Howard to the Southwest to continue the work begun by Colyer. He was instructed to contact Chief Cochise and his band if possible and to make every effort to insure the success of the peace policy.[12]

Howard, sometimes known as "The Christian Soldier," had had a long and distinguished military career. As head of the Freedman's Bureau, he had given devoted service to the advancement of the Negro and was considered entirely competent for the task to which he was now assigned. As a major general he outranked any other army officer in the Southwest, and there was reason to believe that he would have the full co-operation of the military as well as the civil officials of the Department of the Interior and the territorial authorities. General Crook suspended plans for a campaign against the Apache and prepared to co-operate with Howard.[13]

Howard was given almost unlimited powers by Grant and received letters to military and civil officers in Arizona written by the President's own hand. He visited various reservations in Arizona and spent some time with General Crook.[14] He arranged a conference at Camp Grant which was attended by officials and citizens of Arizona,

12 For a full account of this mission, see General O. O. Howard, *My Life and Experiences among Our Hostile Indians,* chaps. VII–XIV.
13 Crook, *op. cit.,* 169–73.
14 *Ibid.*

99

General Crook and other army officers, and the leaders of the Indians assembled on this reservation. All of the children taken captive at the time of the Camp Grant massacre who could be found were restored by Howard's order to their relatives.[15] An addition was made to the reservation at Fort Apache, which eventually resulted in two reservations there: San Carlos and White Mountain, or Fort Apache.

In June, 1872, Howard returned to Washington with a delegation of Apache Indians. A month later he returned to the Southwest, by way of Santa Fé. From there he journeyed to the Navajo country, where he established peaceful relations between the Apache with him and the Navajo. He reached Fort Apache on August 11, to find the Coyotero Apache on the verge of an outbreak. Having settled difficulties there, he journeyed east to the Tularosa Reservation in New Mexico. Extremely eager to have an interview with Cochise, head of the renegade Chiricahua Apache, he secured the aid of Captain Thomas J. Jeffords, a close friend of that Apache chief. Jeffords had formerly been in charge of the mail line from Santa Fé to Tucson. He was very friendly with the Indians and, it was alleged, had sold them arms and ammunition.[16]

While Howard was bitterly criticised by the people and press of Arizona and even to some extent by General Crook, his great personal courage was admirable. Accompanied only by Jeffords, Captain Joseph A. Sladen, and two Apache guides, he penetrated deep into the Dragoon Mountains where he found Cochise and his band of fierce renegade warriors and held a lengthy council with them. An agreement was made by which the Chiricahua Apache were to receive an extensive reservation in the mountains bordering the Mexican province of Sonora. Here the Indians were to live in peace with Jeffords as their agent.[17]

Howard subsequently visited other reservations in Arizona and made further plans for carrying out the peace policy. Convinced that the Camp Grant Reservation was not a suitable location, he ordered that all Indians there be transferred to San Carlos by January 1, 1873.[18] He also abolished the temporary reserves at Fort McDowell, Date Creek and Beal's Spring, apparently with the idea of effecting a greater concentration of the Indians upon the remaining reserva-

15 Ogle, *op. cit.*, 104–105.
16 Howard, *My Life and Experiences Among Hostile Indians.* Also "Account of General Howard's Mission," *Washington Daily Morning Chronicle*, November 10, 1872.
17 *Ibid.*
18 Ogle, *op. cit.*, 109.

tions set aside for the Apache. These reservations, in addition to San Carlos, were Fort Apache and Camp Verde, and the reservation in New Mexico.[19] Howard then returned to Washington, his mission to the Apache ended.

Still the raids went on. Many Apache remained off the reservations; some who came to them left again for the mountains. Accordingly, by the middle of October, 1872, General Crook received from Washington approval of his policy to wage war against those Indians who refused to come to the reservations and persisted in marauding. An active campaign was immediately begun.[20] Crook had used the long period of forced inaction to make careful preparation for the war which he felt was inevitable. He had organized companies of scouts from the ranks of peaceful Apache. A detachment of the scouts was placed with each command of soldiers and six or seven separate columns were sent out to attack the marauders. A considerable number of Indians were killed and the remainder driven back into the remote recesses of the mountains. Crook, however, gave them no rest. Nine columns of troops pursued them to their hiding places, and a number of severe engagements were fought in which a total of at least three hundred warriors were killed. As usual Crook was even more active than his officers.

By April, 1873, the spirit of the hostile Indians was completely broken, and large numbers of them had congregated near Camp Verde begging for peace. Crook was not sure that the time had come to make terms, but fearing that public opinion in the East might interfere if war were continued too long, he arranged a general peace. The Indians agreed to remain upon the reservations and to accept the rule of their agent. Crook, in turn, promised them protection and food. After a sufficient time had been allowed to enable all stragglers to reach the reservations, the General asserted that he would pursue any Indians still remaining in the mountains and kill all those who refused to surrender.[21]

During the next two years nearly all of the Apache were at peace for the first time, perhaps, in centuries. Only in a few cases did some small bands under the leadership of a few irreconcilables flee from the reservation. These Crook hunted down, pursuing and harassing them until, worn out and starving, they would send a messenger with a white flag to beg that they might be allowed to return to the agency.

19 *Annual Report of Commissioner of Indian Affairs, 1872*, 176.
20 Ogle, *op. cit.*, 113-14.
21 *Ibid.*, 116-17.

In such cases Crook sent the answer that before they would be allowed to come back to the reservation, they must bring him the heads of the ringleaders who had persuaded them to leave. Otherwise, he would hunt them down and kill them all.[22] As might be expected, Crook received considerable criticism, but the policy undoubtedly helped to bring peace. No longer did the Apache feel that they could leave the reservation, taking food and arms with them, and engage in depredations until it seemed desirable to surrender and return to be fed again. They began to realize that once they had agreed to remain on the reservation, they must keep that pledge or expect swift and sure punishment from the just but ruthless General.

Crook was severe and at times harsh, but he was fair and impartial and earned the admiration and respect of the Apache more unreservedly perhaps than any other army officer ever stationed among them. They declared later that he had never lied to them and that he had always had their interest at heart.[23]

In 1873 the superintendency of Arizona was abolished. The agents were to purchase their own supplies, in the future, and to report directly to the commissioner of Indian affairs. In order to preserve uniformity of action, however, five inspectors were appointed to visit each agency at least twice a year. In that year a telegraph line was extended from San Diego to Tucson, with a branch reaching to Fort Whipple. This placed Arizona in closer touch with the outside world than it formerly had been and made possible quick communication between officials of the Indian Service there and the commissioner in Washington.[24]

Also, in February 1873, the Apache on the Camp Grant Reservation were removed to San Carlos in accordance with the order issued the preceding year by General Howard abolishing the Camp Grant Reservation. This was the first of a series of movements designed to effect a concentration of Apache at San Carlos.[25]

In 1875 General Crook was transferred to the command of the

22 Crook, op. cit., 181–82. See also Crook to W. S. Schuyler in the Schuyler Letters and Papers, Huntington Library.

23 In 1927 the author as a member of the Indian Survey Staff of the Institute for Government Research was holding council with the San Carlos Apache. One after another the old men in the group arose and said: "I was a scout for General Crook. He told me what I should do and how I should live and ever since I've tried to do just as he said I should." No reference was ever made to any other early officer of the United States, either military or civil, but every old man spoke of Crook with admiration and respect.

24 Ogle, op. cit., 119–20.

25 Annual Report of Commissioner of Indian Affairs, 1873, 289.

Department of the Platte, and on March 22 of that year General August V. Kautz came to the command of the Department of Arizona. Even before the transfer of General Crook, however, difficulties had developed between the civilian agents at the various Apache agencies and the army officers stationed there. Army officers acted as agents pending the arrival of an Indian Bureau agent, and even after the arrival of the latter, the officers had authority to control the Indians, issue rations, and verify by count each day the presence on the reservation of all adult male Indians.[26] This situation resulted in divided authority and, consequently, the speedy development of jealousies and personal animosities. The agents of the Indian Bureau, usually coming from the East, had little knowledge of the frontier or of the problems and responsibilities which were theirs, and army officers had little confidence either in the ability of the civilian agents or in the policies which they sought to carry out.

Conditions on the Camp Verde Reservation under Agent J. W. Williams were fairly good. He planned the construction of an irrigation ditch and sought to interest his charges in farming. Having been at Date Creek previously, he had removed the Indians from that point to Camp Verde until there were more than two thousand of them there. Health conditions were bad, however, and Indians often left the reservation, sometimes in large bodies, and went to the mountains for several weeks. Agent Williams, who had apparently been in good health, became suddenly insane, and the military officers assumed control of the agency, the agency clerk, Oliver Chapman, keeping the records. Chapman was eventually made special agent, but the Indian Bureau in March, 1875, removed the Camp Verde Indians to San Carlos.[27] Thus two of the former Apache agencies in Arizona had been abolished, and a very great concentration of Indians at San Carlos had been effected.

After the transfer of General Crook, the controversy between civil agents and military officials in the Southwest grew increasingly violent. The central figure in the former group was Agent John P. Clum, who had been assigned by the Indian Bureau to the San Carlos Agency in 1874.[28] Clum, who was only twenty-four years of age, found himself faced with problems which might well have perplexed a far older and more experienced man. A few months before his arrival,

26 Ogle, *op. cit.*, 100.
27 *Ibid.*, 149.
28 For a detailed account of Clum's activities as Indian agent, see Woodworth Clum, *Apache Agent: The Story of John P. Clum.*

there had been a violent outbreak, and a large number of Indians fled to the mountains, only to be pursued by Crook's soldiers. They sued for peace, and in accordance with Crook's policy were allowed to return to the reservation when they had brought in the heads of four of their ringleaders.[29]

Clum received the Camp Verde Indians, established them at San Carlos, and sought to keep them contented in their new home. He was able and aggressive, organizing and training a very efficient force of Indian police. With these he felt confident of his ability to control the Indians. In 1875 he engaged in a violent controversy with Captain F. D. Ogilby, in command of the troops at Fort Apache. The agent there was James E. Roberts, who had been nominated by the Dutch Reformed church in December, 1872. Roberts was quite successful at first in encouraging the Indians to engage in farming and stock raising; but it was not long until a conflict had developed with the military which ended in the seizure of the agency by Ogilby, who ousted Roberts and replaced him by J. M. Mickly. When news of these events reached the Commissioner of Indian Affairs, he ordered Clum to take over the Fort Apache Agency. Apparently an armed clash between Ogilby's soldiers and Clum's Indian police was narrowly averted, but the agent refused to be intimidated. Clum then received orders to remove the Apache, numbering some eighteen hundred, from the Fort Apache Agency to San Carlos. This removal was accomplished by Clum and his Indian police without difficulty, and by the autumn of 1875 the young agent had under his jurisdiction at San Carlos about 4,200 Indians.[30] In October, 1875, at Clum's request, all troops were withdrawn from San Carlos by order of General Kautz, and for the first time in twenty years these Apache were left without soldiers to guard them.[31]

In 1874 the Tularosa Reservation was abandoned, and the Indians there removed to Ojo Caliente—just west of the Río Grande, commonly known as the Hot Springs Reservation—the same place from which they had been removed in 1872 because of the threats of citizens in that part of New Mexico.[32]

[29] Report of Agent Clum, August 31, 1874, in *Annual Report of Commissioner of Indian Affairs, 1874*, 296–98. Clum seems to have approved of General Crook's policy even though "Helpless women with babes at their breasts were, despite their tears and entreaties, ordered back to the mountains to await the fulfillment of the general's orders." The agent felt, nevertheless, that such harsh measures were necessary and wise. *Ibid.*, 297.

[30] Report of Agent Clum, *Annual Report of Commissioner of Indian Affairs, 1875*, 215–20.

[31] Clum, *Apache Agent*, 164.

Clum and his Indian police were kept busy by the Indian Bureau. The Indians of the Chiricahua Reservation—set aside in December, 1872, in accordance with the treaty made with Cochise—had for some years remained faithful to their promise not to molest any Americans. There is no doubt, however, that bands from this reservation sometimes raided in Mexico and that they were frequently joined in such raids by visitors to their reservation from other agencies, especially Hot Springs. Unfortunately Cochise died in 1874, and his son became head of the old chief's band, but his influence was never as great as his father's. Inspectors from the Indian Bureau recommended that no reservation should border on Mexico. Agent Jeffords apparently managed the Indians very well, in a loose and unorthodox fashion. In the spring of 1876, however, trouble broke out on the Chiricahua Reservation, caused by a factional dispute among the Indians themselves. An outlaw Apache killed Rogers, a trader on the reservation who had been selling liquor to the Indians, and also murdered the trader's cook, the only other white man at the station. Two or three other whites were killed, and conditions on the reservation became tense. Governor Stafford urged that the Chiricahua be removed either to San Carlos or Hot Springs and declared that Agent Clum was the only man who could do it.[33]

Clum refused to act until a military force sufficient to meet any emergency had been placed in the field. Accordingly, General Kautz, with twelve companies of cavalry and a force of Indian scouts, moved toward the reservation, and when Clum arrived at the Chiricahua Agency, he found most of the Indians were willing to move. One band, under the leadership of Geronimo, Juh, and Nolgee, fled to Mexico, but 326 Chiricahua were transferred to San Carlos.[34] The Chiricahua Reservation was abolished by executive order on October 30, 1876.[35]

Marauding by outlaw bands of Apache continued, nevertheless, and it soon became evident that much of this originated at Hot Springs. Inspector E. C. Kemble, who visited the agency in May, 1876, reported deplorable conditions and recommended the removal of Agent J. M. Shaw. He was replaced in August by James Davis.[36] Learn-

32 *Annual Report of Commissioner of Indian Affairs, 1874,* 310–11. Hot Springs Reservation had been set aside by executive order April 9, 1874, and its boundaries revised December 21, 1875. See *Executive Orders Relating to Indian Reservations,* May 14, 1855, to July 1, 1912, 120–21.

33 Ogle, *op. cit.,* 166.

34 Ogle, *op. cit.,* 167.

35 *Executive Orders Relating to Indian Reservations, 1855–1912,* 5.

36 Ogle, *op. cit.,* 170–72.

ing that Geronimo had returned from Mexico and was at Hot Springs, the Commissioner of Indian Affairs wired Agent Clum on March 20, 1877, to arrest the chief and his renegade band and hold them for robbery and murder.[37] With his force of Indian police, Clum marched to Silver City where he was joined by his former company of police, now in the Arizona National Guard. Without waiting for the arrival of regular troops, Clum arrested Geronimo and his fugitives and put them in irons. Then, at the order of the Indian Bureau, he assembled all of the Indians to be found on the reservation and conducted them to San Carlos. The Hot Springs Reservation was soon after abandoned and returned to the public domain.[38]

When Clum returned to San Carlos with the Apache from Hot Springs, he found an army officer with an escort of soldiers camped near the agency for inspection duty. Angered at what he considered an unwarranted military interference, Clum wired the Commissioner of Indian Affairs that he would volunteer to take care of all the Apache in Arizona if his salary were increased and he could be given two more companies of scouts. The Commissioner refused, and Clum resigned and left San Carlos on July 1, 1877. He was at this time only twenty-six years old, but he had managed the San Carlos jurisdiction with unusual ability for three years, and had concentrated there the Apache from Camp Grant, Camp Verde, Fort Apache, Chiricahua, and Hot Springs.[39]

Clum was succeeded by H. L. Hart. Geronimo and his warriors were released and given rations, in contradiction to Clum's wishes that they be sent to Tucson to be tried and executed for murder. An outbreak of some of the Hot Springs Indians, who in September, 1877, fled from San Carlos and began raiding, interfered seriously with the new agent's work. The bitter controversy between the military and civil administration continued with growing intensity. To Clum's somewhat complacent report of his success in removing the Indians from the Chiricahua and Hot Springs reservations with his Indian police, General Kautz retorted in August, 1877, that only 454 Indians from the former and 325 from the latter reservations had

---

[37] Clum, *Apache Agent*, 204–205.

[38] *Executive Orders Relating to Indian Reservations, 1855–1912*, 120–21; see Clum, *Apache Agent*, 203–49, for a dramatic account of the arrest of Geronimo and the removal of the Hot Springs Indians.

[39] Clum, *Apache Agent*, 253–56. Clum was undoubtedly one of the ablest agents ever to serve in the Southwest. It is unfortunate that the book, *Apache Agent*, is so written as to give the impression that he was egotistical and boastful, as he probably was not.

been removed—a total of 779. Yet previous reports of the Indian Bureau had given the number of Indians at Chiricahua at 2,100 and at Hot Springs at 965, making a total of 3,065, for whom rations and blankets had been regularly issued. The General therefore asked what had become of the remaining 2,286 Indians.[40] The question was embarrassing to the officials of the Indian Bureau. If their earlier figures were approximately correct, then over two thousand Indians from these reservations had fled and were still at large. If Clum, on the other hand, had removed almost all of the Apache on these two reservations, the government had been paying for rations, blankets, and other issue goods for three times the number of Indians on the reservations, which implied graft or at the least gross inefficiency. But officials of the Indian Bureau ignored the question.

The marauding Hot Springs Indians were at length forced by the army to surrender, and after being held prisoners of war for some time, were returned to San Carlos.[41]

Agent Hart was successful for a while, in spite of his difficulty in securing competent employees. Eventually, however, rumors of graft at San Carlos reached the Indian Bureau, and Inspector J. H. Hammond was sent out to investigate. Mining operations were being carried on near the border of the reservation, and prospectors persistently trespassed upon Indian lands. Apparently Hammond and Hart decided to form a mining company in which Commissioner of Indian Affairs Hayt's son, Edward K. Hayt, joined. The result was a scandal which ended in the removal not only of Hart and Hammond from the Indian Service, but of Commissioner Hayt as well.[42]

Captain Adna R. Chaffee was temporarily placed in charge of San Carlos, but in June, 1880, J. C. Tiffany of New York, the candidate of the Dutch Reformed church, was made agent. Rumors of graft and corruption soon began to be heard, and after an investigation had revealed wholesale corruption in every phase of his work, his removal was recommended. There were delays, but he was finally permitted to resign on June 30, 1882.[43]

In the meantime, changes had taken place in the military command. Depredations continued during 1877 and 1878, and General Kautz was harshly criticised by the press and people of Arizona, although he kept troops in the field nearly all the time. On March 7, 1878, he was relieved and General O. B. Willcox became commander

40 Lockwood, *The Apache Indians*, 227.   41 *Ibid.*, 228.
42 Ogle, *op. cit.*, 195–97.
43 *Ibid.*, 212–13.

of the Department of Arizona. His aggressive warfare against the raiding Indians was apparently without too much effect. The feud between the military and the civil officials of the Indian Bureau continued, at times interfering seriously with the administration of the Apache. Many hostiles were still at large and many skirmishes were fought, including the savage Battle of Cibicu in August, 1881, in which six hundred Indians were reported to have been engaged.

In April 1882, General Sherman came to Arizona. He planned a new military department to include both Arizona and New Mexico, but apparently the War Department disagreed with his views, and General Crook was transferred from the Department of the Platte to Arizona where he again took over the command of that Department.[44]

Crook spent several weeks at San Carlos. On his stout mule he rode over the reservation talking with the Apache, holding conferences with small groups, and seeking to learn for himself the needs, wants, and grievances of the Indians. The picture revealed was neither an attractive nor an encouraging one. Nevertheless, Crook set to work with characteristic energy to give relief and help to the peaceful Indians and to wage merciless war upon the hostiles who from their mountain retreats, either in Mexico or southern Arizona, were coming out to plunder and murder settlers and travelers.

It is impossible to give space to any detailed account of the military operations of Crook and his subordinates. In July, 1883, the entire police control of San Carlos was given to the military. Captain Emmett Crawford was given command of all troops on the reservation, with Lieutenant Charles B. Gatewood assigned to the force stationed at Fort Apache. A large number of Indians had been permitted to leave San Carlos and settle in the high, cool valleys of the mountains near that post and still other bands were permitted to join them in 1883.[45] Dual control did not work well, but there were no serious clashes between the military and civil officials. Agent Wilcox objected strongly to what he considered interference with his work by army officers and in September, 1884, resigned, although he remained until the new agent, C. D. Ford, arrived in November to relieve him.[46]

In 1884, Geronimo and his band, who had been for some time in Mexico, returned to the reservation and located in the Fort Apache

44 Ibid., 216.
45 Ibid., 216.
46 Ibid., 229.
47 Ibid., 226.

region.[47] In 1885, however, he once more left the reservation and re-turned to Mexico with a considerable band of followers. Two com-mands under Captains Crawford and Wirt Davis pursued them, since Crook had received orders to follow the hostiles without regard to departmental or international boundary lines. Far down in Mexico, Crawford was killed by some irregular Mexican troops, who fired up-on his men under the impression that they were hostile Indians.[48]

The renegades were so hotly pursued, however, that they at last asked for a conference and agreed to meet General Crook at Canyon de los Embudos, south of the border, if he would come without sol-diers.[49] Despite the obvious danger, Crook met the renegades. The Indians at first refused to surrender except upon the promise that they might return to the reservation and continue to live there. Crook re-fused this, but he agreed that if they surrendered, their lives would be spared, and after two year's imprisonment in the East, they would be permitted to return to the reservation. The Indians refused to give up their arms. However, they marched north with Crook to a point near the border, where some of them became drunk on liquor which they bought from a Mexican rancher just south of the border, and Geronimo, Naches, and some twenty warriors, together with four-teen women and two boys, returned to the Sierra Madre Mountains. The remainder, seventy-seven in number, were brought to Fort Bowie.[50]

Crook wired General Sheridan from Fort Bowie, telling him what had taken place. The latter replied, censuring Crook, questioning the trustworthiness of the Indian scouts, and demanding to know what action was contemplated in the future. Crook replied with dignity, tendering his resignation as commander of the Department of Ari-zona, and on April 12, General Nelson A. Miles assumed command of the Department.[51] By instructions of the Secretary of War, the seventy-seven Apache prisoners that Crook had brought in had been entrained for Fort Marion, Florida, on April 7, under an escort of soldiers to be held there as prisoners of war.[52]

General Miles took command with instructions from General

48 *Ibid.*, 236.
49 Lockwood, *The Apache Indians*, 285–86.
50 *Ibid.*, 286–89. Also see John P. Clum, "Geronimo", *New Mexico Historical Review*, Vol. I, 1928–29, Nos. 2, 3, and 4, for detailed account of Geronimo's ac-tivities.
51 Ogle, *op. cit.*, 236.
52 Lockwood, *The Apache Indians*, 290. The party consisted of fifteen men, thirty-three women, and twenty-nine children.

Sheridan to pursue Geronimo's band vigorously and secure their surrender, without conditions if possible, with conditions if necessary. Commissioner J. D. C. Atkins had paid a visit to San Carlos and, encouraged by the progress of the peaceful Apache there, had approved an appropriation of $67,000 to erect two flour mills and a sawmill and to supply the Indians with livestock and farming implements.[53]

The Chiricahua and Hot Springs Apache who had been brought in by General Crook had been living peacefully on little farms near Fort Apache. They were nominally prisoners of war, although some of them had been scouts under Crook and had rendered excellent service. They were much feared and hated by the people of Arizona and as a whole were disliked by the other Indians of the reservation. Miles regarded them as a menace to progress on the reservation, and in the early summer of 1886, a delegation of thirteen of them was persuaded to go to Washington to discuss a proposal to remove the entire band to some point remote from Arizona. They refused to consider a home in Indian Territory, however, and were eventually ordered back to Arizona. Miles' superiors had by this time reached a decision to remove all the Chiricahua to Fort Marion, Florida, to join the little band of Geronimo's followers previously sent there. Orders were accordingly issued to stop the members of the delegation at Fort Leavenworth, Kansas, and hold them there as prisoners, pending arrangements to remove their kinsmen at Fort Apache.[54]

Miles concentrated a strong military force about Fort Apache, and on August 29 the Chiricahua, who were assembled as usual for roll call, were surrounded by soldiers, seized, disarmed, and closely guarded. On September 7, the entire group of some four hundred persons was started with a strong escort of troops for Holbrook, Arizona, where they were placed on board a train and sent to Fort Marion.[55]

[53] Ogle, op. cit., 238.

[54] Ogle, op. cit., 239.

[55] Lockwood, The Apache Indians, 313–16. The exact number is given by Ogle as 382, while Lockwood says that there were 428 Chiricahua on the reservation. On September 12, the Secretary of War ordered the members of the Apache delegation confined at Fort Leavenworth to be sent to Fort Marion to be held there as prisoners and, with the exception of the little band of renegades in Mexico, the Chiricahua were all held as prisoners in Florida. General Miles is authority for the statement that one man escaped from the train after it had passed St. Louis and a year later reappeared on the Fort Apache reservation. Here he lived as an outlaw, capturing and murdering several women until he was finally alleged to have been killed by soldiers. Nelson A. Miles, Personal Recollections, 529.

In the meantime, Miles had sent out Captain H. W. Lawton with an expeditionary force which chased Geronimo's renegades for more than a thousand miles. Finally, on July 14, 1886, the scouts succeeded in making contact with the hostiles and defeating them. Captain Gatewood, who had been sent to join Lawton for the purpose of entering Geronimo's camp and demanding his surrender, at last met the chief and his little band on August 24, 1886. Geronimo wished to return to the reservation, but upon learning that the Chiricahua were all being sent to Florida, agreed to meet Miles near the border for a final surrender. He did this on September 4, 1886, and the surrender was arranged. The Indians were marched to Fort Bowie and from there to Bowie Station, where they were placed on board a train and sent under a strong guard to Fort Marion. Miles had promised the Indians that they might join their families there, but President Cleveland had demanded an unconditional surrender. The party of fifteen men, eleven women, and six children was stopped at San Antonio, Texas, and held there for several weeks while an investigation was being made. By order of the Secretary of War, the men were sent to Fort Pickens to be confined while the others of the band were delivered at Fort Marion.[56]

With the surrender of Geronimo and his little band of thirty-two persons, the Apache wars in the Southwest came to an end. They had been shockingly destructive of life and property, and almost unbelievably costly to the United States government. General Crook had three thousand soldiers during his second period as commander of the Department of Arizona, and Miles had received two thousand more. This large military force had been utilized in 1886 for operations against a mere handful of Apache warriors and for police duty on the various reservations. Indeed, ever since the close of the Civil War, military and Indian contracts had been the chief means of support for the civilian population of Arizona. Considering that the white population of Arizona in 1870 was less than ten thousand, it is hardly surprising that General Sherman should have written the Secretary of War suggesting that all troops be withdrawn from the region and that it be given back to the Indians.[57] By 1886, however,

---

[56] Lockwood, The Apache Indians, 308–13. Also Miles, Personal Recollections, 527–29. A small band consisting of Chief Mangas, two warriors, three women, and six children, were later captured and sent to Florida. They were renegades from Fort Apache, but had apparently been living peacefully in Mexico for some time. Ibid., 530. Miles devotes one hundred pages to his activities against the Apache in Arizona.

[57] Ogle, op. cit., 73.

the work of the army in the Southwest was almost over, except for police duty. Later relations of the federal government with the Apache were peaceful and may be considered a part of the general policy for the protection and advancement of other tribes of New Mexico and Arizona.[58]

[58] The lot of the 498 Chiricahua sent to Florida as prisoners of war was a hard one. Seventeen hostile warriors were confined at Fort Pickens, and the remainder of the adults were kept in camp under guard at Fort Marion, near St. Augustine. In April, 1887, the families of the prisoners at Fort Pickens were sent to them, and the rest of those at St. Augustine were removed to Mount Vernon Barracks near Mobile, to which the Fort Pickens group was brought in 1888. One hundred and twelve children were sent to Carlisle School in Pennsylvania, where thirty of them died in less than two years. In addition eighty-nine of those held as prisoners in the South had died before January 1, 1890. The Indian Rights Association and humane people from various parts of the country urged better treatment of the Chiricahua, and after a long investigation they were removed in 1894 to Fort Sill, Oklahoma, and located on the military reserve. In 1914 they were released from their nominal captivity and 138 returned to the Mescalero Reservation in New Mexico, while the remainder received allotments of land and remained in Oklahoma. Lockwood, *The Apache Indians,* 320–30. A young woman of these Oklahoma Apache, who is a descendant of Mangas Coloradas and a grand-niece of Geronimo, was in 1948 graduated from the University of Oklahoma.

VIII

Peaceful Relations in Arizona and New Mexico, 1869–1900

WITH THE EXCEPTION OF THE APACHE, the Indians of Arizona and New Mexico were not troublesome during the last three decades of the nineteenth century. The Navajo had learned their lesson, and most of the other tribes of the region were traditionally peaceful. For years there were some depredations by hungry Ute, Mescalero, and Jicarilla Apache; and, just as in white communities, a few lawless men were found even among such tribes as the Pima and Papago. The civil administration of the various tribes in this expansive region, during the period from 1869 to 1900, has been described by many persons. Every Indian agent in this area made an annual report on his jurisdiction. In addition there were reports of army officers, inspectors, special commissioners, accounts of contemporary teachers, and technical monographs, all of which comprise an overwhelming amount of data. The accounts are filled with details of minor squabbles, caused by personal jealousies, and with examples of political intrigue, graft, and mismanagement. The quarrel between the civil and military authorities was always a complicating factor, and its intensity was increased by a strong and concerted effort to return the Indian Bureau to the Department of War.

When President Grant established his policy of appointing army officers to superintendencies and agencies for the Indian Service, there were but three agencies in Arizona. These were the Gila River, Colorado River, and Moqui, or Hopi, agencies. No reservation had been created for the last-named tribe; hence there were but two reservations in all Arizona. New Mexico had five agencies—Navajo, Pueblo, Abiquiu, Cimarron, and Southern Apache—but reservations had been established only for the Navajo and each of the some twenty villages of the Pueblo. Most of the Indians of both territories, therefore, had not had lands reserved for them, and the greater part of the

113

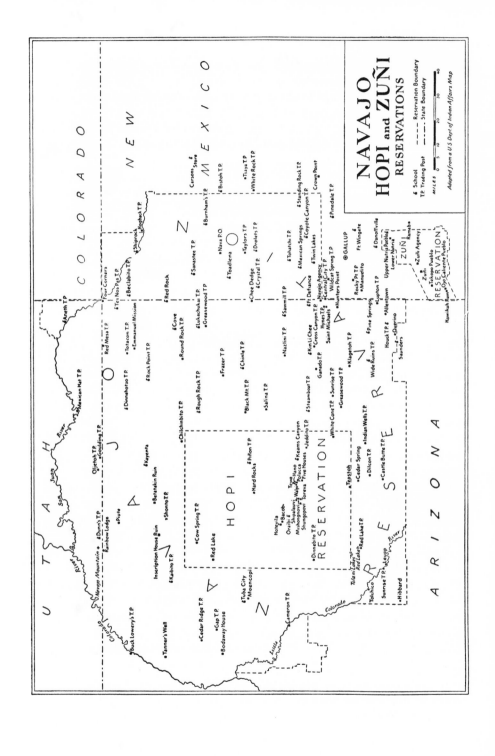

NAVAJO
HOPI and ZUÑI
RESERVATIONS

   School
T.P. Trading Post

------ Reservation Boundary
-·-·-· State Boundary

MILES
0   5   10   20   30   40

Adapted from a U S Dept of Indian Affairs Map

Indians in Arizona and a large number of those in New Mexico were not even nominally under agency supervision and control.[1] The agent for the Hopi was stationed at Fort Wingate and visited his charges only for brief periods three or four times a year to give them farming implements and have all who were willing vaccinated for smallpox.[2] The agencies for the Ute and Jicarilla Apache at Abiquiu and Cimarron, as well as the southern Apache agency, at Fort Craig, were only feeding stations to which the Indians came from time to time to receive rations and issues of blankets and clothing. While the agent tried to exercise some supervision and control over the Indians under his jurisdiction, and to minister to their needs as far as possible, it is doubtful whether he did much except feed them enough to prevent their preying upon the livestock of the ranchmen.

By 1870, or even before, it was becoming increasingly clear that the Indians should be given definite reservations from which all whites must be excluded and which the Indians should not be permitted to leave. While they were allowed to roam at large, clashes between them and the whites were inevitable. The reservation policy has been harshly criticized. The reservations have been referred to as "concentration camps," and critics have pointed out the injustice of forcing a people so long accustomed to complete freedom of movement to reside within a restricted area. Such theorists, however, have never suggested any real alternative. As a matter of fact, there was none. With a white population penetrating every part of the Southwest, the Indians could not avoid contact with ranchmen, prospectors, and settlers. Few of these whites had any respect for the rights of the Indian, and many of them regarded the aborigines as deadly enemies —not without reason. A people like the Apache, who for centuries had lived chiefly by plunder, did not readily change. The settler, returning from his work to find the horribly mutilated bodies of his wife and little children lying among the smouldering ashes of what had been his home, did not stop to theorize about what wrongs inflicted upon the Indians had caused them to turn their hands against the whites. He merely felt that all Indians were fiends, to be slaughtered without regard to age or sex. Gathering together a company of his friends and neighbors, he began reprisals in which the innocent suffered for the sins of the guilty, just as they had already done in the case of his own family.

1 See *Annual Report of Commissioner of Indian Affairs, 1870*, 114–40 and 144–62, for reports on these agencies.
2 *Ibid.*, 132–36.

The policy of placing tribes upon reservations was therefore necessary for the Indians' own protection. But in the Southwest the federal government delayed far too long the establishment of such reserves. There were definite reasons for this delay. White settlers and territorial officials objected to having large tracts of land withdrawn from settlement and set aside for the sole use and benefit of the Indians. Congress was slow to make the necessary appropriations. The Indians were reluctant to leave their homes. Consequently, it was not until 1887 that reservations for all tribes of Arizona and New Mexico had been established, and long after that date it was found necessary to add to some of these.

It should have been plain to officials of the Indian Bureau long before 1870, however, that agencies for Indians who had no fixed reservation could never accomplish much. The Abiquiu and Cimarron agencies were on private land grants, and even if the Indians had been willing to cultivate the soil and establish farms, they would not have been permitted to do so by the landowners. It was impossible for an agent to maintain any adequate control over wandering bands or to check their numbers for the purpose of issuing rations, blankets, and clothing. Enterprising individual Indians from other jurisdictions would visit Cimarron, for example, in order to receive rations and clothing, only to hurry back to their own agency to share in the issue at home. A light-footed young Indian with a flair for travel might receive issues of rations and goods from three or four agencies each year. The surplus could be traded for liquor or useless trinkets.

The first objective of Vincent Colyer and General Howard in carrying out the peace policy of President Grant was, therefore, the establishment of reservations. They confined their efforts primarily to the warlike Apache, leaving other less troublesome tribes for later consideration.

The next step was the abolition of the temporary reserves and the abandonment of Camp Grant, Camp Verde, Chiricahua, and Warm Springs reservations. By 1877 the Indian reservations in Arizona and New Mexico had been reduced to about the same number as had been in existence in 1869, with the addition of the huge White Mountain, or Fort Apache, Reservation, first established in 1871, upon which many of the Apache had been concentrated, and a small reservation of slightly over sixty thousand acres set aside in 1874 for the Papago.[3]

As the Apache menace was reduced and more settlers arrived, it

[3] *Executive Orders Relating to Indian Reservations, 1855–1912*, 23.

became increasingly difficult to maintain an agency for Indians who had no reservation. More reservations were created, and by the time of the surrender of Geronimo in 1886, reservations had been created and assigned to every important tribe or group of Indians in the two territories. There were nine reservations administered from the three agencies in Arizona, including the Yuma, across the Colorado in California, first under the jurisdiction of the Colorado River Agency, but later transferred to the Mission Agency in California. The Colorado River Agency also administered the affairs of the Hualapai and Havasupai reservations. The first, established by executive order, January 4, 1883, contained 730,880 acres, on which lived about 620 Hualapai.[4] The second, created in 1880–82, was a small reservation lying largely within Cataract Canyon, occupied by about 200 Havasupai.[5]

The San Carlos Reservation of 2,528,000 acres, with a total population of five thousand Apache, was the sole responsibility of the San Carlos Agency.[6]

The Pima Agency, at Sacaton on the Gila River, had charge of the Gila River Reservation, 357,120 acres, the Salt River Reservation, 46,720 acres, set aside on June 14, 1879, the Gila Bend Reservation, 22,391 acres, established in 1882, and the Papago Reservation created in 1874.[7] About 5,300 Pima and Maricopa were on the Gila River and Salt River reservations, and a few hundred Papago were at Gila Bend. The Papago numbered from six to seven thousand, but only a few hundred lived on the comparatively small reservation near the old mission of San Xavier del Bac. Most of them lived in small villages in the region between the reservation and the northern boundary of Mexico. The only other reservation in Arizona was that of the Hopi, a separate agency until 1886, when it was placed under the jurisdiction of the Navajo Agency in New Mexico. The total area of all nine reservations in the territory was 6,603,191 acres, including the Hopi, which alone had over two and a half million acres. The total Indian population of the territory in 1886 was 21,163, of which all but 2,464 were definitely under agency control.[8]

4 Alice C. Fletcher, *Indian Education and Civilization*, Washington, 1888, 200–201. Hereafter referred to as Fletcher.

5 *Ibid.*, 201. In 1896, however, the Hualapai and Havasupai were made a separate agency.

6 For the various orders and other documents relating to this reservation see Fletcher, *op. cit.*, 208–15.

7 *Ibid.*, 202–208. Also 22 *Stats.*, 299.

8 See Fletcher, *op. cit.*, 198–215 for statistics and other information relative to all agencies and reservations in Arizona.

By 1886 nearly all of the Indians of New Mexico had also been placed on reservations, but in some cases this had been delayed for a long time.

After the army officers acting as agents in New Mexico had been relieved by civilians—appointed largely upon the recommendation of the Presbyterian church board—the Indians would have benefited if it had been possible to keep the same officials for any length of time. But agents became discouraged and resigned, or were removed, and changes of administration came with bewildering frequency. Almost every agent at Abiquiu, Cimarron, or Mescalero urged that the Indians be given reservations, but the difficulty of finding an area to which the Indians were willing to move caused delay. Congress eventually authorized the opening of negotiations with the Utes. A commission headed by Felix Brunot concluded an agreement with the various bands of Utes to move to Colorado, and this agreement was ratified by Congress on April 29, 1874.[9] An agreement was made with some of the Jicarilla chiefs to accept a reservation along the San Juan River, east of the Navajo country, and this area was set aside by executive order on March 24, 1874.[10] This did not, however, mean the removal of these Indians. Reluctant to leave their homes, they remained, receiving rations from the Cimarron and Abiquiu agencies. Inspector John McNulta, who visited Cimarron in 1875, declared that the Indians there were "an unmitigated nuisance" and should be removed to the reservation.[11] This was not done, however, and the following year the Jicarilla Reservation was restored to the public domain.[12]

In the meantime the Utes of Abiquiu Agency, in common with the band attached to Cimarron, continued to prove troublesome. On October 1, 1876, Ben M. Thomas, agent for the Pueblo, was also given jurisdiction of the Cimarron Agency. He reported that the 749 Indians there were all vagabonds and there was no hope of improving their condition so long as they remained in their present location.

The Indian Appropriation Act of March 3, 1877, provided for a new agency on the southern part of the Ute Reservation in Colorado,[13] to which the Utes of New Mexico could be removed. In 1874 and 1875 a reservation for the Mescalero Apache had been established in the

9 Frank D. Reeve, "Federal Indian Policy in New Mexico, [1858–80]," *New Mexico Historical Review*, Vol. XIII, No. 2 (April, 1938).

10 *Executive Orders Relating to Indian Reservations, 1855–1912*, 121–22.

11 *Annual Report of Commissioner of Indian Affairs, 1875*, 38–39.

12 *Executive Orders Relating to Indian Reservations, 1855–1912*, 122.

13 19 Stats., 288.

mountainous region about one hundred miles north of El Paso.[14] Agent Thomas urged that the Jicarilla should be transferred to this reservation,[15] but there were delays until 1878, when Congress directed that the Utes and Jicarilla Apache be removed at once.[16] So far as the Utes were concerned, removal was not difficult. The issue of rations at Abiquiu Agency was stopped and the Indians were told that no more would be issued except at the new agency in Colorado. After some of them had waited for a month or so, hoping government officials would relent, the entire tribe moved to the Southern Ute Agency in Colorado. The Cimarron Ute removal waited for an escort of troops, which failed to appear, and at last Agent Thomas and Inspector Watkins moved them in July, 1878.[17] The Utes thus passed out of New Mexico history.

Only about thirty of the Jicarilla Apache left for the Mescalero Reservation. The rest of the tribe refused to go because they felt that the Lincoln County War had created such disturbed conditions among the whites as to make it unsafe for them to live there. In addition, they were told that an epidemic of smallpox had broken out among the Mescalero. Many of them drifted up to the region about the old Abiquiu Agency, but the Indian office was prohibited by law from issuing rations to the Jicarilla after July 20, except at Mescalero. Therefore, three to four hundred of these Indians were forced to live by hunting or raiding.[18] In 1880 a reservation was established for them, but in 1883 they were forced to join the Mescalero, and their own reservation was returned to the public domain. The Jicarilla were very unhappy at Mescalero, however, and gave the agent a great amount of trouble. Finally, in May, 1887, they were returned to northern New Mexico, receiving a grant of land just south of the Colorado state boundary.[19]

By 1887, therefore, the reservation policy in Arizona and New Mexico had largely been established, and except for a large part of the Papago tribe, most of the Indians of these territories were on lands of their own. From this time until after 1900, New Mexico had three agencies. These were the Mescalero Agency, with jurisdiction

14 *Executive Orders Relating to Indian Reservations, 1855–1912*, 117–18.
15 *Annual Report of Commissioner of Indian Affairs, 1877*, 162.
16 *80 Stats.*, 84 and 232.
17 *Annual Report of Commissioner of Indian Affairs, 1878*, XL–XLI.
18 *Ibid.*, XLI. See Also Reeve, "Federal Indian Policy in New Mexico [1858–80]," *New Mexico Historical Review*, Vol. XIII, No. 2 (April, 1938), 189–91.
19 See *Executive Orders Relating to Indian Reservations, 1855–1912*, 122–23 for these various orders. Boundaries of the reservation were changed somewhat in 1907 and 1908. *Ibid.*, 123–24.

over the Indians of the Mescalero Reservation, the Navajo Agency, to which was also attached the Hopi, and the Pueblo Agency at Santa Fé, having supervision of some twenty little Pueblo grants and also of the Jicarilla Apache. The total number of Indians in the Territory of New Mexico after the removal of the Utes was about 29,000, and the total area included in the various reservations in 1886 was ten million acres.[20] Of this land 691,805 acres had been confirmed to nineteen Pueblo groups, while the original Navajo Reservation had been increased by executive orders in 1878, 1880, and 1884 by the addition of 1,769,000 acres in Arizona and 967,680 acres in Utah, giving the Navajo a total area of 8,205,440 acres.[21]

Years before the policy of placing all tribes upon reservations had been fully carried out, Congress and officials of the Indian Bureau began to consider the idea of allotting lands in severalty to tribal members. The movement for allotment was sponsored by various organizations in the East, including the Indian Rights Association. It finally resulted in an act of Congress, approved February 8, 1887, commonly known as the General Allotment Act. This authorized the President to provide for the allotment in severalty of the lands of any reservation. The patents to such allotted lands were to be held in trust by the United States for twenty-five years, and this period of time might be extended by the President. After allotment of any reservation had been completed, the President was authorized to negotiate with the tribe for the purchase of its surplus lands to be disposed of to settlers.[22]

The passage of the Allotment Act, however, had little effect upon the Indians of the Southwest. Mention has already been made of the allotting of certain small reservations of the Mission Indians in California, and allotments were eventually made of irrigated lands for the Pima and some other tribes. As a whole, however, the character of the land and climate in Arizona and New Mexico made the holding of lands by Indians in severalty impracticable if not impossible. The

[20] Fletcher, *op. cit.*, 501.

[21] *Ibid.*, 501 and 508. After 1892, the reports of the Navajo agents are published under Arizona instead of New Mexico.

[22] 24 *Stats.*, 388. There has been much discussion of the Allotment Act and wide differences of opinion respecting it. Generalizations with respect to the policy are dangerous, but it seems reasonably certain that the results of the act were far less beneficial to Indians in every case than those responsible for its enactment had hoped, and in many cases were positively harmful. What the individual Indian needed was not a farm of his own, as the proponents of the act seemed to believe, but education, in the broader sense of the term, which would make him capable of utilizing a farm for his own economic advancement.

wide stretches of deserts and mountains of the Navajo and Apache reservations had to be utilized for common pasturage, under such local regulations as the Indians might devise for themselves, if they were to be utilized at all. Only in the case of irrigated lands would it have been possible to justify allotments in severalty. The Pueblo, however, and most other tribes were so wedded to their old system of common ownership that it would have been almost impossible to induce them to accept any other form of land tenure. The land, moreover, was undesirable for white settlement, and there was no incentive to accept allotments in order to provide surplus land for sale to whites.

The internal history of the various agencies from 1869 to the middle eighties, and, indeed, up to the end of the century, will be considered very briefly. Largely it is a story of petty squabbles, of orders sent from Washington with little conception of the difficulties to be overcome in carrying them out, and of efforts on the part of various agents to preserve order on the reservation, prevent the introduction of liquor, and keep their charges sufficiently well-fed to prevent depredations. Agents, as well as the commissioner of Indian affairs, were changed so frequently as to prevent the formation of any long-term program.

By far the most important tribe in the two territories, with the possible exception of the Apache, was the Navajo. To Captain Bennett, appointed in 1869, fell the task of beginning to carry out the provisions of the treaty of 1868 with this tribe. He constructed agency buildings, utilizing logs cut by the Indians from the reservation. He distributed fourteen thousand sheep and one thousand goats and issued seed wheat, corn, and garden seed. He fitted up a schoolroom and employed a young woman who gave instruction to thirty-five or forty children.[23] Bennett found the Navajo eager to remain at peace with the whites and stated that in many cases when lawless young Indians stole livestock, the chiefs would bring the animals to him to be returned to the owner before the agent had ever heard of the theft. He declared that white thieves and outlaws stole animals from the Indians and that perhaps a thousand Navajo children were held as slaves in the Mexican settlements of New Mexico. He sent Lieutenant Ford to try to arrange for the return of these captives, and later went himself, but the Mexicans would not even talk about it. He urged that

---

23 *Annual Report of Commissioner of Indian Affairs, 1870*, 148–51. This first teacher was Charity A. Gaston. She reported only indifferent success. *Ibid.* 153–54.

a special police force of Navajo be organized to preserve order on the reservation and arrest criminals.[24]

James H. Miller, who relieved Captain Bennett as agent in February, 1871, found himself in a difficult situation. The Navajo crops had failed the year before, and no appropriation had yet been made to feed the Indians. He secured corn from the quartermaster at Fort Wingate, however, and Superintendent Pope provided him with a loan of beef, but in spite of his efforts there were raids made by hungry Indians, and it was necessary to call out troops from Fort Wingate to recover stolen livestock and arrest the guilty Navajo. The chiefs and the tribe as a whole co-operated with the agent and did their best to restrain the few unruly tribesmen.[25]

On June 11, 1872, Agent Miller, while on a trip to the San Juan River to look for suitable farming land for the Navajo, was murdered by two Utes. He had left the agency in charge of Thomas V. Keam, a trader on the reservation, and General Howard, who reached the Navajo country about that time on his second visit to the Southwest, appointed Keam as special agent. He remained in charge until September 1, 1872, when he was succeeded by W. I. Hall, although Keam was retained for another year as temporary subagent to establish a post in the San Juan Valley. Keam, acting under authority granted by General Howard, had established a Navajo police force of 130 members to capture thieves and recover stolen livestock.[26]

Hall was relieved at the end of a year by "the perennial W. F. M. Arny," who had been agent for the Pueblo and had held various other positions including that of territorial secretary. Arny continued the police force, which was a great service in maintaining order. The Navajo at this time were reported to have about 125,000 sheep and were fast becoming a pastoral people. Little had been done to provide them with schools, although their population had increased to about eleven thousand, and some nine thousand of them were living on the reservation. Agent Arny complained that the recent act of Congress limiting the total amount of the salaries of all employees at any agency to $6,000 a year had made it necessary to reduce the number of his employees and in some cases to decrease the pay of those remaining. He urged that the physician's salary "be increased to $1400 annually."[27]

Arny insisted that white "squawmen" were the source of much

[24] Ibid.   [25] Ibid., 1871, 376.
[26] Ibid., 1872, 302–304.
[27] Ibid., 1874, 306–308.

trouble and urged that a law be enacted making it a criminal offense for a white man to live with an Indian woman unless legally married to her, and that when so married, he should be prohibited from residing on the reservation. Like most agents in the Southwest during this period of years, he complained of lack of military co-operation and even of positive interference with his work upon some occasions by officers and troops of the regular army.[28]

Alexander G. Irvine, who succeeded Arny in 1876, urged the removal of the agency from Fort Defiance to the valley of the San Juan River, where there was a larger area of good farming land. He stated that the Navajo council of twenty-six chiefs was a source of trouble. Since the treaty of 1868 would expire in 1878, he urged that before that time the Navajo should be made self-sustaining.[29]

Irvine was followed by John C. Pyle in 1878. He was enthusiastic about the progress made by the Navajo in the ten years since they had left Bosque Redondo. He agreed that the agency should be removed to the valley of the San Juan, which had remained unused because of the proximity of the Utes in southern Colorado. He said that the removal of either the agency or of the Utes from Colorado would enable the Navajo to utilize this large body of arable land. Irvine believed that the time had come to discontinue rations except to a few old and infirm people and that government gifts in the future should be cattle, sheep, or agricultural implements, all of which would help the Navajo to help themselves.

By the time of the expiration of the treaty in 1878, the Navajo were a very different people from the miserable band of paupers who left Bosque Redondo ten years before. Their numbers had greatly increased, and they owned hundreds of thousands of sheep, goats, and horses, and a considerable number of cattle. Large additions made to their reservation in 1878, 1880, and 1884 had extended it by some two million acres; subsequent additions in 1886, 1900, and 1901 had made it still larger, and even after this it was increased.[30]

One agent followed another at the Navajo Agency in rapid succession from 1869 to 1900, and the same was true at almost all other agencies in New Mexico and Arizona. This was the fatal weakness of the Indian Field Service, but it was only a reflection of what happened in Washington, where most commissioners of Indian affairs found their tenure equally brief and uncertain. From 1868 to 1897

28 *Ibid., 1875*, 330–33.
29 *Ibid., 1878*, 107–109.
30 *Executive Orders Relating to Indian Reservations, 1855–1912*, 17–18.

the average term of a commissioner was only two years. Consequently, it was impossible to formulate any long-term program. Among the Navajo some licensed traders—such as John Lorenzo Hubbell, who had established a post at Ganado in 1876—had a greater influence over the Navajo and did more to promote their welfare than any agent did. Unfortunately many traders, especially those operating off the reservation but near its border, were not of Hubbell's type, and these were a bad influence upon the Indians.[31]

From 1878 to 1897 no less than eight agents served at Fort Defiance. That the Indians recognized the evil of this constant change is shown by the fact that the Navajo offered to add one thousand dollars to the salary paid Agent Riordan by the government if he would remain as their agent.[32]

Despite the evils incident to frequent change of agents, and regardless of frequent crop shortages due to drought, the economic condition of the Navajo steadily improved. Within fifteen years after leaving Bosque Redondo, they owned more than a million sheep and thirty thousand horses. Their great need was more land and water, for the reservation was badly overgrazed. Homesteaders had occupied a few tracts about the reservation boundaries, however, and the government had granted alternate sections to the Atlantic-Pacific Railroad passing near the southern boundary of the Navajo country, so that it was difficult to enlarge the reservation without including such lands within its limits. Trouble with whites over grazing rights was common, but in 1877 a permanent police force was organized, and in 1891 a "court of Indian offenses"—a tribal court to try petty cases— was set up.[33]

Lieutenant E. H. Plummer, who was agent for a time, took a number of Navajo to the World's Fair at Chicago in 1893. These Indians returned deeply impressed with what they had seen and fully convinced that the Navajo must eventually learn more of the white man's civilization by sending their children to school. The federal government had made little effort to carry out the provision of the 1868

[31] Hubbell declared that the Indian trader was everything from merchant to father confessor, justice of the peace, judge, jury, court of appeals, chief medicine man, and de facto czar of the domain over which he presided. He said that for nearly half a century he had been known locally as the king of northern Arizona. John Lorenzo Hubbell, as told to John Edwin Hogg, "Fifty Years an Indian Trader," Touring Topics, Vol. 22, No. 12 (December, 1930). Quoted in Reeve, "Federal Indian Policy in New Mexico," New Mexico Historical Review, Vol. XIII, No. 2 (April, 1938), 43 n.

[32] Dane and Mary Coolidge, The Navajo Indians, 259.

[33] Ibid., 256–57.

treaty which guaranteed the establishment of schools, probably because the Navajo had until now shown little disposition to send their children to the few schools that had been established. As a rule it had been necessary to send out police to bring children in, and in some cases the parents had bitterly objected to placing their children in boarding schools, in one case, at least, attacking and injuring an agent who sought to bring children into school.[34]

At the close of the century the Navajo were a peaceful, pastoral people, more than twice as numerous as they had been thirty years before. Their chief wealth was in their flocks of sheep, in the care of which they showed remarkable aptitude. "The white man has sheep in his head," an old Navajo once remarked, "but the Navajo has sheep in his heart." In addition to the money derived from wool and lambs, the Indians also had considerable income from the rugs and blankets which they wove and sold to traders, and from the sale of piñon nuts that grew in abundance on parts of their reservation.[35]

The federal government's relations with the Navajo from 1869 to 1900 may be regarded as typical of its relations with the other tribes of Arizona and New Mexico during this period. Everywhere the same rapid shifting of agents was found, and at every agency the resources provided by Congress and the Indian Bureau were inadequate. "Too little and too late" might well be said of funds and supplies provided for the Indians of every jurisdiction. There was a universal complaint of insufficient money for rations, clothing, blankets, tools, seeds, and livestock, as well as of low salaries for employees and the failure to provide them with decent living quarters and other buildings required for carrying on the work of the agency.[36] Seeds often arrived after the planting season had passed, and blankets and warm clothing sorely needed in winter sometimes did not arrive until spring. The Indian Bureau blamed the niggardly attitude of Congress, while the latter felt that the Indian Office and its agents did not always make

34 Coolidge, *op. cit.*, 247. Even in the twentieth century an old Navajo father complained that he had six boys and had given five of them to the agent to place in school, but the latter now wanted the sixth son. "It is not just," observed the old Indian. "I need this last boy to herd sheep. If I give the agent five, it seems to me he should let me keep one at home to help in my work."

35 In checking figures on Navajo income in 1927, the author was surprised to find that they received a larger total sum from the sale of piñon nuts than from the sale of rugs and blankets.

36 The act of Congress creating an Indian police force fixed the salaries of officers at eight and of privates at five dollars a month, which was far too low. Also, one thousand dollars a year seems an absurdly low salary for doctors, even in the last quarter of the nineteenth century.

the best use of the funds they had, that employees were inefficient, and money was wasted, or even stolen. Thus a vicious circle was created. Not enough money was provided for the agent to do a good job, and because he did a bad one, larger appropriations were not made.

In the general administration of Arizona and New Mexico, the superintendencies were abolished in 1873 and 1874 respectively, H. Bennett being the last superintendent of Arizona and L. E. Dudley of New Mexico. After these dates the agents reported directly to the commissioner and such integration of agencies as seemed necessary was maintained by means of inspectors. At all other agencies the tenure of agents was usually as brief as at the Navajo. There were, however, a few exceptions. J. H. Stout at Gila River came to the agency in 1871 and remained for ten years, but few of the agents following him remained more than two or three years. All of them tell essentially the same story of insufficient land and water for the Pima and Maricopa. Early agents complained that the Pima had absorbed the vices of the whites, that the use of liquor was widespread, and that moral conditions were bad, although Agent Young in 1897 gave a glowing account of the progress made by the tribe during the three years he had served as agent.[37] A day school had been opened in 1871, and ten years later Agent Wheeler established a boarding school, which opened with an enrollment of 75 and by 1900 had 190 pupils.[38]

The Papago had an agent of their own from 1871 to 1876, when they were placed under the jurisdiction of the Pima Agency, but they received little from the federal government. Most of them spoke Spanish and long after 1900 still had a veneer of Spanish culture and civilization.

The Colorado River Agency was far less important than the Pima, and the Indians belonging to it were much lower in the scale of civilization than were the Pima, Maricopa, and Papago. For some years the Indians under its jurisdiction were widely scattered. Perhaps fourteen hundred Mojave around Needles and Fort Mojave were nominally under the jurisdiction of this agency, but they persistently refused to come to the reservation. The Hualapai and the little band of Havasupai living on their reservations were so remote from the agency that it could not maintain any great measure of control over them. Accordingly in 1896, the Hualapai Agency was created for these two tribes and placed under an industrial teacher, Henry P. Ewing,

[37] *Annual Report of Commissioner of Indian Affairs, 1897*, 108–11.
[38] *Ibid., 1900*, 198.

who was still in charge in 1900.[39] The Havasupai lived by farming small patches of irrigated lands. They still remain the most remote and inaccessible Indian tribe in the United States. Since their reservation cannot be reached by automobile, all visitors must come on horseback, and goods have to be brought in on pack animals. Therefore their contact with the whites prior to 1900 was slight, and it remains slight today. The Hualapai Reservation, bordering the Grand Canyon, is largely barren desert, but the people provide part of their living from farming small tracts, raising cattle, and making baskets. Unlike the Indians of some other reservations in Arizona, they were not addicted to the use of liquor to any great extent at this time, although this was not true of those living about Needles.

Colorado River Reservation had a boarding school established in 1881 but it enrolled only 25 pupils out of a school population of 285.[40] Eventually, however, the number was considerably increased, and by 1900 there were 103 pupils enrolled.[41] Lack of water for irrigation made the growing of crops difficult. The federal government had to provide some food, but perhaps five-sixths of the subsistence of the people came from their own efforts. In 1899 the government provided a powerful pump, by means of which the area of irrigated land was greatly extended.[42] The Indian Office had earlier spent a large sum for an irrigation canal, and had provided additional funds from time to time to extend it and to make repairs. The earlier agents reported a great deal of disease, especially syphilis, and predicted that the tribe would soon become extinct.[43] By 1900, however, the population was increasing and health conditions were greatly improved.

The third Arizona agency, that of San Carlos, has been discussed to some degree in the preceding chapter. Up until the surrender of Geronimo in 1886, civil administration had been greatly hampered by intermittent warfare with the Apache and constant quarrels between military and civil officials. Even during these years, the greater part of the Indians under this jurisdiction were peaceful, and their agents had aided them in opening little farms and producing crops. Nevertheless a very large part of their subsistence was provided by the federal government. The agency had two divisions and jurisdiction over two separate groups of Apache, since Agent Clum had not removed all of the Fort Apache group to San Carlos, and many of those he moved had been permitted to return. Because of the size of the agency, the San Carlos agent usually maintained an official to

39 *Ibid., 1900*, 200–204.   40 *Ibid., 1882*, 1–3.
41 *Ibid., 1900*, 185–88.   42 *Ibid., 1899*, 145–49.   43 *Ibid., 1871*, 116.

look after the Indians in the vicinity of Fort Apache. In 1889 it was reported that there were over 3,200 Indians on the San Carlos division of the agency and about 1,700 living in the mountains around Fort Apache.[44] Boarding schools were established by the federal government on both divisions of the reservation. The Apache, unlike the Navajo, preferred cattle to sheep,[45] and the government in 1884 purchased over six hundred cattle for them. The erection of a sawmill and gristmill by the government also helped the Indians, and gradually they began to make some economic advancement.

In 1897 the Fort Apache Indians were separated from those at San Carlos, and their territory was made into a separate reservation.[46] The Indians of the two jurisdictions remained primitive, despite efforts to advance them in white civilization. In 1900, and even a quarter of a century later, most of them lived in grass tepees, farmed a little when water could be had for irrigation, worked in the mines and for the railroads, and eked out a scanty living. They remained peaceful after the final surrender of the Geronimo band, but occasionally there were individuals who embarked on a career of crime, the most notorious being the "Apache Kid," who in 1893 committed a series of robberies and murders.

The Jicarilla and Mescalero Apache have already been discussed. The first named, at last receiving a permanent reservation, remained under the jurisdiction of the Pueblo Agency at Santa Fé. Their reservation had extensive areas covered with valuable pine timber. Allotments were made to a number of these Indians after the passage of the Allotment Act, but the agent later reported that, because of the confusion of names, it was impossible to determine to whom the patents belonged. The tribe numbered about 850. After the establishment of nonreservation boarding schools in the Southwest, a few Jicarilla children were sometimes sent to the school at Fort Lewis, Colorado, but in 1897 the agent reported that of the 171 children between the ages of six and sixteen, not one was in school.[47] A school for these Indians was completed about the close of 1900, however, and thereafter a large part of the children were kept in school. In 1900 issues of food were still made twice a month to the Jicarilla, and they derived not more than one half of their livelihood from their own efforts, the remainder being supplied by the government.[48]

[44] *Ibid., 1889*, 121–23.
[45] *Ibid., 1884*, 7.   [46] *30 Stats.*, 64.
[47] Report of Acting Agent C. E. Nordstrom in *Annual Report of Commissioner of Indian Affairs, 1897*, 194–202.
[48] *Annual Report of Commissioner of Indian Affairs, 1900*, 292–97.

A Hopi Leader

Papago family on the Papago Reservation in Arizona. The
house is made of ocotillo wands and has a mud roof

After the establishment of the Mescalero Reservation in 1873, these Indians remained on it continuously, with the usual rapid changes in agents. During the seventies, they were troubled frequently by whites who stole from them. Some white homesteaders had lands within the limits of the reserve, and their places became a refuge at times for white thieves and outlaws.[49] While the reservation contained nearly 475,000 acres, little of the land was tillable, and even in 1886, it was estimated that 85 per cent of these Indians were subsisting on government rations.[50] Early in the next year, however, the Jicarilla were removed to northern New Mexico and thereafter only some six hundred Mescalero occupied the reservation. From the date of the establishment of the reservation in 1873 until 1900, there were more than a dozen agents, only two of whom served as much as four years. These were William H. Llewellyn, 1882 to 1885, and Lieutenant V. E. Stottler, who served from 1895 to 1898. After the conflict between two factions of white ranchers and business men, known as the Lincoln County War, which ended in the summer of 1878, the Mescalero had less difficulty with their white neighbors and the agents' problems were considerably lessened.[51]

In 1884 a boarding school had been established for the Mescalero which that year enrolled 15 children. The number remained small for some years, but by 1897 the agent reported that 116 children, which constituted the entire school population of the reservation, were in the boarding school.[52] In 1899 the Indians were so nearly self-supporting that the agent stopped issuing rations to all except members of the Indian police force and a few old or infirm people.[53] By 1900 the Mescalero seemed in a fair way toward becoming completely self-supporting, although they were later to experience want due to drought and crop failures.

Since the story of the Pueblo Indians lies largely outside the limits of this book, these peaceful agricultural people may be dismissed with only a brief statement. Their agency during the period under consideration was at Santa Fé, and from that place their agent sought to maintain contact over their scattered reservations, extending from Taos in the north to Isleta in the extreme south and reaching as far west as Zuñi near the Arizona–New Mexico line. As a rule, the Pueblo caused the Indian Office and its agents little trouble. Accustomed for

49 *Ibid., 1877*, 154–58.   50 Fletcher, *op. cit.*, 502.
51 There are many printed accounts of the Lincoln County War, but few, if any, of these give any discussion of the effects of this struggle upon the Indians.
52 *Annual Report of Commissioner of Indian Affairs, 1897*, 192–94.
53 *Ibid., 1899*, 243–44.

centuries to live from the produce of their small, irrigated fields, they asked and received little from the government. Their chief problem was the encroachment of settlers, for the boundaries of the reservations had not been surveyed and were frequently the cause of disputes. Lack of sufficient water for irrigation, or of land to which water could be brought, sometimes constituted a further problem. Schools were soon established for them, and by 1885 there were three day schools supported in part by the government.[54] The agent that year urged that more children from his jurisdiction be sent to Carlisle or to boarding schools in Santa Fé and Albuquerque. By 1889 Agent W. P. McClure reported that eighty or ninety Pueblo boys and girls were at Carlisle.[55] The number of day schools was steadily increased, but the people of several pueblos, especially Santo Domingo, were for a long time reluctant to place their children in school. These Indians were industrious and thrifty, however, and their agent reported in 1900 that they had that year cultivated over eighteen thousand acres of land and produced nearly 70,000 bushels of wheat and over 97,000 bushels of corn, in addition to large quantities of melons, fruits, and vegetables.[56] These crops should, it seems, have provided an adequate supply of food for a people numbering only about eight thousand and should even have given some surplus for sale. While agents came and went with surprising frequency, one Pueblo agent, Ben M. Thomas, remained from 1875 to 1882.[57]

The Hopi, dwelling on their mesas in the desert region of northern Arizona, lived in much the same fashion as did the Pueblo of New Mexico. From 1870 to 1883 the Hopi Agency was maintained as a separate jurisdiction. In 1883 it was again placed under the jurisdiction of the Navajo agent, who usually made a separate report each year on the Hopi. Like the Pueblo, the Hopi asked little from the federal government. Day schools were established for them, and a boarding school was opened at Keams Canyon, but the Hopi objected to sending their children to it and it later became a Navajo school. The federal government also did some excellent work in drilling wells and developing springs for the Hopi and Navajo alike, although the major part of this water development came after 1900. An appropriation of $7,500 made by Congress in 1887 for this work was very helpful.[58]

[54] *Ibid., 1885,* 158.
[55] *Ibid., 1889,* 262–64.   [56] *Ibid., 1900,* 293.
[57] See *Annual Report of Commissioner of Indian Affairs,* for these years.
[58] *Ibid., 1887,* 177–78.

The Pueblo and the Hopi had a civilization of their own which they considered superior to that of the whites. In consequence, they clung very closely to their old customs and institutions and therefore changed less in the half century following the acquisition of the Southwest by the United States than did some of the wilder and more warlike tribes. The Navajo were the traditional enemies of the Hopi, and the agent was often troubled by petty quarrels over range, water rights, trespass, minor thefts, and a number of other things. After the passage of the Allotment Act, a zealous agent allotted land to a large number of Hopi, but these allocations were not confirmed, and it soon became evident that individual ownership of lands by these people would not solve any of their problems. By 1900 most of the Hopi Reservation was used largely by the Navajo for grazing sheep and these pueblo dwellers devoted themselves largely to growing crops about the mesas on which their villages stood, and to the making of pottery and baskets.[59]

On the whole there had been much progress prior to 1900 by the Indians of this region, despite the brief tenure of most agents, the quarrels between military and civil officials, the hostility of much of the local white population toward Indians, and the great amount of graft and corruption on the part of political appointees of the Indian Bureau.

Many grave problems, however, remained unsolved. On several reservations the Indians were extremely poor, and a large part of them were dependent upon government issues of food and clothing for much of their living. Few of the children of some tribes, particularly the Navajo, were in school, many Indians of all tribes clung tenaciously to their old customs. Most of them refused to accept the services of agency physicians, calling in the medicine man to treat any persons who became ill. Between 1900 and 1948 many of these problems were solved, but the complete solution of all of them lies in the more or less distant future.

[59] As late as 1927, the author was holding council with the Hopi at Walpi and was surprised at the bitter complaints directed against the Navajo. Several speakers asserted that the Navajo was a natural thief and robber and insisted that the Hopi reservation should be given to the Hopi alone and the Navajo forced to move from it.

IX

Utah and Nevada, 1869–1900

THE INDIANS OF UTAH AND NEVADA were fewer and a great deal lower in the scale of civilization than the Indians of Arizona and New Mexico, and, with the exception of the Utes, there were no great, warlike tribes similar to the Navajo and Apache. Thus they could not resist the whites, and must accept without too much question whatever decision officials of the United States Government made concerning them. Much of the region they occupied was so barren and uninviting that it discouraged white settlers.

When Grant became president, there was but one Indian reservation in Utah—the Uintah Valley Reservation of over two million acres set aside by executive order in 1861, and established on a permanent basis by the act of Congress approved May 5, 1864. The Uintah Valley Agency was located on the reservation, which was so remote from any white settlements that it was very difficult to obtain supplies for it, or even for the agent to maintain contact with the world outside his own jurisdiction.[1] Various bands of Utes lived permanently upon this reservation and others came in temporarily, during the winter, and were given rations by the agent.[2] Since not more than five or six hundred Indians were permanent residents, it is clear that most of the Indians of Utah were scattered widely over the territory, living as best they could.[3]

The two large Indian reservations in Nevada—Walker River and Pyramid Lake—had not been formally set aside in 1869, but had

[1] The agency was about two hundred miles from Salt Lake City from which all supplies must be brought over a high mountain pass blocked by snow for several months each year.

[2] *Annual Report of Commissioner of Indian Affairs, 1870*, 143.

[3] See Report of Superintendent J. E. Tourtelotte, *Report of Commissioner of Indian Affairs, 1870*, 141–44, for numbers and distribution of the various tribes and bands of Utah.

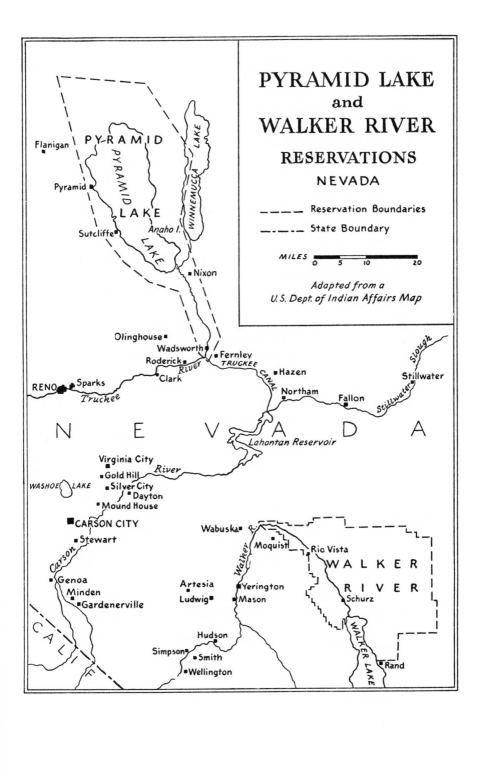

PYRAMID LAKE
and
WALKER RIVER
RESERVATIONS
NEVADA

– – – – Reservation Boundaries
– ·– ·– · State Boundary

MILES 0 5 10 20

*Adapted from a
U.S. Dept. of Indian Affairs Map*

merely been recognized as lands reserved for Indian use by the commissioner of the General Land Office upon the recommendation of the commissioner of Indian affairs.[4] As for the so-called "timber reserve" previously mentioned, apparently all claim to it was soon abandoned by the Indian Office, if, indeed, there had ever been any real claim asserted. As in Utah, most of the Indians of Nevada were scattered, and even the comparatively small number on the reservations frequently left them to hunt or gather native products in the mountains.

In accordance with his policy of appointing army officers to most positions in the Indian field service, President Grant designated Brevet Colonel J. E. Tourtelotte superintendent of Indian affairs for Utah, and Major H. Douglas superintendent for Nevada. For the Uintah Valley jurisdiction Lieutenant George W. Graffam was named as agent, although he did not establish himself at the agency but at Fort Bridger, in Wyoming. In 1870, however, J. J. Crichtlow was made agent at Uintah and reached Salt Lake in December of that year, arriving at the agency the following February. His first impression of his post was far from favorable, and he frankly reported to the Commissioner that if he had known of its situation and condition, he would never have accepted the position.[5] Apparently Crichtlow was the only agent in Utah until early in 1872 when George W. Dodge arrived as special agent for the Northwestern Shoshone Agency which presumably had jurisdiction over a number of bands of Indians so scattered that Dodge had to spend much of his time in locating his charges.[6]

The federal government seems to have been more concerned about the Indians of Nevada than those of Utah as more officials were sent out to the former jurisdiction. In addition to the appointment of Major Douglas, Lieutenant J. M. Lee was appointed special agent to travel over Nevada and report upon the condition of the Indians, and Captain R. H. Fenton was sent to the bands of Indians living in the extreme southeastern part of Nevada, who had hitherto never had an agent.[7] The latter reported that there were some 3,500 Indians in this area, in bands of from 25 to 250. They were more destitute and degraded than any people he had ever seen, living on lizards, snakes, sunflower seed, and piñon nuts; and those Indians in near

4 Fletcher, op. cit., 494.
5 Annual Report of Commissioner of Indian Affairs, 1871, 545.
6 Ibid., 1872, 294.
7 Ibid., 1870, 113–14.

settlements were existing by depredations made on the whites. A few planted small crops, but they had no agricultural implements and used sticks to dig the ground for planting and knives to harvest their grain.[8]

After the passage of the act prohibiting army officers from holding civil positions, the office of superintendent was discontinued in both Nevada and Utah, which were made independent agencies. Reverend George Balcolm was made special agent for the Pyramid Lake Indians, but his tenure was brief, and on August 17, 1871, he was relieved by C. A. Bateman, who had been appointed Indian Agent for Nevada.[9]

Bateman remained in this position for four years and apparently did very good work, considering the difficulties he was forced to meet and the meager appropriations of Congress for the Indian Service in Nevada. In 1872 no tribe of Indians in Nevada had any treaty relations with the federal government; there was not a school for Indians in the entire state, and the total appropriation for an Indian population estimated at 13,000 was $15,000 a year.

The situation of the Indians in Utah and of those charged with their administration was not much better. The Northwestern, Western, and Goship bands of Utes, numbering in the aggregate about three thousand, had made treaties with the United States in 1863, by which the first bands were to receive $5,000 each and the Goship band $1,000 annually for twenty years. This provided less than four dollars per capita each year for these Indians which certainly was not adequate for subsistence, clothing, and other needs. Since proper supervision over such widely scattered groups was impossible, it became the primary objective of the Indian Office to concentrate the roving bands in Utah upon the great Uintah Valley Reservation.

The reservation was large enough to furnish a home for all the Indians of Utah, but there were very definite reasons why no large number could be induced to remain there permanently. In fact, for many years the population of the reservation was only six or seven hundred, although at times other bands would come in and remain for a few weeks or months in order to receive rations, or issues of goods. Unfortunately, appropriations by Congress were so meager that the agent seldom had much to give even to those residing there permanently. Consequently the Indians were always short of food and were frequently forced to go long distances to hunt for game and such

8 *Ibid.*
9 *Ibid., 1871,* 558–61.

135

native products as the forests and mountains afforded, in order to avoid starvation. This interfered with their farming, but a hungry people could not wait for crops to mature. It now seems clear that most of Utah's Indian problems might have been solved by very generous appropriations of funds for the Uintah Valley Agency. If a boarding school, medical service, and sufficient money to provide food, clothing, farming implements, and livestock for every Indian willing to work had been provided, it might have been possible to concentrate almost all of the Indians of Utah under this agency. Such a plan would undoubtedly have gone far toward advancing their civilization.

Obviously there were many hindrances to such a program, and perhaps it is not surprising that neither Congress nor the Indian Bureau showed a disposition to undertake it. Transporting rations and goods such a distance involved great difficulty and enormous expense. The Indians were so remote from white settlements that it was difficult for them to market the furs and buckskins taken by hunting or trapping, or any surplus livestock, farm products, or handmade articles. Also, the lives of the six or seven agency employees must have been intensely lonely, and it is not strange that few were willing to remain long. Agent Crichtlow declared that officials of the Mormon Church deliberately sought to prevent a large concentration of Indians at the Uintah Agency by urging certain bands to remain where they were. This was facilitated, the agent said, by the leaders' jealousies and their unwillingness to risk a loss of authority by bringing their people to a location where they might fall under the influence of some rival leader.[10]

Despite his first unfavorable impression of Uintah Agency, Crichtlow remained in charge of it for more than twelve years, until July 21, 1883, when he was succeeded by Elisha W. Davis.[11] Crichtlow's long tenure established a record for Indian agents in this region, and his work was excellent. Only a man with a real missionary spirit and a deep devotion to the welfare of the Indians could have remained so long at such a remote post with only a half-dozen white associates, and with so many difficulties and hardships to be faced. The advancement of his charges must have seemed to him exceedingly slow, but apparently he never grew discouraged. He established a sawmill and a gristmill, opened an agency farm, encouraged the Indians to grow

[10] Report of Agent Crichtlow, *Annual Report of Commissioner of Indian Affairs, 1877*, 181–86.
[11] *Annual Report of Commissioner of Indian Affairs, 1883*, 139–41.

crops, and earnestly sought to secure a physician and a school for the agency. Although no appropriation was made for a physician, a school was finally opened in 1874.

Before the end of Crichtlow's term of service, many changes had taken place in the Indian situation in Utah. These changes, caused primarily by the Ute War in Colorado and its aftermath, resulted in the removal of most of the Utes of that state to Utah, some to a new reservation and the remainder to the Uintah Valley Reserve.

The removal of the New Mexico Utes to Colorado and the establishment of Los Pinos Agency was keenly resented by many citizens of Colorado. The Ute lands at that time extended over an enormous area, including much of the western part of the state. Far to the north of Los Pinos Agency was the White River Agency, while far to the south was the agency for the Southern Utes. Since miners and prospectors operating in this part of Colorado often trespassed upon the Indian reservation, and Indians hunted both on and off the reservation, clashes between Indians and whites were not uncommon. Settlers and state officials insisted that the Utes should be removed and their lands opened to settlement.

In September of 1879, N. S. Meeker, agent for the White River Ute, who was unpopular because of his arbitrary acts, was attacked by an Indian. Meeker, finding the situation very tense, called for military aid, and Major T. T. Thornburgh left Fort Fred Steele, Wyoming, September 24, with some two hundred troops and marched toward the agency. On Milk River, some thirty miles away, Thornburgh's force was ambushed by the Utes, and the commanding officer together with nine of his men were killed, and forty-three men were wounded. The remainder of the force was able to withstand the Indians for six days, until General Wesley Merritt arrived with reinforcements. In the meantime, the Utes attacked the agency, killed Agent Meeker and seven employees, and took Mrs. Meeker and two other women captive. Chief Ouray, who was always friendly to the whites, was away on a hunting trip when this massacre occurred. It was through his efforts that further hostilities were averted and the captives released.[12]

The Meeker massacre increased the demands of the people of Colorado that the Utes be removed at once from the state. Accordingly, the Ute Commission was appointed to negotiate with these Indians for their removal to Utah, and after long discussion, came to an agree-

12 See J. P. Dunn, *Massacres of the Mountains*, for an extended account of the Meeker massacre. For a brief account see *Dictionary of American History*, III, 371.

ment on March 6, 1880. It was found impossible to fix responsibility for the massacre upon any individual, and the tribe eventually purchased immunity from punishment by agreeing to cede their lands in Colorado and move to the Uintah Reservation in Utah. Also the Uncompahgre Ute, formerly known as the Tabequache, whose agency was at Los Pinos, ceded their reservation and agreed to move to a new one to be created for them just east of the Uintah Reserve. Only the Southern Ute, who had given no trouble, were allowed to retain their comparatively small reservation in Colorado.[13] The agreement was ratified by Congress on June 15, 1880, and the White River Utes removed to Uintah, where they were to receive allotments in severalty when the lands had been surveyed.[14] The reservation for the Uncompahgre was set aside by executive order on January 5, 1882.[15] It consisted of nearly two million acres, mostly mountains and desert, but a small part of the land was suitable for agriculture if water for irrigation could be provided. The reported number of Uncompahgre was about twelve hundred and fifty. They were poor and showed little disposition to accept white civilization. For years there was no school and no missionary work among these Indians and even after a school was established, the agent had great difficulty in getting the children to attend it.

The Ute agreement provided that the White River Utes and Uncompahgre combined should receive a cash payment of $50,000 annually to be distributed individually. Strictly speaking, the Uintah were not included in this annuity, but it was agreed that they should share in it when they admitted the White River Utes to the Uintah Reservation. The amount of money was about fourteen dollars per capita for the Uintah and the Uncompahgre, but a large sum was deducted from the White River share to pay pensions to the families of the Meeker massacre, leaving to the latter tribe only six or seven dollars each. In some cases the Indians agreed to allow part of this annuity to be used for the purchase of cattle for the tribe, but as a rule they demanded a cash payment. By 1885, however, the Uncompahgre had a tribal herd of over twelve hundred head.[16]

13 This reservation is, in 1948, the only one in Colorado. It is known as Consolidated Ute, and the agency is at Ignacio near the southern boundary of the state.

14 21 *Stats.*, 199. The commission was abolished by act of Congress, March 3, 1883; its work was to be continued by an official of the Department of the Interior. 22 *Stats.*, 499.

15 *Executive Orders Relating to Indian Reservations, 1855–1912*, 170–71.

16 *Annual Report of Commissioner of Indian Affairs, 1885*, 176–80.

Elisha W. Davis, who succeeded J. J. Crichtlow at the Uintah Agency in 1883, remained in charge until near the end of 1885 when he was succeeded by T. A. Bynum. The agency buildings at Ouray were very poor and there was no room to maintain a separate agency there; therefore, on July 1, 1886, Ouray and Uintah were consolidated, under Bynum. In the future only a subagency was maintained for Ouray, sometimes in charge of an Indian Service farmer.[17]

The problems of the agent for Uintah were vastly increased by the addition of this huge area; he now had the responsibility for more than two thousand Indians scattered over a region embracing over four million acres. Moreover, there were jealousies among these three tribes; the Uintahs did not like the White Rivers and neither of them showed any fondness for the Uncompahgre. At times various bands of Indians grew restive and troublesome, and in one or two cases the agent felt that his life was in danger. Since white ranchmen trespassed on the Uintah Reservation, Robert Waugh, who became agent in July, 1890, began to collect a grazing tax from whites who pastured cattle on the Uintah Reserve, thus providing the Indians with additional funds for food, clothing, and agricultural implements.[18] A few months later, the leasing of Indian lands for grazing or mining was authorized by Congress, and in 1893 Agent Waugh leased 675,000 acres in the western part of the Uintah Reserve for grazing for five years at an annual rental of $7,100.[19] That year a school was opened at the Ouray subagency and three brick buildings were provided, but it was possible to secure only twenty pupils. The Uncompahgre at this time were receiving 450,000 pounds of beef annually besides flour, sugar, coffee, tea, salt, and baking powder, as well as blankets, overcoats, shawls, ginghams, and other goods. Since the tribe numbered little over one thousand, it is clear that they derived nearly all of their support from the federal government.[20] The Uintah and White Rivers were somewhat more self-supporting, but even they derived approximately half of their subsistence and clothing from the United States Government.

After the act of February 8, 1887,[21] allowing for allotments in severalty, officials of the Indian Office apportioned lands to individual Indians on the various reservations as rapidly as possible. It was felt

17 *Ibid., 1887,* 199–201.
18 Report of Agent Waugh, *Annual Report of Commissioner of Indian Affairs, 1890,* 214–16.
19 *Ibid., 1893,* 316–20.
20 *Ibid.*
21 24 *Stats.,* 388.

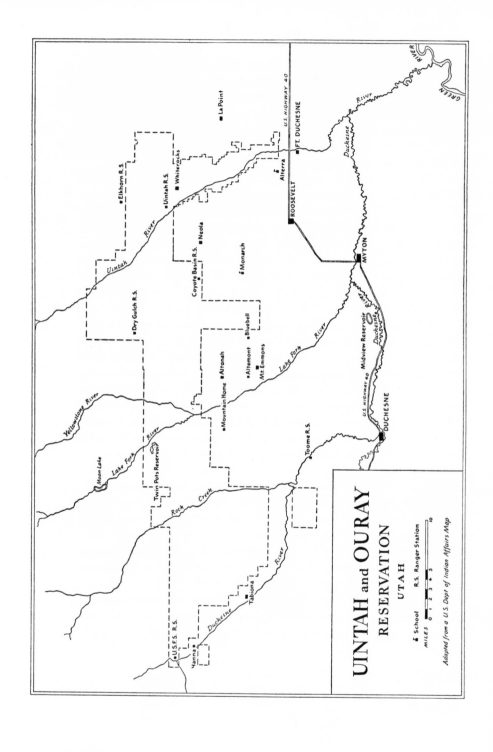

UINTAH and OURAY
RESERVATION
UTAH

🏫 School   R.S. Ranger Station

MILES 0 1 2 3 4 5   10

Adapted from a U.S. Dept of Indian Affairs Map

that once the Indian had received a farm of his own, he would speedily become an industrious self-supporting farmer. Nothing of the sort took place. Even if an Indian's allotment had a considerable area of land suitable for farming, he usually had no work animals, tools, seeds for planting, or, in fact, any of the things needed to transform a tract of raw land into a real farm. Most important of all, he lacked both the desire to farm and the knowledge of even the first principles of agriculture. In most cases he refused to live on his allotment and roamed about in exactly the same fashion as he always had. Yet, the Indian Office and members of Congress were slow to understand this, and many more years elapsed before there came a tardy realization that the allotment act had frequently proved a distinct evil, rather than an advantage, to large numbers of Indians. Nevertheless, a commission was sent out from Washington in 1895 to assign farms to the Uncompahgre and to negotiate with the Indians of the Uintah Reserve to cede a portion of their fertile lands.[22]

The Indians on the Ouray Reservation were opposed to such allotments, and none were made until Congress specifically directed the secretary of the interior to allot lands to the Uncompahgre and to open all unallotted agricultural lands of the Ouray Reservation after April 1, 1898, to white settlement. James F. Randlett (agent from 1895 to 1898) asserted that this act was the work of certain whites who sought possession of valuable asphalt deposits on the reservation and who had been urging Congress to take such action for four years. He felt that the act was unfair to the Indians and urged that Congress reconsider it.[23]

H. P. Myton, who became agent in 1898, also reported that the Uncompahgre had been badly treated and that, although their reservation had been taken from them and opened to white settlement, not a single homestead entry had been made on these lands. He recommended that the lands be returned to the Indians.[24] This was not done, but since no whites settled there, the Indians continued to use the former reservation as a hunting ground.[25]

In the meantime most of the Indians of Nevada, like the Indians in Utah, were on no reserve, but roamed about, working for the

[22] Annual Report of Commissioner of Indian Affairs, 1895, 309–12.

[23] Ibid., 1897, 285–86 and 1898, 292–96. The work of allotting lands to these Indians was done by the Uncompahgre Commission, the chairman of which was G. F. Barge.

[24] Ibid., 1899, 351–52.

[25] See H. M. Tidwell, "Uintah and Ouray Indian Agency," Utah Historical Quarterly, Vol. IV, No. 1 (January, 1931), for sketch of this agency.

whites, or making a living as best they could. Charles F. Powell, who had been appointed special agent for the Indians of southeastern Nevada, strongly recommended a reservation for them, and in 1873 his successor, G. W. Ingalls, was able to accomplish this.[26] Work at this new Moapa Reservation started well: a school was established and a physician employed. The number of Indians on the reservation declined so rapidly, however, that before 1900 only a few families made it their permanent home. It was under the control of the Nevada agent, but since it was some six hundred miles from the agency, he could exercise little supervision over it.

C. A. Bateman remained as Indian agent for Nevada from 1871 until 1875. Although Moapa and western Shoshone were nominally under his authority, his jurisdiction was primarily Pyramid Lake and Walker River reservations, both of which were given a permanent status in 1874, being set aside by executive order as Indian reservations.[27]

The Nevada Agency was located on the Pyramid Lake Reserve a few miles north of Wadsworth, a little town on the Union Pacific Railway on reservation lands. Each reservation had an area of some 320,000 acres, and each included the waters of a large lake. It is difficult to determine the number of Indians who resided permanently on these reservations; for many of the Indians left them frequently to gather piñon nuts in the mountains, or to go on hunting expeditions, or to work for the whites. As a rule, however, each reservation had only five or six hundred Indian residents and at times even less, although the numbers increased somewhat in later years.[28]

Bateman's successor, A. J. Barnes, who had spent five years at Moapa River, remained in charge of the Nevada Agency for over five years. He erected a sawmill on the Pyramid Lake Reserve in an effort to provide better housing for the Indians and also established a school which opened on March 1, 1878. Western Shoshone Agency was under the supervision of an Indian service farmer for some years after its establishment. He issued rations and annuity goods to his widely scattered charges but was eager to have a reservation created for them. Some lands near Elko were reserved as farms for the Shoshone in 1877,

[26] *Executive Orders Relating to Indian Reservations, 1855–1912.* Set aside first by executive order, this was changed in 1874; by an act of Congress, March 3, 1875, the reservation was reduced to 1,000 acres.

[27] *Ibid.,* 114–15. Walker River was established March 18, and Pyramid Lake, March 23, 1874, by order of President Grant.

[28] See *Annual Reports of Commissioner of Indian Affairs, 1877,* 150–51, and *1878,* 102–104.

but two years later this grant was cancelled, and the lands were returned to the public domain because a new reservation was created for them: Duck Valley, established by executive order April 16, 1877, with an area of 243,200 acres.[29] It was near the northern boundary of the state, extending across the state line into Idaho. Some Shoshone occupied it, but these Indians were slow to move to the reservation, and Levi A. Gheen, farmer in charge of the Western Shoshone Agency, urged that all issues of rations and supplies be made on the reservation as an incentive to the Indians to take up their permanent residence there.[30]

Joseph M. McMaster succeeded Barnes in Nevada; he sought to encourage the Indians of Pyramid Lake and Walker River to do more farming despite the fact that not over nine thousand acres on both reservations were suitable for agriculture. McMaster pointed out that the Indians regarded all food as common property. Consequently any hungry Indian felt free to dig and use potatoes planted by one of his fellow tribesmen, or to appropriate corn or vegetables grown by another Indian just as if such crops were native products.[31] This Indian custom of regarding both land and food as common property was almost universal and still persists. In 1884 Congress had passed the Indian Homestead Act allowing Indians to take homesteads which were to be inalienable for twenty-five years,[32] but efforts to persuade the landless Indians of Nevada to take such homesteads were unavailing, as had been efforts to induce the Indians to take allotments. None were made prior to 1890, although about fifty Indians received them the following year.[33]

McMaster constructed additional dams and ditches on the Pyramid Lake Reserve, but there was not sufficient fertile land under irrigation at either Pyramid Lake or Walker River to provide a living for the Indians. Those at Pyramid Lake derived a large amount of income from the sale of fish, sometimes marketing annually as much as 90,000 pounds of Pyramid Lake trout at an average price of six cents a pound.[34]

On the whole the Indians of the Pyramid Lake and Walker River reservations made considerable progress during the decade of the

29 *Executive Orders Relating to Indian Reservations, 1855–1912*, 109–10. The reservation was somewhat enlarged on May 4, 1886.
30 *Annual Report of Commissioner of Indian Affairs, 1878*, 104–105.
31 *Ibid., 1881*, 130–32.
32 *23 Stats.*, 96.
33 *Annual Report of Commissioner of Indian Affairs, 1891*, 298–302.
34 *Ibid., 1889*, 249–51.

1880's, though their advancement was doubtless hindered to some extent by too frequent changes of agents. McMaster had established a boarding school at Pyramid Lake and a day school was in operation at Walker River; both seemed to be fairly well attended although there were many objections on the part of Indian parents to sending their children to boarding school.[35] Since about one-fourth of the Pyramid Lake Indians lived in Wadsworth, a day school for their children was established there.[36]

In 1891 came the beginning of the so-called "Messiah Craze," which was to extend to many tribes throughout the United States and to result in grave difficulties with the Sioux. This was started by Jack Wilson of the Pyramid Lake Reservation, who eventually was visited by delegations of Indians from tribes all over the country. These delegations often had letters from their agents authorizing such visits and Agent Warner protested to the Indian Office against issuance of such letters. Curiously enough, the Messiah Movement, or Ghost Dance religion, caused little trouble among the Indians of the reservation where it originated, or even in Nevada as a whole. It was in far-off Dakota and Montana that it created excitement, culminating in bloody warfare.[37] This indicates that even among Indians "a prophet is not without honor save in his own country."

The Indians of Western Shoshone Agency were making further progress. The treaty granting these Indians an annuity expired in 1883, but the federal government continued to supply them with rations, clothing, and other goods. They depended upon hunting for a living, and it was difficult for the agent to keep them on the reservation or to induce them to take much interest in farming. A tribal court and police were established at the agency, but usually there was little work for either. In 1884 the Indian Office inspector urged that the reservation be abandoned and the Indians removed to the Fort Hall Reservation in Idaho, but the tribe was unwilling to leave Duck Valley.[38]

---

[35] Ibid.

[36] Ibid., 1891, 298–302. On October 17, 1891, the Indians of Pyramid Lake Reserve agreed to cede a strip of land on the southern part of the reservation where the town of Wadsworth was located for $25,000 to be invested in cattle. The agreement was not ratified by Congress, however, and the white people of Wadsworth became uneasy over their situation since they held no title to the lands on which their homes and business houses had been built. At last, in 1899, by the Indian Appropriation Act, Congress gave the citizens of Wadsworth the right to acquire from the Indians title to 640 acres of land on which the town was located, finally settling an irritating problem of long standing.

[37] Ibid. [38] Ibid., 1889, 128–30.

Indian turkey grower, Walker River Reservation, Carson Agency

Courtesy Milton Snow, Navajo Service

Navajo shepherds

John B. Scott, who became agent at Western Shoshone in 1885,[39] urged the federal government to issue fewer annuity goods and less "tepee cloth" and more lumber to build houses for the Indians. He also felt that some means should be devised to compel parents to keep their children in school. Apparently this agency was neglected by the Indian Office, for by 1889 the buildings were badly in need of repair, and when this was reported to the commissioner by Inspector F. C. Armstrong, Agent Scott replied with considerable heat that his requests for funds had been repeatedly ignored. Scott also intimated that there had been gross mismanagement and waste of government funds by the Indian Office in purchasing beef for this reservation. He declared that $12.40 a hundred was the price paid the contractor but that the latter sublet the contract to someone who purchased beef from Indian cattle owners for less than half that price.[40]

Scott was succeeded in 1889 by William I. Plumb, who served for four years, and was followed by four other agents within seven years. During this time, the day school was converted into a boarding school, a physician was secured, a hospital erected, and rations, in limited quantities, were issued regularly to the Indians. No great change in conditions at the agency took place, and advancement in civilization was slow.

There was a growing demand for the establishment of a large nonreservation Indian school in the state to which Indian children from the entire area might be brought. Eventually the state legislature of Nevada appropriated $10,000 for such a school, provided the federal government would establish one. Accordingly, Carson School, first known as Stewart Institute, opened its doors to students on December 17, 1890, beginning with thirty-seven pupils. By January 1, 1891, the number had increased to ninety-one, and soon thereafter to more than one hundred.[41]

In 1895 a bill was introduced in Congress providing for the cession of Walker River Reserve by the Indians and the transfer of those residing there to Pyramid Lake Reservation. Albert K. Smiley, of the Board of Indian Commissioners, visited Nevada, and reported that the bill was promoted by officials of the Carson and Colorado Railway, which crossed the Walker River Reservation. They sought the approval of the Indians by promising them free transportation

---

39 *Ibid.*, 251–53.

40 Report of Agent Scott, *Annual Report of Commissioner of Indian Affairs, 1889*, 251–53.

41 *Annual Report of Commissioner of Indian Affairs, 1891*, 571.

of their products and by giving Indians of the Walker River Reserve passes to ride on their trains. Smiley, as well as the Indian agent, urged that the bill be rejected by Congress because it would benefit only the whites.[42] As a result of these protests the bill was defeated.

On April 1, 1897, Walker River Reserve and the Indians belonging to it were removed from the jurisdiction of the Nevada Agency and placed under the superintendent of Carson School. This left only Pyramid Lake under the direct control of the Nevada Agency, although it also had nominal jurisdiction over the little Moapa River Reserve, some six hundred miles away, and also over the landless Indians of the state.

At the close of the century officials responsible for the administration of Indian affairs would have been forced to admit that their efforts to advance the Indians of Utah and Nevada had not been too successful. Most of the Indians of the Great Basin were still landless and still very poor; those on the reservations depended for a living largely upon rations and "annuity goods" furnished by the federal government.

Lack of progress was due to the remoteness of a region composed largely of deserts and mountains, where the aboriginal inhabitants had always been very poor and low in the scale of civilization. Added to this were the activities of greedy and unscrupulous settlers and local political leaders. As in all other parts of the country, the Indian Service in Utah and Nevada during this period was hampered by governmental red tape, inadequate appropriations by Congress, inefficient and, at times, corrupt officials, and a great many other things. Yet progress had been made. There were comparatively few Indian outbreaks in the period from 1869 to 1900, and depredations by Indians upon the whites were seldom serious. Schools had been established at Uintah Valley and Ouray in Utah, at Pyramid Lake, Walker River, and Western Shoshone in Nevada, and the important non-reservation school near Carson City had been created and was growing rapidly. The Indian Bureau had not been able to resist the pressure for opening the lands of the Uncompahgre Ute, or Ouray Reserve, to white settlement, but Walker River Reservation had been saved for the Indians.

[42] See Smiley's report, *ibid.*, *1895–96*, 101–103.

X

Indian Administration in the Southwest
1900–33

By THE TURN OF THE CENTURY, improvements in communications— railroads, wagon roads, bridges, telegraph lines, and a postal service— had brought the various sections of the Southwest into closer contact with one another and with the outside world. The administration of Indian affairs reflected this change, and the story of the entire area henceforth need not be divided regionally but can be surveyed as a whole. In spite of mistakes and painfully slow progress, by 1900 the Indian Bureau had accomplished a great deal, which becomes evident when we remember how savage and primitive the tribes had been a half century earlier, how remote and arid the country was, how inadequately Congress had provided funds, and how shortsighted the Washington policy makers had been. Taking over the administration of many tribes of varying degrees of culture, scattered over a vast, unknown, and remote region, the federal government had by 1900 established agencies and reservations, inaugurated an educational system, provided a health service, and changed many of the Indians from fierce and lawless nomads and hunters to peaceful farmers. Rations, clothing, blankets, and other "annuity goods" had been dispensed. Great tribal herds of cattle and sheep had been established. Field matrons had been sent out to teach the women housekeeping and child care. Principles of hygiene and sanitation had been taught. Indian police had been trained and tribal courts established to maintain order.

In 1901 the only Indian agency in Southern California was that for the Mission Indians located at San Jacinto. In 1903 the jurisdiction was divided into two agencies, one remaining at San Jacinto, the other established at Pala.[1] There were thirty-two Mission Indian reservations, including the Tule River, and the Indians numbered

1 See Chapter VI.

3,002.[2] Some Indians resided in Owens Valley, where three day schools had been established under the jurisdiction of the Carson School (Walker River) Agency in Nevada. Most of the Indians of southern and central California, however, did not live upon any reservation. In Arizona there were eight separate Indian jurisdictions: Yuma, Colorado River, Pima,[3] Hualapai, San Carlos, Fort Apache, Hopi, and Navajo. In addition there was the Phoenix nonreservation school, which was also given control of the little Fort McDowell Reservation when the latter was established in 1903.[4] There were thirteen distinct reservations, on which lived some forty thousand Indians.

By 1900 the Navajo were all under the control of a single agency, but the great size of the reservation and the rapidly increasing numbers of the Navajo tribe made administration from a single center difficult. Accordingly on July 1, 1901, the western portion of the reservation was set aside as a separate jurisdiction, and Milton J. Needham, superintendent of the western Navajo Industrial School, was placed in charge.[5] Additional lands added to the Navajo Reservation soon caused further subdivision, with the establishment of an administrative center for Navajo Extension at Canyon Diablo, and for the Northern Navajo at Ship Rock, New Mexico.[6] Further subdivisions were later made, but in 1934 administration of the Navajo was again concentrated at a single center with the establishment of a new agency at Window Rock, only a few miles from Fort Defiance, which since that time has had control over all the Navajo country and people.

New Mexico had but four Indian agencies: the two Pueblo jurisdictions, one administered from Santa Fé and the other from Albuquerque, the Mescalero Agency and reservation in the southern part of the territory, and the Jicarilla Agency in the extreme north. Utah had, at that time, but one important jurisdiction, Uintah and Ouray, a huge reservation inhabited by only a few hundred Indians; but there were one or two small reserves with schools, as Shivwits and Panguitch. Nevada had three agencies: Carson School, which also had jurisdiction over Walker River Reservation, the little Fort Mc-Dermitt Reserve, and three day schools in California; Nevada Agency,

---

[2] *Annual Report of Commissioner of Indian Affairs, 1901,* 195–201.

[3] In 1902, San Xavier, formerly under Pima Agency, was made a separate jurisdiction and an acting agent appointed. *Ibid., 1902,* 167–69.

[4] *Ibid., 1905,* 173. Yuma was sometimes reported to be an agency of California and at other times of Arizona.

[5] *Ibid., 1900,* Vol. I, 164–66.

[6] *Ibid., 1904,* 144, 252.

which administered the Pyramid Lake Reservation and Moapa River Reserve; and Western Shoshone, in charge of the Duck Valley Reservation which extended across the line into Idaho. In southern Colorado was the Consolidated Ute Agency at Ignacio near the New Mexico border. The total number of Indians in the five states and territories dealt with in this study was given by the Indian Bureau in 1900 as 71,536.[7]

Such was the Indian situation in the Southwest at the beginning of this century; it remained almost the same throughout the period from 1901 to 1933 and was not greatly changed even in 1948.

Critics of the Indian Service have pointed at instances of shameful neglect, of treaties made and never kept, of agreements ignored, and of corruption and graft and incompetence. But these instances were, on the whole, outweighed by other examples of patient effort on the part of agents of the Service who wrought great changes for bettering the condition of their charges. The mistakes that were made were due mainly to ignorance on the part of officials in Washington, and even of agents in the field, about the nature of the Indian. The allotment of land in severalty, for instance, proved to be a mistake because of the very nature of the region and the Indian's attitude toward ownership. By 1920 more than 96 per cent of the Indian land was still held in common ownership.[8]

Another mistake was the overlavish issuance of rations and annuity goods, which, after some years, the Indians came to accept as theirs by right. The idea that the United States Government owed them a living became so firmly implanted in their minds that many refused to make any effort to support themselves. Large groups, sometimes entire tribes, were pauperized by the ration system. A great many Indians traded the blankets and other necessities issued to them for liquor or jewelry. In 1901 orders were sent to reservation superintendents to reduce the issue of clothing and food in order to induce

---

7 *Ibid., 1900,* Vol. I, 638–52. These were distributed as follows: Arizona, 40,189; California (including Yuma and those Indians in the central and northern portions of the state) 11,431; Nevada, 8,321; New Mexico (exclusive of the Navajo), 9,480; and Utah, 2,115. Comparable figures for 1920 are Arizona, 42,400; California, 16,241; Nevada, 5,900; New Mexico, 21,530 (now includes part of Navajo tribe formerly counted in Arizona); and Utah, 3,057.

8 By 1911 the total Indian population of Arizona, California, Nevada, New Mexico, and Arizona, had increased to 85,071. These Indians owned a total of 23,304,877 acres of land, of which 919,157 acres had been allotted. In 1920 the number of Indians in these states was 89,128, with land holdings aggregating 26,195,-297 acres, of which only 964,780 had been allotted. *Annual Report of Commissioner of Indian Affairs, 1911,* 54, 95–98; *1920,* 64, 82–85.

the Indians to support themselves.[9] Indian agents found it difficult to comply. To the Indian it was unthinkable that anyone with food should deny it to someone else who was hungry. A week's rations distributed to the old, sick, and helpless was freely shared with the young and able-bodied. As a result, whatever was distributed was consumed within a day or two and all starved together for the remainder of the week. This communal use of food constituted one of the gravest of the agent's problems when he began to apply the rule of feeding only those unable to work.

To assist the Indian to help himself, the government employed farmers to teach him how to grow crops and care for livestock. "Reimbursable funds" were provided to purchase cattle and sheep. Additional funds were made available to build roads, construct irrigation dams and ditches, to drill wells, and to erect sawmills. Jobs were found for Indians who were not engaged in these pursuits.

Some of the mistakes sprang from a misinterpretation of the term "civilization." To some officials and agents civilizing the Indian meant giving him a house to live in, and making him wear white men's clothing. The government built houses which the Indians used for storing hay while they continued to live in grass tepees. Indians cut the legs off the trousers to wear as leggings, discarding the rest of the garment. The Indians who received allotments of land continued to live anywhere they chose and failed to improve the land granted them. In 1896 an order went out from Washington that all male Indians should be required to wear their hair short.[10] Fortunately most of the superintendents refused to take the order too seriously, and it was later countermanded; but it is said that a quarter of a century later visitors at the Duck Valley Agency might still see the iron shackles that were clamped upon the legs and arms of Western Shoshone while their locks were being shorn by an agency barber. In 1902 Agent Charles E. Burton included in his annual report the comment: "Their long hair is the last tie that binds them to their old customs of savagery and the sooner it is cut, Gordian like, the better it will be for them. I am in full sympathy with the original order and regret that there was any backward step in the matter."[11]

Notwithstanding the efforts to make the Indians self-supporting, the ration system could not be too suddenly discontinued. The de-

9 *Ibid., 1901,* 6.
10 See *ibid., 1900,* 291, for reference to difficulties of the agent of the Mescalero in carrying out this order with respect to his Indian police.
11 *Ibid., 1902,* 153.

struction of the game by whites had removed an important source of the Indians' former food supply, and the lands granted to them were largely of a type which the white man did not want because he could not derive a living from them. It was doubly difficult for the Indians to farm these lands with their meager knowledge of agriculture. Periods of drought and crop failure, moreover, often made it necessary to provide some tribes with temporary subsistence. As late as 1910 the Jicarilla Apache were issued in one year 150,000 pounds gross weight of beef, or slightly over 200 pounds for every member of the tribe.[12] The total value of all rations issued in the Southwest by 1911 had dwindled to $57,889.87 annually, or around sixty cents each.[13] And there was little reduction in the issuance of rations during the next ten years.

However, the federal government spent large sums in helping the Indians in other ways. The total appropriation for the Indian Service in 1901 was $9,040,479.80.[14] This had increased to considerably more than $10,000,000 by 1910, after which appropriations consistently rose with occasional fluctuation, until in 1932 they amounted to more than $26,000,000, about $1,250,000 of which was for the Indians of Alaska.[15] While a part of these increased funds were spent for administration, the greater part of them was expended for irrigation and water development, the purchase of lands, livestock and implements, and education, hospitals and medical service, for the Indian.

The outbreak of the first World War greatly affected the Indians and their relations with the federal government. Many of them entered the armed forces, serving ably and well; others, attracted by high wages, left the reservation to work on the railroads or in mines, shops, or factories. The inflation in prices which occurred during the war and continued for some years after its close affected the Indians of the region in much the same fashion that it affected the whites. Higher prices for food, clothing, transportation, furniture, the construction of buildings, and of irrigation works were to a large extent responsible for the need of greatly increased appropriations for the Indians.

Although this was a period of great scientific advancement which brought about radical changes in the manner of living of most of the people of the United States, it brought comparatively little change in the life of the Indians of the Southwest, or in the methods pursued

12 *Ibid., 1910,* 128.   13 *Ibid., 1911,* 154.
14 *Ibid., 1901,* 7.   15 *Ibid., 1931,* 26.

by the federal government in administering their affairs. The Indian, always conservative and wedded to his old customs, progressed with what seemed to many persons an astonishing slowness. Critics of the Indian Bureau, including such organizations as the Indian Defense Association, complained that despite greatly increased appropriations, the solution of the Indian problem seemed no nearer than it had been a generation before. They asserted that due to allotment in severalty, the issuance of fee patents, and the sale of heirship lands, the Indian was rapidly being deprived of his patrimony, and that another generation would find a large portion of the Indians of the country landless paupers, a charge upon the public, and a perpetual source of annoyance and trouble to their white neighbors. They protested that the health conditions of the Indians were deplorable, their schools and hospitals were substandard and badly administered, and that inadequate protection against selfish and unscrupulous whites had been afforded them by the federal government.

The widespread criticism eventually prompted Secretary of the Interior Herbert Work to make an honest effort to learn the truth about conditions among the Indians of the United States as a whole, to what extent the federal government was responsible for any existing evils, and what it might do to correct them. Accordingly, on June 12, 1926, he formally requested the Institute for Government Research in Washington, D. C., to make a survey with special reference to relations with the federal government and to report to him its findings and recommendations.

The Institute was "an association for co-operating with public officials in the scientific study of government with a view to promoting efficiency and economy in its operations and advancing the science of administration."[16] Dr. W. F. Willoughby, its director, agreed to undertake the survey, provided he could secure the necessary funds and recruit a staff largely outside the Institute, since it would be able to provide only a technical director. The necessary funds were secured from private sources, and a technical staff was formed. The staff consisted of a specialist in each of the fields of education, health, sociology, economics, agriculture, statistics, and law.[17]

After a month of preliminary work in Washington, formulating

[16] It has since been merged with the Brookings Institution.

[17] The personnel consisted of Lewis Meriam of the Institute for Government Research, technical director; Ray A. Brown; Henry Roe Cloud; Edward Everett Dale; Emma Duke; Herbert R. Edwards; Fayette Avery McKenzie; Mary Louise Mark; W. Carson Ryan, Jr.; and William A. Spillman. For personal data on each, see Lewis Meriam *et al, The Problem of Indian Administration*, 79–85.

plans and collecting data on the various jurisdictions to be visited, the survey staff spent over seven months in field work. During this time, one or more of its members visited ninety-five different jurisdictions. In the Southwest, all agencies and jurisdictions were visited except Camp Verde and Kaibab in Arizona and Moapa River and Western Shoshone in Nevada.[18] While the time spent on most reservations was necessarily brief, it was possible to accomplish much, since each specialist devoted his entire time to his particular field. The data he collected was assembled by the field secretary. Councils with the Indians were held at most agencies, many of them being arranged by the full-blood Indian member of the survey group, Henry Roe Cloud. Transportation over the reservation was furnished by the Indian Service, and agents and school superintendents supplied members of the staff with lodging during their stay if hotel accommodations were not available, but all other expenses were borne by the private agencies which subsidized the survey.

After completing the field work, the group returned to Washington and spent some three months in formulating a rough draft of the report, which was completed by Lewis Meriam, technical director. It was published in 1928 with the title of *The Problem of Indian Administration*, but it is generally known as the "Meriam Report."

The report declared that emergencies existed with respect to some phases of the administration of Indian affairs, and presented a few recommendations for immediate action. One of these was the establishment of a Division of Planning and Development, for which an appropriation of $25,000 should be sought from Congress at the earliest possible moment. An additional $75,000 should also be secured as soon as possible for the employment of six medical specialists, a senior personnel officer and an assistant, a senior statistician, statistical clerks, and equipment for their work.[19] Another recommendation was that an appropriation of five million dollars be sought from Congress for the general improvement of the Indian Service. Finally, it urged that the matter of securing promptly an adequate supply of properly qualified employees be taken up at once with the United States Civil Service Commission.[20]

These recommendations were particularly applicable to the Indian Service in the Southwest where careful planning by experienced specialists was necessary. That the Indian Service had for many years been forced to operate upon grossly insufficient funds was the settled opinion of every member of the survey staff, and this was especially

18 *Ibid.*, 65.   19 *Ibid.*, 52.   20 *Ibid.*, 54.

true in the Southwest. The arid nature of that region necessitated the expenditure of large sums for irrigation, and the extension of the boundaries of reservations such as that of the Navajo, and the improvement in breeds of livestock, were necessary before the Indian could be expected to maintain himself according to even minimum standards of health and decency. The Southwest was, moreover, the "full blood area" where many tribes had much further to go than did some others of the country before their members reached a standard of living commensurate with that of the whites.

It was obvious to all members of the survey group that salaries in the Indian Service were far too low. This again applied with peculiar force to the Southwest, where the hardships, loneliness, and inconvience incident to living and working (often at a distance of from seventy-five to a hundred miles from any railroad or town) required extra compensation if the Service was not to lose many of its ablest and most efficient employees.[21] Living quarters were lamentably poor in 1928, and large sums for repairs and new construction would be necessary to provide adequate housing of Indian Service employees.

It was painfully apparent that low salaries and poor living conditions were reflected in the quality of personnel of the Indian Service. Most agency employees were intelligent, faithful, and conscientious in the performance of their duties, but a very large number of them lacked adequate training for the work they were expected to do. The reservation superintendents, on the other hand, were almost without exception men of good education and great administrative capacity, devoted to their work and alert to the needs of the Indians. In fact, it seemed surprising that the Indian Bureau had been able to secure officials of such high qualities. The report also proposed the maximum practical decentralization of authority to give to those officials dealing directly with the Indians the largest possible measure of initiative and responsibility.[22]

The Meriam Report constitutes an important landmark in the history of the administration of Indian affairs by the federal government. Soon after its appearance the Secretary of the Interior appointed a committee of six officials from his department, including certain prominent members of the field force of the Indian Bureau, to study this report and submit to him its own findings and recommenda-

[21] Tuba City, at that time the site of Western Navajo Agency, is about a hundred miles from any railroad or town; Keams Canyon, the location of the Hopi Agency, is nearly as far; and Kayenta subagency much farther.

[22] For a full discussion of its recommendations, see Meriam *et al., op. cit.,* 113–54.

tions.[23] The committee met on November 12, 1928, and, on December 5, submitted its report in the form of a monograph of thirty-nine mimeographed pages. While it did not take up in detail each of the recommendations included in the Meriam Report, it stated that the committee fully agreed with most of them.[24] It then offered its own recommendations, divided into two groups—the plans that could be carried out without further appropriations and others which would require additional funds from Congress. It gave in broad, general terms an analysis of the problems to be solved in promoting Indian welfare as seen by persons who had, in some cases, spent the greater part of their lives in the Indian Service.

On July 1, 1929, the Commissioner of Indian Affairs, Charles H. Burke, who had served in that capacity for more than eight years, was succeeded by Charles J. Rhoads of Pennsylvania. Commissioner Rhoads was a very different type of man from his predecessors, almost all of whom had been political appointees. He was a successful banker with wide experience in the administration of a number of important business enterprises. In addition he was a scholar and was especially well-known for his philanthropy. He accepted the position reluctantly, but gave to the difficult task his best efforts, bringing to bear all the resources of a well-trained mind together with his broad experience as an executive. As rapidly and as fully as possible, he sought to put into operation the chief recommendations of the Meriam Report, but no sudden change in the general condition of the Indians could be made by new policies or by new methods of administrative procedure. It required patient and persistent education, in the broadest sense of the term, over a long period of time. After some months of conscientious effort, Rhoads confessed that "the appointment as Commissioner of an experienced business executive with little knowledge of Indian affairs and in consequence, no preconceived ideas might be excellent in theory but not so good in practice."[25] He declared that he was appalled by the intricate nature of the Indian situation and the mass of detailed information necessary to arrive at even a reasonable understanding of all of its complexities.

Mr. Rhoads served as commissioner of Indian affairs until early

[23] The chairman of this committee was John A. Buntin, district superintendent and also superintendent of the Kiowa Agency in Oklahoma.
[24] *Report of the Interior Department Committee on "The Problem of Indian Administration,"* 1. The committee especially stressed the need for additional funds and strongly endorsed the recommendation for the creation of a scientific "Division of Planning and Development."
[25] Statement of Commissioner Rhoads to the author.

in 1933 and did a great deal to promote the welfare of the Indians of the Southwest and of the entire country. During his tenure both the schools and the health service were much improved, and more scientific methods in the work of the Bureau and in the administration of the various agencies were adopted.

The United States Senate also ordered an investigation of conditions among the Indians. The committee consisted of Senators Lynn J. Frazier of North Dakota, Robert M. LaFollette of Wisconsin, Burton K. Wheeler of Montana, and Elmer Thomas of Oklahoma. Senator Frazier was named chairman, and Senator W. B. Pine of Oklahoma served for a time as a member of the subcommittee. In addition, the senior senator of the state concerned in the hearings became a member ex officio. The committee was empowered to hold hearings in Washington and in the field, to summon witnesses, to receive and record their testimony, and to publish the same for the use of the Senate Committee on Indian Affairs. The work was begun in 1928 and was not completed until 1933.[26] During the recess periods of Congress, the committee, often accompanied by Assistant Commissioner of Indian Affairs J. Henry Scattergood and some other officials of the Indian Bureau, traveled extensively throughout the West and held hearings at numerous places. In the Southwest these included San Francisco and Riverside, California; Salt Lake City, Utah; Reno, Nevada; Albuquerque and Santa Fé, New Mexico; and Ignacio, Colorado.

The committee summoned officials of the field force of the Indian Service, including the superintendents of reservations and schools, livestock men, agency farmers, nurses, physicians, and those employees in charge of forests, irrigation, and water development. Testimony was also taken from Indian leaders, licensed traders, and white citizens familiar with conditions among the Indians. Scores of Indians clamored to be heard. One who reads through the twenty-six volumes of those Hearings, aggregating nearly fifteen thousand pages, must be struck by the childish nature of the complaints made by many of the Indians about almost everyone with whom they came in contact. They demanded that their claims against the federal government be settled and that something be done to improve their situation. The more prosperous and better satisfied Indians seldom appeared unless called upon to do so, or unless they were tribal leaders who felt a responsibility for presenting the viewpoint of their people.

[26] *Survey of Conditions of the Indians of the United States: Hearings of a Sub-Committee of the Committee of Indian Affairs of the United States Senate.*

It is apparent, too, that the tempers of some members of the committee, whose nerves were frayed by the discomforts of field work and the gruelling nature of their task, occasionally flared.[27] There was even bickering within the committee itself, particularly when an ex officio member within whose state the hearing was held felt that his colleagues had criticized his state's treatment of the Indians.[28]

The Hearings of the committee added to the Meriam Report, furnish an invaluable source of information for the student about conditions among the Indians of the Southwest. The committee gave patient and conscientious labor to its task and derived a great deal of knowledge from its investigations. Its members were political leaders, however, who had given comparatively little scientific study to many of the subjects which had to be considered. Consequently, there is little evidence that the information secured greatly affected future legislation.

[27] *Ibid.*, 9407.
[28] *Ibid.*, 9074–76 and 9408.

XI

The Agent and His Wards

THE INDIAN AGENT was the representative of the federal government in all its dealings with the Indians within his jurisdiction. Except for such limitations as might be imposed by statute and the orders or regulations of his superior officers, his word was largely law on the reservation which he administered. In a sense, he was the father of a great family numbering from a few hundred to many thousands of persons, who looked to him for protection and aid in every emergency. Upon his shoulders rested the responsibility of seeing that they were fed, clothed, and provided with shelter. He must maintain law and order; care for the old, the sick, the helpless; provide education for the children; and use every effort to advance the welfare of the Indian and to make him capable of supporting himself and his family.

The agent's office, before which floated the flag of the nation he served, was a clearing house for grievances concerning the trespasses of whites, problems of domestic relations, complaints about the traders, petty squabbles between individuals, questions involving the maintenance of order, demands for emergency issues of rations or clothing, and scores of other matters.

The Indian agent, however, could not spend all of his time in his office. He must travel over a reservation, sometimes extending over millions of acres, visiting various communities to inspect the work of his subordinates, to adjust difficulties, and to acquire the information necessary to enable him to understand conditions. During the nineteenth century and early part of the twentieth, such trips must be made on horseback, or in a buckboard, or in some other horse-drawn vehicle; even after the use of automobiles had become almost universal, the government cars were usually open models, far from comfortable for long journeys in bad weather over the rough trails known, by courtesy, as roads. Nevertheless, the agent must go where duty called, often parched by heat and thirst during the torrid summers, or chilled in winter by the harsh winds which so often swept over the high, bleak plains and mountains.

His office was frequently only a room, bare of everything except the few most necessary articles of furniture; most agency buildings were crude structures of logs or rough lumber.[1] His living quarters were usually small and uncomfortable, inadequately furnished, and lacking in all modern conveniences. Often the agency was remote from any town or even from any white settlements. If the agent brought his family to the post to which he had been assigned, there was seldom adequate school facilities for his children and almost never opportunity for recreation or social activities for his wife. They were often lonely. But the agent who had no family or had left his wife and children in more congenial surroundings was even more lonely, and he sometimes gave up his position in a very short time. Until almost the last decade of the nineteenth century, there were times when the agent's life was in real danger from hostile Indians.

Until some years after the passage of the Civil Service Act in 1884, most agents—with the exception of army officers and officers nominated by the various churches—were political appointees. They secured their positions not because of special qualifications or training for the job but by virtue of their services to the political party in power. Probably a majority of them were conscientious and intelligent men, eager to do the work to which they had been assigned well, but many were inefficient and a considerable number were unscrupulous or dishonest.

To the last-named type, an appointment as Indian agent afforded ample opportunities for graft. Ranchmen pasturing their herds on the public domain along the borders of a reservation were often willing to pay generously for the privilege of grazing their cattle on Indian lands when the pasturage elsewhere became poor. Beef contractors who supplied the Indians with a certain number of animals each week for slaughter some times took advantage of the opportunity to turn a dishonest penny by corrupting the agent. Scales were at first seldom available to weigh the cattle, and their weight had to be estimated by the agent or someone appointed by him. If the estimates were consistently too high, who could say that it was not an honest mistake? Any gains accruing to the contractor in such fashion were usually shared with the official of the federal govern-

[1] *Annual Report of Commissioner of Indian Affairs, 1874,* 288, 298; and *1877,* 155.

ment who had made them possible. The government undoubtedly paid for far more beef than the Indians received, and this particular form of thievery was very difficult to detect.[2]

The receipt and distribution of other rations or annuity goods gave the dishonest agent an opportunity to increase his income, which he might also augment because he often had on deposit large sums of money in tribal or individual funds. Indian traders were occasionally willing to pay for the privilege of defrauding the Indian, and bootleggers or whiskey peddlers once in a while sought to arrange for protection. Lumber companies or tiemakers might, for a consideration, be permitted to cut timber growing on the reservation, especially if its boundaries were not clearly marked. In short, there were many ways by which a crooked agent could add to his meager salary, and it is in no sense condoning such criminal practices to state that the temptation must at times have been great.

It is not the purpose of this chapter, however, to deal with those comparatively few agents who secured an appointment as Indian agent primarily for the purpose of enriching themselves. It has seemed necessary to point out that there were some dishonest agents, but most of them were able to conceal their corrupt acts even at the time, and the passing years have still further obliterated all traces so that it would be almost impossible to furnish conclusive proof of the dishonest activities of any particular individual, even if it seemed worth while to do so. It is far more profitable to consider here the work of that great number of the Indian agents of the Southwest who were honest, conscientious, and at least reasonably efficient, and to discuss the chief problems with which they were confronted in dealing with the people under their jurisdiction. Schools and the Health Service will be treated in succeeding chapters. Some phases of the agent's duties and responsibilities have been touched upon in preceding chapters, but in most cases so briefly as to require further elaboration. Others barely mentioned must be given far more consideration in order to give anything like an adequate picture of the relations of these representatives of the federal government with the Indians of the Southwest.[3]

From the very first the Indian agent found that the physical wel-

[2] In 1870, Congress ordered an investigation of Commissioner Ely S. Parker's administration of Indian affairs. One charge was neglect concerning the weights of cattle. See argument of N. P. Chipman, in *Investigation into Indian Affairs before Committee on Appropriations*, U. S. House of Representatives, Washington, 1871.

[3] See Flora Warren Seymour, *Indian Agents of the Old Frontier*, for a general account of the agent's work. Chaps. VI, IX, and X deal with Southwestern agents.

The Window Rock, site of the Navajo Agency

Guy B. Dickerson, principal, Moencopi Day School,
in his classroom (note Indian designs)

fare of the people under his charge constituted the gravest problem. Contrary to popular opinion, the Indian, prior to the coming of the whites, did not live in primitive luxury in a Utopian land of peace and plenty, and certainly not the Indians in the American Southwest. The first agents of the United States Government sent to that region found the people of most tribes wretchedly poor. The Pueblo and Pima, and perhaps other sedentary Indians in normal times, were not in serious want of such necessities as food, clothing, and shelter; but unfortunately they were subjected to perennial raids by the predatory Navajo and Apache, who frequently seized or destroyed their livestock, grain, and other food supplies, leaving numbers of them to face real need until the next harvest. The Indians of most other tribes lived a hand-to-mouth existence and were perpetually hungry and nearly naked, dwelling in temporary shelters of grass, brush, or cactus. The commissioners in California and most of the earliest agents gave the Indians presents consisting of food, clothing, and trinkets, to induce them to sign treaties, as a bribe to remain peaceful, or simply to prove the good will of the Great White Father in Washington whose children they should now acknowledge themselves to be.

The earlier agents appointed in the Southwest journeyed to the area over which the Indians nominally under their jurisdiction roamed, and set up a headquarters which they called an agency. In a few instances the agent was embarrassed by not being able to find any of the people to whom he had been assigned; they were away in the mountains hunting or gathering food. Eventually some of them learned of his presence by the "moccasin telegraph" and drifted in, especially if rumors had reached them that he might have presents of food and clothing to give them. As already indicated, such an agency was merely a sort of "feeding station" to which the Indians of the surrounding territory came to receive rations or to secure the sympathy and help of the agent in adjusting some minor grievance. Fortunately this type of agency was short lived. The establishment of the reservation policy gave the agent a definite territory over which to preside, and on which he was expected to see that the Indians remained. It was then possible to locate an agency at a suitable spot, erect permanent buildings, and provide assistants to carry on the agent's work.

The reservation system was designed for the protection of both the Indians and the whites. If it were to prove successful, the Indians must not be allowed to leave the territory set aside for them except by special permission of the agent, and, likewise, white people must not be allowed to trespass on it. In the earlier years of federal administration in the Southwest, this constituted one of the agent's more important problems. Human nature is extremely jealous of the right to complete freedom of movement. A man may have every intention of spending the day in his room, but if someone locks the door to compel him to do so, he will break down the door or smash through a window or a wall if necessary in order to achieve his liberty. The Indian, because of his roving nature, is even more impatient of restraint than the average person. If, in the past, certain Indians had been accustomed to spend their time in an area which had not been included within the limits of the reservation later set aside, it was certain that they would continue to do so despite the best efforts of the agent to keep them on their own lands. Indians and whites alike, if in pursuit of game, were not likely to turn back when they reached the imaginary boundary.

Little bands of adventurous young warriors would sometimes slip away under cover of night to raid white settlements, returning to the reservation with their plunder before they were ever missed by their agent. Such activities kept the white population in a state of anxiety. Knowing that the Indians were expected to remain on the reservation, they often assumed that any found off it were hostiles and started shooting without stopping to ask questions, although these Indians might be quite friendly and only seeking game or an opportunity to trade. For several years the agent of any jurisdiction whose tribes had formerly waged war on the settlers insisted that the Indians must not leave the reservation without first securing a permit signed by himself. Many tribesmen did not bother to do this, however, and even those who did were sometimes attacked by the rough-and-ready frontiersmen who felt that it was better to take no chances and so fired upon the Indians without waiting to see whether or not they carried permits.[4]

If the Indian agent had difficulty in keeping his people within the limits of the territory assigned to them, he also found it nearly impossible at times to prevent trespassing upon the reservation by white ranchmen seeking pasturage, or by hunters and trappers, timber cutters, and prospectors.[5] Much of the trouble arose because the reservation boundaries were not carefully surveyed and marked.[6]

[4] Many examples may be found in the *Annual Reports of Commissioner of Indian Affairs.*

[5] See *ibid., 1885,* 4, for one example.

[6] Agents' reports frequently urge the survey of boundaries or complain of trespassers. For one example, see *ibid., 1892,* 321.

Before 1885 most of the Indians of the Southwest had been definitely located upon reservations and the period of warfare had ended. Therefore, the agent had an opportunity to devote more attention to the physical welfare of the people. The regulations regarding absence from the reservation were relaxed and Indians were allowed to go and come as they pleased so long as they did not prove an annoyance to whites or get themselves into serious trouble.[7]

Rations and issue goods were dispensed with generosity up to the end of the nineteenth century and for some years thereafter. In 1885 the federal government purchased 2,500,000 pounds of beef on the hoof for the Indians of the San Carlos Agency and 850,000 pounds for those of the Mescalero jurisdiction.[8] Quite early, however, it became clear to the intelligent agent that the federal government could not continue indefinitely to support able-bodied Indians in idleness. Long before the final surrender of Geronimo had closed the period of warfare in the Southwest, earnest attempts were made by many agents to induce and aid the Indians to maintain themselves.[9] Lists of tools and agricultural implements purchased for the Indians were printed in some of the annual reports of the commissioner of Indian affairs, and they are so lengthy that they resemble the invoice sheets of a hardware and implement store.[10] The agent of every important southwestern jurisdiction had the help of one or more agency farmers to assist him in encouraging and teaching the Indians to plant and cultivate crops and to acquire and care for livestock. In 1885 the government disbursed $25,000 in salaries to farmers at the Indian agencies throughout the country.[11]

Such tribes as the Pima and Papago, agricultural Indians for many centuries, often lacked tools and seeds. Cattle and sheep were purchased for the tribes occupying reservations consisting of grazing lands, and were either distributed among the Indians or placed in a tribal herd. This herd became a reservoir from which animals were drawn each year to be sold to individuals of the tribe.

Up until the last decade of the nineteenth century there was no legal authority for leasing Indian lands for grazing, but in 1883 the Secretary of the Interior announced that persons desiring to pasture

---

7 *Ibid., 1902,* 282, states that the "pass system" at Mescalero Agency was abolished in 1898 and the Indians given freedom to go and come as they pleased.

8 *Ibid., 1885,* 412 and 418.

9 On the subject of rations, see Schmeckebier, *op. cit.,* 252–55.

10 See *Annual Report of Commissioner of Indian Affairs, 1885,* 520–37 and 618–22.

11 *Ibid.,* 308.

THE INDIANS OF THE SOUTHWEST

cattle on certain reservations might make the necessary arrangements with the Indians themselves. The Department, however, reserved the right to remove the ranchmen and their animals whenever, in its judgment, their presence on the reservation was against the best interests of the Indians.[12] Such a policy proved entirely impractical, and a few years later Congress enacted legislation authorizing grazing leases of Indian lands.[13] It then became one part of the duties of the agent to recommend such leases as he thought proper, and to collect the money and disburse it to the Indians. The practice of leasing lands has continued up until recent years, especially on the San Carlos and Fort Apache reservations. It was the purpose of most agents, however, to make it possible for the Indians to utilize all of their lands for pasturing their own livestock, and through the use of tribal herds and by means of reimbursable loans, earnest efforts were made to reach this objective.

On the Navajo Reservation there was no question of leasing lands to white ranchers. The Navajo were born shepherds and their agent soon found that the number of their sheep had increased to such a point as to threaten the entire reservation with overgrazing. It was apparent that the Navajo needed a great deal more land in order to supply sufficient pasturage for their flocks, particularly since the Navajo population was increasing rapidly. The reservation superintendents sought to improve the breeds of sheep, since a well-bred animal producing a heavy fleece eats no more grass than an inferior one does. Numerous wells were drilled throughout the Navajo country, and springs and pools were developed, making considerable areas of waterless lands available for regular pasturage.[14] Overgrazing eventually caused serious soil erosion, and the situation became so bad that in 1928 Congress made an appropriation of $200,000 to purchase additional lands for the Navajo and authorized additional expenditures aggregating a million dollars (largely from tribal funds) to acquire land.[15] Within three years over three-quarters of a million

[12] Teller to Fenlon, April 4, 1883, 48 Cong., 1 sess., *Senate Ex. Doc. 54*, Vol. IV, 99.

[13] Feb. 28, 1891, 26 *Stats.*, 795.

[14] In 1927 one agency employee devoted his full time to the task of greasing and keeping in repair nearly a hundred windmills on the reservation that were used to pump water for sheep. To visit and inspect each of them, it was necessary to travel approximately a thousand miles. By 1945 there were 234 deep wells, drilled by the federal government, which were pumped by windmills, in addition to 56 flowing wells, 579 shallow wells, 685 springs, and 1,085 reservoirs for stock water. Superintendent J. M. Stewart to E. E. Dale, October 11, 1946.

[15] 45 *Stats.*, 899.

acres in Arizona, New Mexico, and Utah had been purchased and added to the Navajo Reservation.[16]

Agents of such sedentary tribes as the Pima, Pueblo, and Colorado River Indians secured large sums of money for building dams and ditches, since little could be grown except by irrigation.[17] *Charcas*, or water holes, were constructed on the Papago Reservation by the agent, with the use of government funds, in order to provide a water supply for livestock and for domestic use. The Hopi who depended largely upon rainfall to grow their little crops of corn, beans, and squashes were often supplied with seed. The springs below their mesas were excavated and lined with rock or cement to insure an adequate supply of pure water for household use, and cisterns were constructed to catch the rainfall. For much of the work involved in water development, building roads, and freighting goods from the railroad to the agency, Indian labor was employed.

Indians were also hired for the services they were able to perform in the operation of the agency, including work at the schools and hospitals. Much Indian labor was utilized in the construction of buildings and in caring for the buildings and grounds, working in the laundry, the employees' mess, the bakery, or the shops. As they became better educated, young men and women were employed as teachers, matrons, nurses, and clerks.[18] Sawmills were erected on some reservations—San Carlos, Fort Apache, and Uintah—and operated by Indian labor. The lumber produced was used largely in constructing Indian homes or additional buildings for the agency. The agent of almost every jurisdiction in the Southwest increased the material welfare of a considerable number of Indians by keeping them on his agency payroll.

The agent on the most remote reservations seldom had much contact with white employers of labor. At some agencies such contacts were established and a way found to secure employment for a great number of Indians on the railroads, or in their shops, as well as in mines and factories or in the construction of dams and irrigation works. Jobs were found for other natives in the beet fields, in picking cotton and fruit, in the hay fields and market gardens, and, in some

16 Office of Indian Affairs, *Indian Administration Since July 1, 1929*, 33.

17 See Schmeckebier, *op. cit.*, 237–42, for discussion of irrigation of Indian lands.

18 The act of Congress of May 17, 1882, provided that preference be given to Indians in the employment of help on the reservations and about the agencies, 22 *Stats.*, 88. This was reaffirmed in 1894, 24 *Stats.*, 313.

cases, the agent furnished the Indians transportation.[19] The wise agent recognized that there was a certain educational value in many of the tasks performed by Indians, and gave close supervision at first to Indians placed on the government payroll for work at the agency or on the reservation. Later they were given a larger measure of responsibility. By such means the program of adult education was advanced, while the Indian was given the opportunity of earning money to maintain himself without having to depend upon rations and clothing issued by the government.

The program of adult education was extended to Indian women, a great many of whom were employed at the agency or in the schools and hospitals. Field matrons were hired to visit the homes of the reservation and teach women cooking, housekeeping, the care of children, and the more elementary principles of hygiene and sanitation. Much of the work in handcrafts was also done by women, and the agent, field matrons, and other agency employees encouraged and helped men and women alike to produce more and better pottery, blankets, baskets, and silver jewelry. Regulations were made to afford protection to Indian craftsmen against competition. A stamp guaranteeing the genuineness of handmade articles was devised and affixed to the products of Indian craftsmanship, with heavy penalties for its use by others. The Navajo derived a great deal of their income from the sale of rugs and blankets, while the Hopi and Pueblo sold pottery, silver jewelry, and baskets. The Pima, Apache, and Mission Indians also made beautiful baskets, as did the Walker River Utes. For years the baskets made and sold by the Hualapai brought in a considerable income to a number of families, while the prosperity of the little Pueblo village of San Ildefonso rested largely upon the black pottery made by a few clever craftsmen. Most agents gave all possible aid and encouragement to such work. They sometimes arranged credit for the purchase of dyes, paints, beads, and other materials and found markets for the finished products.[20]

While most agents endeavored to turn the Indian away from hunting and trapping as a means of livelihood, Indians were occasionally supplied with guns or traps to destroy predatory animals and to add deer and rabbits to their supply of food. The Department of War in earlier years complained that the guns and ammunition supplied by officials of the Indian Service were used for attacks on white settlers.

[19] In 1905 the Indian Service established an employment service for Indians. Schmeckebier, *op. cit.*, 251.

The Indians derived a portion of their income from the sale of furs, and the meat and buckskin secured from hunting added to their supply of food and clothing. Agents also helped the Indians in gathering and marketing certain native products. The Navajo, in particular, had an excellent income from the sale of piñon nuts, and the agency furnished wagons or trucks to haul these nuts to market.[21]

As already indicated, the Indians of the Pyramid Lake Reservation consumed large quantities of fish and sold many thousands of dollars' worth annually to whites. It was a part of the agent's duty, not only to assist the Indians in utilizing all such resources of the reservation for their own profit, but also to preserve these resources for the sole benefit of the legal owners by keeping white poachers off the Indians' lands.

Added to his responsibility for the physical welfare of the Indians, the agent had other equally important duties. Since he had control of all schools and educational work in his territory and, until recent years, of all the health and medical services rendered to his people, a large share of his time was given to labor in these two fields. This will be made more apparent in succeeding chapters. He was also charged with maintaining law and order on the reservation, not always an easy task.

The Indian police, who appear quite early in the history of the federal administration of the Indians of the Southwest, were eventually used on every important reservation in the entire region.[22] Mention has been made of the police force organized by Agent Clum of the San Carlos Agency and used to arrest the formidable Geronimo and to bring the turbulent Apache bands from the Hot Springs and Chiricahua agencies to his reservation.[23] The Indian police were used not only to arrest Indians guilty of crimes or misdemeanors but also to bring in children to fill the schools, to return those who ran away, to remove white trespassers from the reservation, and to curb the liquor traffic. Unfortunately the pay offered these police—eight dollars a month for privates and ten dollars for officers—was totally inadequate.[24]

20 Statement of C. E. Faris, superintendent of Northern Pueblo, and others.
21 The piñon nuts yielded the Navajo an income of $390,000 in 1945, which is more than the combined value of both rugs and silver which they produced. Superintendent J. M. Stewart to E. E. Dale, October 11, 1946.
22 Indian police were authorized by an act of Congress, approved May 27, 1878. 20 Stats., 86.
23 See Chap. VII.
24 Annual Report of Commissioner of Indian Affairs, 1887, 36–37.

So far as any generalization is possible, Indians are reasonably tractable, and the number of lawless or criminal persons in any tribe was probably no larger than would be found in a white community of equal size. For many years the agents in the Southwest settled controversies and dispensed justice arbitrarily. Offenders could be thrown into the agency jail, and Indians who persisted in violating regulations might be punished by withholding rations or issues of goods.[25] The lack of any body of law, or of courts to try criminal cases and to settle civil disputes, made the work more difficult. Federal courts have held again and again that an Indian reservation is not a part of any state within the meaning of the United States Constitution.[26] Therefore, state laws did not apply in the case of crimes committed by one Indian against another on Indian lands.

A decision of the United States Supreme Court in 1883 that an Indian who murdered another on a reservation could be punished only by the Indians themselves[27] led to the enactment of a law giving the federal courts jurisdiction over seven major crimes when committed by an Indian on Indian lands.[28] There were many minor crimes and misdemeanors, however, over which no court had jurisdiction, and no court existed for the settling of minor civil controversies or domestic relations.

It was to meet this situation that the tribal courts, commonly known as Courts of Indian Offenses, were organized. Authority for them did not rest upon any action of Congress unless appropriations made by that body for their support could be so construed. They were merely organized and maintained by virtue of an administrative order issued by the Secretary of the Interior in April, 1883.[29] The Court of Indian Offenses did not exist at all agencies in the Southwest, but it was freely used at many of the more important ones and was of great service in assisting the agent to maintain order.

The Court usually consisted of two or three judges appointed by the agent. He selected them from among the older men of the tribe, always seeking those who had long been leaders among their people and in whose wisdom and judgment most of the Indians had

25 Schmeckebier, *op. cit.,* 77.
26 *Worcester* v *Georgia,* 6 Peters, 557 (1832).
27 *Ex parte Crow Dog* (1883), 109 U. S., 556.
28 March 3, 1885, 23 *Stats.,* 385. The crimes were murder, manslaughter, rape, assault with intent to kill, arson, burglary, and larceny. An eighth crime, assault with a dangerous weapon, was later added. See 29 *Stats.,* 487, and 35 *Stats.,* 1151. Two others were later added.
29 Schmeckebier, *op. cit.,* 76.

confidence. No sharp distinction was made between civil and criminal law, and the trial procedure was quite informal although characterized by great dignity. An Indian accused of some offense was brought before the court usually sitting in a large room in one of the agency buildings, and witnesses were summoned and interrogated by the judges. There were no formal rules of evidence and no attorneys. It was a "common-sense court," in which the judges merely sought by diligent questioning of witnesses to arrive at the whole truth. When all evidence had been submitted, the judges retired for a conference and then reappeared and rendered their decision. This was valid only when approved by the agent, who in some cases modified the sentence imposed. It was the duty of the agent to see that the sentence was carried out.[30]

Civil disputes, or cases involving problems of domestic relations were tried in exactly the same way. In criminal cases the punishment imposed was usually a jail sentence of from ten to ninety days. This often meant that the offender was merely locked up in the agency jail at night and spent the day in work about the grounds, mowing the grass, spading up flower beds, or other useful labor.[31]

In the Pueblo jurisdictions of New Mexico, every village together with the lands of the little reservation lying about it constituted a separate unit. The governor and his council, nominally elected by the people of the Pueblo but often chosen and controlled by the caciques, or religious heads of the community, tried persons accused of minor infractions of the law and also adjudicated civil and domestic disputes. By thus taking care of their own local troubles, they relieved the agent of some responsibility, but at times they created problems for him. Punishments administered were usually fines or whippings, and since most Pueblos were divided into two or more factions, the person punished, together with his friends and relatives, often complained to the agent and demanded that he take action.[32]

[30] For a discussion of the Court of Indian Offenses, see Meriam *et. al., op. cit.,* 769–73.
[31] The author once attended the trial of a young Indian who was brought before the Court of Indian Offenses charged with deserting his wife and fleeing with another woman to the Uintah and Ouray Reservation. When he returned some months later, he was arrested on the complaint of his wife. The decision of the court, consisting of two dignified old judges, neither of whom spoke English, was that he be considered divorced from the wife he had deserted, married to the woman with whom he had fled, and that he be sentenced to sixty days in jail on general principles.
[32] Meriam *et al., op. cit.,* 774–75.

Many cases brought before the Court had to do with drunkenness or the sale of liquor to the Indians. In fact, the liquor problem was a very important one for many Indian agents in the Southwest. Traders on the reservation very seldom sold liquor to the Indians and in most cases dealt fairly with them in all business transactions. Some traders who remained for many years on a reservation, often through the administration of several agents, had enormous influence on the Indians and greatly assisted the agent. Other traders sometimes set up their posts just outside the reservation boundaries, however, and over these the agent had no control. Some of them did not hesitate to sell liquor, but sufficient proof to secure their conviction under federal laws was difficult to secure. Even those who avoided the sale of liquor often made a practice of cheating and defrauding the Indians at every opportunity.[33]

In certain instances, homesteaders had perfected title to a few small tracts of land which were later included within the boundaries of an Indian reservation. Over these small areas the agent obviously had no authority; and if one of them fell into the hands of an unscrupulous individual who established on it a store or trading post, it sometimes became a rallying point for evil-disposed persons, Indian and white, from the reservation and the surrounding region, who constituted a grave source of trouble for the agent.[34]

In addition to the licensed traders and the government employees, the only other white persons who resided permanently upon an Indian reservation were the missionaries. Their work began quite early with some tribes in the Southwest, while in the case of others no mission station was established until late in the nineteenth century. The missionary, like the honest and conscientious trader, should have been of great assistance to the Indian agent and often was. The objectives of both were the same—the advancement of the welfare and civilization of the Indians. Some missionaries established schools, while others gave their chief attention to preaching the Gospel; and most of them sought by example and precept to develop a higher standard of living and to induce the Indians to practice such virtues as cleanliness, sobriety, and unselfishness.[35]

This was very helpful to the authorities of the reservation, but there were some jurisdictions where missionary activities added to

[33] See Schmeckebier, *op. cit.*, 264–67 for discussion of Indian traders.

[34] *Annual Report of Commissioner of Indian Affairs, 1877*, 155.

[35] See Meriam *et al.*, *op. cit.*, 812–47, for a detailed discussion of missionary activities.

the worries and perplexities of the already overburdened head of the agency. Where there were three or four missionaries on a reservation, each representing a different faith, they sometimes became involved in disputes among themselves, thereby defeating the good which they might otherwise have been able to accomplish. One talked to the Indian of salvation by works and another of salvation by grace. One asserted that immersion was the only correct form of baptism, and another declared that sprinkling was equally correct. One believed in the celibacy of the clergy and wore long black robes, and another had a wife and three or four children and dressed in the ordinary garb of the white man. In the midst of so much conflicting testimony, the poor Indian decided that perhaps after all the old religion of his forefathers might be best!

The position of the missionary was sometimes difficult. If he discovered that certain Indians were not conforming to the regulations or orders of the agent, should he report that information to the latter and so run the risk of jeopardizing his own influence with the people that he had come to serve? Particularly, should he do this when he felt that these regulations, or orders, were unwise? Most missionaries were idealists, but the agent was a practical man of affairs, and some of their ideas were almost certain to clash. Sometimes the missionary felt that he could not support the policies and activities of the agent without compromising his own principles. If he chose to criticize the agent and his policies in the presence of the Indians, he speedily became a disturbing influence on the reservation. The agent, too, could not risk offending the powerful denomination which the missionary represented by seeking his removal from the jurisdiction.

Active opposition to the agent's policies and methods of administration by any white man who was a permanent resident of the reservation and who had some influence over the Indians might soon become a major problem. Mention has already been made of the factionalism usually found in every one of the New Mexico pueblos. The same factional differences were apparent in almost every important jurisdiction in the Southwest. We have already seen how the Mescalero objected so strongly to occupying the same reservation with the Navajo that they left Bosque Redondo en masse and fled back to their native mountains; and how the Hopi living in the midst of the Navajo country developed an intense dislike of the latter.

Indeed, most tribes were divided into two or more parties or factions. Sometimes the division was due to the rivalry of leaders, each of whom had his followers, but in most cases the tribe was split into parties, which might be called the "Progressives" and the "Conservatives." The former believed in the advancement of the Indian toward white civilization, education, medical care by the agency physician, and a higher standard of living to be achieved by their own efforts. The latter clung tenaciously to old Indian customs and ways of life, objected to sending their children to school, called on the medicine man for treatment when ill, refused to work for their own economic advancement, and insistently demanded to be supported by the government. While the former co-operated with the agent, the latter opposed him and complained of his interference with their freedom.

The agent was sometimes faced with the less serious but almost equally irritating problem of dissension within his own official family. Unfortunately perhaps, he lacked authority either to choose or dismiss agency employees, except laborers and temporary appointees. Had the agent been given large powers in hiring and firing, he might have surrounded himself by his own friends and favorites and thus have created a small machine of great power; but such a situation could hardly have been worse than that which occasionally developed. Most agencies were located at remote spots where the employees saw no other white person than members of their own little group for weeks at a time. They often began to get on one another's nerves and sought relief from boredom in petty intrigues and bickering among themselves. Dissension grew, factions developed, and minor capacities for leadership asserted themselves. This lack of harmony among the employees must at times have interfered with the work and caused the agent much worry and annoyance.

On the whole, the lot of the average Indian agent in the Southwest could hardly be called an enviable one. He had to make endless reports and sometimes became entangled in the red tape so freely issued by Washington. He had to try to carry out blanket orders and instructions of his superior officers which, regardless of how correct they might be when applied to jurisdictions in other parts of the country, sometimes did not fit the particular situation at his own agency. Recognizing the fact that conditions varied widely throughout the region in which the Indian Field Service operated, the survey staff of the Institute for Government Research urged giving the largest possible measure of initiative and responsibility to officials in direct contact with the Indians.[36]

Every agency was visited from time to time by traveling inspec-

36 Meriam *et al., op. cit.,* Chap. X.

tors, who frequently did not remain long enough to gain more than a superficial view of conditions.[37] Consequently their reports to the Bureau were likely to be based largely upon those things that were readily apparent rather than upon intensive study. If, for example, the agency buildings and grounds appeared neglected, the inspector might not realize that this was caused by the agent's giving his time to other work more beneficial to the Indians than improving the appearance of the agency plant.

The varied duties and responsibilities of the Indian agent called for a man of unusual capabilities. Ideally, he should be a diplomat, an able executive, and a skilled social worker. At best, his relation to his wards was that of a wise and sympathetic father, a real "guide, philosopher and friend," who at all times dealt with them kindly and with infinite patience and understanding but who could be firm and unyielding if necessary. At worst, the agent, even if not corrupt, was a petty tyrant with neither sympathy nor understanding of the people committed to his care who soon lost the confidence and respect of the Indians. This type was rare and usually did not remain long at a jurisdiction. Unfortunately, he was sometimes transferred to another agency in the hope that under different conditions he might succeed when it should have been apparent that his failure was caused not by a particular situation but by his own lack of the qualities necessary for successful administration.

Every agent in the Southwest must have felt at times that he was a sort of "animated wailing wall" to which came all sorts and conditions of people to voice their grievances. He must listen not only to complaints of the Indians on a multitude of subjects but to those of the whites hostile to the entire Indian race who believed that the sooner it perished from the earth the better off the world would be. Some of the persons complained that the Indians were being pampered and spoiled by the wasteful use of government funds. He must listen, too, to the complaints of "professional friends of the Indians," usually residing in the East, who asserted that all Indian peoples were being either neglected or oppressed and who seemed far more ready to criticize than to offer real help.

The position of the agent nevertheless offered certain compensations for all its hardships and difficulties. Much of the work was outside, in the open air of a land of sunshine and matchless scenery. Often he was able to indulge in such recreation as fishing or hunting. So

[37] For the laws creating the office of inspector, see 17 *Stats.*, 463 (1873) and 18 *Stats.*, 422 (1875).

long as he kept within the regulations of the Indian Bureau, he had complete freedom of action, and his power inside the limits of his jurisdiction was enormous. Most important of all was the opportunity for service to a people in real need and the satisfaction derived from seeing their advancement as the result of his labors.

Those familiar with the Indian administration in the Southwest during the past half century will agree that a large number of agency heads were outstanding and that by their energy, initiative, and resourcefulness they accomplished much for the Indians under their control. Such men, where their resources permitted, literally fed the hungry, clothed the naked, healed the sick, ministered to the helpless and unfortunate, and diligently sought to educate the illiterate. To them not only the Indians but all the people of America owe a deep debt of gratitude. One who looks back over the century can hardly escape the conclusion that the Indian agents of this region have greater cause to be proud of their work and its results than have those officials in Washington who were responsible for obtaining appropriations and formulating the policies and regulations under which the Field Service operated.

XII

Education and Schools

IT IS SOMETIMES SAID that the Indian cannot be educated because the federal government has been trying to do it ever since the formation of our republic and has met with little success. Such a statement is quite incorrect. For three-quarters of a century after the adoption of the Constitution there were virtually no Indian schools supported and administered by the government of the United States, and even a hundred years after that event, the program of the federal government for the schooling of Indian children was only begun.

Until the time the American Southwest came into the possession of the United States, Indian education was almost entirely carried on by missionary groups. In 1819 Congress appropriated the sum of ten thousand dollars annually for the industrial and scholastic education of Indians,[1] but since no administrative machinery existed for supervising Indian schools, this money was distributed among various missionary organizations to be used in their educational work.[2] When other funds became available later through treaty provisions, they too were paid over to missionary organizations. This system was still in operation in 1848.

From the first, Indian agents in this region pointed out the need for schools,[3] and this need became more apparent to officials of the Indian Field Service when they became more familiar with the tribes of the Southwest and the conditions under which they lived. Agents were not slow to realize the truth of the proverb about the difficulty of teaching an "old dog new tricks," because their own customs were so deeply ingrained in the adults that it was exceedingly difficult to

[1] 3 *Stats.*, 516.
[2] This appropriation was continued until 1873 when the act was at last repealed. 17 *Stats.*, 461.
[3] Calhoun to Medill, July 29, 1849. Abel (ed.), *op. cit.*, 19.

change them. If the Indian was to be advanced, it must be through education begun at an early age and continued persistently for many years. Even then, this desirable objective could not be reached in a single generation. However, through education the time must come when racial differences would be largely blotted out, and Indians and whites could live together on an equal basis with mutual confidence and respect.

The federal government was slow to establish Indian schools in the Southwest. Almost no educational work was done prior to 1870, and very little for ten years after that date. The treaties of 1868 with the Navajo and Utes each contained a provision that the Indians would induce all children from seven to eighteen years of age to attend school and that the United States would provide schools for every thirty children of these tribes.[4] In accordance with this provision a teacher was employed in the autumn of 1869 to establish the first Navajo school at Fort Defiance. This teacher, Miss Charity A. Gaston, made her first report in 1870. She stated that she left Santa Fé for Fort Defiance on October 2 and arrived at her post on October 12. No building was available for her use at that time, and school was not actually opened until December 1. Behind the brief statement of the report, the imaginative reader can visualize the discomforts and hardships of the ten days' journey by wagon or buckboard from Santa Fé to Fort Defiance. The enforced wait of more than six weeks while a school room was being made ready must have been discouraging, and the task of teaching children, most of whom knew not a single word of English, was no doubt even more dismaying. The teacher seemed well satisfied with results, however, and reported an average attendance of twenty-two during the term and more than thirty pupils on several days.[5]

The education of the Navajo has, from that day to the present, progressed with an astonishing slowness. In 1874 their agent reported that although day schools had been in operation ever since the Navajo had been removed from Bosque Redondo five years earlier, almost no benefit had resulted because of the irregularity of attendance. In 1878 the agent stated that thousands of dollars had "been spent on transient teachers and even more transient scholars and not a solitary Navajo can either read or write."[6] This was caused primarily by the pastoral pattern of Navajo society. The children did not remain in

---

[4] 15 Stats., 619–23 and 667–71.
[5] Annual Report of Commissioner of Indian Affairs, 1870, 153–54.
[6] Ibid., 1878, 108.

Hopi sheep, Second Mesa

Indian cattle crossing Gila River, San Carlos
Apache Reservation

any one place long enough to attend a day school for a lengthy period of time. Day schools established on other reservations, especially those occupied by sedentary tribes, were more successful. By 1878 there was a school on the Uintah Reservation, one on the Mescalero Reserve, two on the Gila River Reservation for the Pima and one for the Papago, conducted by Sisters of the Order of St. Joseph, who were employed by the federal government. No school was in operation at Colorado River, but one had been authorized, while the day school established a few years earlier for the Hopi had been closed in 1876.[7]

Officials of the Indian Service in the Southwest agreed that day schools contributed little to the education of Indian children and should be replaced by boarding schools. They also urged that vocational education was especially desirable for Indians, but at this time vocational schools in the United States were few. In 1878 the federal government made a contract with Hampton Institute by which that school was to receive and train Indian students, and that year a considerable number were enrolled. Very few of these were from the Southwest, but the opening of Hampton to Indians furnished a precedent for the establishment of new Indian boarding schools of the vocational type at places remote from the homeland of the pupils who attended them.[8]

The following year, 1879, Carlisle was opened by Captain R. H. Pratt, who for three years had been in charge of a large group of Cheyennes and Kiowas held as prisoners of war at Fort Marion, Florida. His management of these Indians won him widespread recognition. With the aid of Mrs. Pratt and a group of ladies of St. Augustine, he had established and conducted a prison school which was so successful that in 1878, when their three-year prison sentence had expired, a number of young Indians expressed the wish to remain in the East and secure further education. It was mainly because of the wish to provide schooling for them that Hampton opened its doors to Indian students.

The Secretaries of War and of the Interior were both so impressed by Pratt's work that with their aid he was able to secure the buildings of the old military post at Carlisle, Pennsylvania, for use as an Indian school. Also, the act appropriating funds for the War Department carried a provision that an officer not above the rank of

---

[7] *Ibid.*, 4, 9, 107, 110, 127.

[8] For thirteen years after Indian students were first admitted to Hampton, only fifteen pupils from Southwestern tribes seem to have enrolled. These were mostly Pima, Papago, and Apache. Record of Indian Students Returned from Hampton Institute, 52 Cong., 1 sess., *Sen. Ex. Doc. 31*, 32–51.

captain should be detailed for Indian education. The school was opened on November 1, 1879, with a comparatively small number of students. By 1885 the enrollment had grown to 543, of which 6 were Navajo and 92 Pueblos.[9] In 1902 a total of 1,284 students from eighty-eight tribes had been enrolled during the year. The grades taught were from the first to the tenth and there were three pupils listed in "higher education."[10] For many years Carlisle had approximately a thousand students and was the largest and most important boarding school in the entire Indian Service. Apparently at no time did any large percentage of its student body consist of pupils from the Southwest, although there were at times a considerable number of Pueblo, as well as some Pima, Papago, Mission Indians, Navajo, and others. Also the children of Chiricahua Apache held as prisoners of war in Florida were sent to Carlisle, and they, together with a few Apaches already there, gave the school for two or three years nearly a hundred students of that tribe.

Carlisle continued to operate until 1918, when it was finally closed. Its importance to Indian education in the Southwest is not so much due to the number of students from that region who attended it but to its becoming the model for all other large Indian boarding schools, a number of which were established throughout the Southwestern area within ten or fifteen years after Carlisle was founded.

Pratt had very definite ideas about Indian education and strove with remarkable energy and ability to put them into execution. He believed that large boarding schools should be established—preferably as remote as possible from the homeland of its students—to which Indian children should be brought and kept for a number of years. During this time they were not to return to the reservation or have any personal contact with their families or friends residing on it. He felt that it was far better to take the Indian to civilization than to attempt to carry civilization to the Indian. Consequently he developed a slogan: "To civilize the Indian, put him in the midst of civilization. To keep him civilized, keep him there."[11]

In the furtherance of this idea, Pratt originated the so-called "outing system" which received the enthusiastic commendation of Commissioner Leupp and other officials of the Indian Bureau. This was the placing of students with white families during the summer

[9] *Annual Report of Commissioner of Indian Affairs, 1885*, 214.
[10] *Ibid., 1902*, 467–68.
[11] For a discussion of Pratt's work at Carlisle, see Seymour, *op. cit.*, Chap. XIII, or Elaine Goodall Eastman, *Pratt, the Red Man's Moses*.

vacation instead of permitting them to return to the reservation. In these white homes they lived and worked, usually on the farm or in domestic service, thereby earning wages and at the same time learning much that would be of benefit to them when they had farms or homes of their own. At the close of the vacation period the student returned to school, often with a snug little sum of money earned during the summer; sometimes he remained with the white family and attended public school, doing sufficient work to pay for his board and room. Pratt and the proponents of his system believed that if the student had no contact with his family and the reservation for several years, he would lose all of his old Indian ways of life and become, in everything except the color of his skin, exactly the same as a white person.

There were serious flaws in this argument, but they were not apparent to most officials of the Indian Service and, until comparatively recent years, the federal government largely followed Pratt's policy and depended to a great extent upon boarding schools modeled upon Carlisle for the education of Indian children. It was asserted that a three months' summer vacation spent on the reservation with the child's own family was likely to nullify much of the nine month's teaching at school. As for the day schools, some officials declared that the child's home and family undid most of the good accomplished by the school during the six or seven hours each day that it had control of its pupils.

In 1926, out of a total of 24,591 pupils enrolled in government schools, 20,092 were in boarding and only 4,499 in day schools.[12] Even as late as 1944 when the movement to establish day schools had been going on for ten years, more than one-third of the pupils in government Indian schools were in the boarding schools.[13]

Carlisle was operated as a vocational or industrial school, each student giving half the day to academic subjects and the other half to work on the school farm or in the shops and in the duties necessary to the operation of the institution. While some hired labor was used, most of the work in the barns, dairy, laundry, kitchen, dining room, and dormitories, as well as in maintaining the buildings and grounds, was done by students.

It is unfortunate, perhaps, that the founder of Carlisle was a soldier with a firm belief in the value of maintaining strict military

12 Schmeckebier, *op. cit.*, 216.
13 Exact figures are 11,712 in boarding schools and 21,342 in day schools. *Statistical Supplement to the Annual Report of Commissioner of Indian Affairs, 1944*, 14.

discipline in his school. This may have been necessary at first, although it seems a little doubtful, but Pratt was a martinet in his insistence upon all of the details of a rigid military regime. Superintendents of other boarding schools that sprang up throughout the West followed his example and imposed upon their pupils regulations and forms that were not only unnecessarily severe but were a hindrance to the formation of a warm human relationship between teachers or other school employees and pupils.

Among the Indian boarding schools founded in the Southwest were Fisk Institute, or Albuquerque Indian School—operated earlier as a church institution—opened as a government school in 1884. Others were Santa Fé School, Fort Mojave in Arizona, and Carson School in Nevada, all established in 1890; Phoenix School, opened in 1891; and Perris School at Perris, California, founded in 1892. The last named was replaced soon after 1902 by Sherman Institute, completed that year and located a short distance from Riverside, California. This was eventually to become one of the most important educational institutions in the Indian Service. Haskell Institute at Lawrence, Kansas, and Chilocco Indian School at Chilocco, Oklahoma, both opened in 1884, also enrolled a considerable number of students from the Southwest.[14]

All of these were nonreservation schools which might receive students from any tribe or agency so long as room could be found for them. Each was an independent jurisdiction not under the control of any agency but reporting directly to the commissioner of Indian affairs. Funds for the operation of each were provided by Congress, usually as a separate item in the Indian Appropriation Act. All the larger nonreservation schools had students from many tribes, but acts of Congress prohibited sending a child to a school outside the limits of the state in which he resided without the written consent of his parents, guardian, or next of kin.[15] These schools at first received pupils of all grades, but later their enrollment was largely limited to those of the sixth grade or above. Most of them eventually offered some high school work, and some offered a full four-year high-school course, while a few gave special work in music, business, or methods of teaching to students who had completed the regular high school course.

The establishment of these nonreservation schools was accom-

14 See *Report of Commissioner of Indian Affairs, 1892,* 48, for a list of schools in existence at that date.
15 28 *Stats.,* 313 and 906, and 29 *Stats.,* 348.

panied by the creation of many reservation boarding schools in the Southwest. By 1892 those in Arizona were Colorado River, opened in 1872, Navajo Agency, and Pima, both established in 1881, and Keams Canyon in 1887. California had Fort Yuma, opened in 1884; Nevada had Pyramid Lake, founded in 1882, and Western Shoshone, which became a boarding school in 1892.[16] New Mexico had in 1892 only one reservation boarding school, that for the Mescalero Apache founded in 1884, and Utah only the Uintah school opened in 1881.[17] There were also by that date a number of day schools in the Southwest, including eight among the Mission Indians, one each at San Carlos and White Mountain reservations, two in Nevada, at Walker River and Wadsworth, and at least four among the Pueblo.[18]

Additional reservation boarding schools were established in the Southwest after 1892, although more slowly than in the earlier period, until by the close of the first quarter of the twentieth century there was one or more in almost every important jurisdiction in the entire region. Reservation schools were under the control of the agency within the limits of which they were located. Each was administered by a principal responsible to the agent. Funds for the maintenance of such schools usually came from the general Appropriation Act which was the rule in the case of the nonreservation school. Ordinarily they did not educate any students beyond the sixth grade, and those desiring further schooling were sent to a nonreservation school.[19] They thus tended to become feeders for the latter type of school, which gradually dropped the elementary grades, although in some instances they were retained until 1925, or even later.

The methods employed were essentially the same in all government boarding schools whether they were of the reservation or nonreservation type. All were organized on a military basis, with the pupils dressed in uniforms and placed in platoons and companies under the command of student officers appointed by the principal or superintendent. The children devoted a half day to work in the school room and the other half to so-called vocational training, often frankly productive labor—the girls, washing dishes, scrubbing floors, or feeding sheets through a mangle, and the boys, working in the fields and

16 The author who in 1927 observed the fare of the children in nearly every boarding school in the Southwest could not avoid feeling that several of them at that time might have been aptly called "semi-boarding schools."

17 *Annual Report of Commissioner of Indian Affairs, 1892*, 51–52.

18 *Ibid.*, 53.

19 Some of the larger ones eventually gave instruction up to the ninth grade or even higher. Schmeckebier, *op. cit.*, 211.

181

gardens of the school farm, milking cows, patching shoes, or mowing the lawns. Doubtless many of the pupils learned much that would prove useful in later life, but a large part of the work had little educational value after they had acquired a reasonable amount of skill.

Schools were established so rapidly that great difficulty was often experienced in filling them. Some parents objected to sending their children to school, and the children objected even more strenuously to going. Agent after agent reported that it was exceedingly difficult to induce parents to place their children in school and urged that they be compelled to do so. Apart from the desire of officials of the Indian Field Force to see that Indian children received an education, there were financial considerations involved in keeping the schools filled. Funds for the support of every school were allotted on the basis of the number of pupils in attendance. For several years the boarding schools were granted $167.50 annually for each student in attendance; this was later raised to about $225.00 to $250.00, where it remained until about 1928.[20] Obviously, a school could not operate, for monetary reasons, unless it could enroll and retain a reasonably large number of pupils. Accordingly, officials made every effort to secure as many students as possible, limited only by their accommodations. Many boarding schools, however, disregarded the limitations of their facilities and overcrowded their schools, in many instances their enrollment being 20 per cent more than their rated capacity.

For many years after their founding, however, many schools in the Southwest were poorly attended, and their officials put forth every possible effort to induce parents to accept the educational facilities provided. As early as 1892, the commissioner of Indian affairs was authorized to enforce regulations to secure the attendance of Indian children of suitable age and health.[21] This authority was strengthened the following year by two separate provisions in one act. These authorized the secretary of the interior to withhold rations from parents who did not send their children to school.[22] Such acts were apparently never fully enforced, for in 1920 Congress re-enacted the provisions of the act of 1892.[23] In 1921 an order was issued providing for the adoption of the compulsory school laws and regulations

[20] The act of June 30, 1919, limited the expenditure to $225 per capita in schools of two hundred or more pupils and $250 per capita in schools of less than two hundred pupils. The average attendance was used as a basis for determining the amount of the allotment and was determined by dividing the total daily attendance by the number of days the school was in session. 41 *Stats.*, 6.

[21] 27 *Stats.*, 143.   [22] 27 *Stats.*, 628 and 635.

[23] 41 *Stats.*, 410.

of each state as a part of the rules governing the Indian Service. Superintendents were instructed to impose upon Indians not under state laws the same penalty for violation of such regulations that the state imposed upon its own citizens.[24]

It was easy for Congress to pass compulsory school laws, but for officials of the Indian Service to enforce them was very difficult, especially in the Southwest. A number of tribes, such as the Navajo, were receiving so small an amount of rations, that there was none to withhold. If agents sent the police to bring the children in by force and to pursue and return any that ran away, they not only created resentment among the Indians but were nearly certain to bring upon themselves harsh criticism from many sentimentalists whose interest in Indian welfare was great enough to cause them to be regarded as outstanding friends of the Indian. These friends criticized harshly the inhumanity of officials who were willing to "kidnap" children or tear them from their mothers' arms and take them away to the strange environment of the boarding school.[25] On the other hand, if officials allowed the children to remain out of school, these same critics complained bitterly that Indian children were allowed to grow up in ignorance despite the fact that funds had been appropriated for their education. In such a dilemma, the school superintendent or agent merely did the best he could and by constant pleading, persuasion, and threats sought to induce parents to allow their boys and girls to be brought to school.

Bringing children in by force must have been sickening work for the kindhearted and sympathetic agent or principal, regardless of the fact that he knew how much better off these children would be in school than in the squalid surroundings of their camp or village. The youngsters fled and hid themselves, or were concealed by their parents, at the first glimpse of the police or school officials. Some children sought refuge in the hills or thickets, and some of the village dwellers secreted their children in dark storehouses or corn cellars beneath piles of sheepskins or anything else that seemed to afford covering.[26] Even when parents were willing for their children to go to school, and the youngsters did not object too much, they were often in no hurry about getting started. The average Indian refuses to be a slave to the calendar or the clock. Schools opening in September were frequently not filled to capacity until November.[27]

---

24 Schmeckebier. *op. cit.*, 223.
25 Leo Crane, *Indians of the Enchanted Desert*, Chap. XIV.
26 *Ibid.*

By the end of the second decade of the twentieth century, however, the situation was greatly improved. Parents had become reconciled to having their children educated, and older students often came willingly enough, bringing in their younger brothers, sisters, and friends. Eventually there came a time when some fathers and mothers seemed all too willing to shift to the federal government the responsibility for their offspring during a large part of the year, although this was not often true in the Southwest.

When the children reached school, they were given a physical examination, often of a ·very perfunctory character; a bath, a hair cut, and a "delousing" treatment were given to those who needed it. They were then issued uniforms, shoes, and other clothing, organized into platoons and companies, and assigned beds and lockers in the dormitories. In the larger schools there were separate dormitories for the older and the younger girls, and the same was true for the boys. Each of these buildings was under the supervision of a matron, who was responsible for the students assigned to her as well as for the cleanliness of the building and the orderly arrangement of its furnishings.

Students were aroused each morning about six by the bell or the notes of a bugle. They dressed quickly and hurried outside to line up under the watchful eyes of their student officers, who conducted the march to breakfast. As soon as it was over, they were marched from the dining room, halted in line and half of them were detailed to work and the other half sent to the school rooms. At noon they marched back to the dining room for lunch, after which those who had worked during the morning were sent to the class rooms and those who had spent the morning hours in school were placed on work details for the afternoon. School was dismissed around four o'clock and the pupils had an hour and a half or two hours of freedom for play and recreation until dinner, served about five-thirty or six. After dinner there was another hour or more for recreation, but usually pupils had to be in study hall for an hour or two before nine when they returned to the dormitories to make ready for bed. About nine-fifteen taps sounded the warning for lights out, and the Indian student's day ended.

In most schools, especially the larger ones, an attempt was made

27 Pablo Abeita once said: "All white people are slaves to the clock. Their masters tell them when to get up in the morning, when to eat, when to go to work, when to quite work, and when to go to bed. Almost without exception they are slaves to the clock. Even the President of the United States must obey his master."

to provide students with some recreation and entertainment. Usually the school had a band or an orchestra, or both, and occasionally a glee club. Athletic sports were organized, and basketball, baseball, boxing, and football were popular. Practicing for the athletic teams, as well as for the band and orchestra, gave some relief from study hall or other boresome work, and attending games, concerts, and occasional parties lightened dull routines.

School regulations were enforced by an official known as the "disciplinarian." Penalties for infraction of the rules were usually demerits which had to be worked off by additional hours of labor, and until these marks were removed, the student was denied most of the privileges accorded others. Sometimes corporal punishment was administered, but there is little evidence of brutality in its application; and, even prior to 1900, it was probably more common in the public schools. The children in the boarding schools were evidently happy, in spite of poor clothing and bad housing. It is true that many children ran away, and authentic stories tell of small children trudging, with catlike instinct, across the desert to their homes seventy or eighty miles away.

Most larger schools had a "lockup" in which persistent runaways or others who were not amenable to ordinary methods of discipline were confined for a few days. Although rigid military discipline and the "highly institutional" character of the boarding school were not conducive to warm personal relationships between teachers and students, many school employees were kind and sympathetic in their attitudes and won the complete confidence, respect, and often the real affection of their charges. Other officials were never able to break through the protective wall of reserve with which the typical Indian, young or old, often surrounds himself.

School authorities, as often as Indian agents, were handicapped in their work by senseless orders from Washington. On July 16, 1887, an order went out to all reservation agents and all representatives of societies having contract schools for Indian education, calling attention to the rule forbidding instruction in any language except English. It stated that: "Instruction of Indians in the vernacular is not only of no use to them but is detrimental to the cause of education and civilization and will not be permitted in any Indian school over which the government has any control. . . . You will see that this rule is rigidly enforced. . . ."[28] The Commissioner of Indian Affairs further stated that: "Every nation is jealous of its own language and none

[28] *Annual Report of Commissioner of Indian Affairs, 1887*, xxii, xxiii.

should be more so than ours." In addition, he pointed out that only English was taught in the lands we had acquired from Mexico and Russia and that the Germans had forbidden the teaching of French in either the public or private schools of Alsace and Lorraine. The Commissioner ended his argument with a paragraph which reveals the warped thinking so often apparent among Indian Bureau officials in Washington:

> It is believed that if any Indian vernacular is allowed to be taught by missionaries in schools on Indian reservations it will prejudice the pupil as well as his parents against the English language. . . . This language which is good enough for a white man or a black man ought to be good enough for the red man. It is also believed that teaching an Indian youth in his own barbarous dialect is a positive detriment to him. The impracticability, if not impossibility, of civilizing the Indians of this country in any other tongue than our own would seem obvious.[29]

Freely granting that American public schools were not too good in 1887 and that many crimes, or at least misdemeanors, were committed in the name of education by our own people during the latter part of the last century, it still is obvious that the Indian Field Service was under an enormous handicap in being directed by an official with such distorted ideas as the above quotation indicates. Apparently it had never occurred to the Commissioner that an Indian nation might also be "jealous of its language" or that the greater part of the white and black peoples of the world do not speak English. Nor could he foresee a time when his commendation of the policy of the Germans in Alsace and Lorraine would seem to most people of our country especially mistaken.

Fortunately, later commissioners showed greater intelligence in matters concerning education than some of the earlier ones had shown. Nearly all of them had the best intentions, and some of them were very capable men, but all were political appointees seldom having any technical knowledge of education, social service, or even business administration. Very few commissioners when appointed were experienced enough with Indians to have any understanding of their characteristics and habits. Of the thirty-one men appointed to the office of commissioner of Indian affairs from its inception in 1832 to the accession of Commissioner Collier in 1933, only seven came

[29] Commissioner J. D. C. Atkins, *ibid.*, XXIII–XXV.

from a state west of the Mississippi.[30] A few commissioners became conversant with Indian culture by traveling among the Indians studying their problems, and administered the office with wisdom and discretion. Their tenures were, unfortunately, brief.[31] The nature and problems of the Indian Service were so involved that most heads of the Bureau despaired of mastering all of the intricate details and decided merely to follow established precedents and carry on the work just as it had been carried on in the past. What these precedents and former methods were could be learned from the clerical staff, or minor officials, who after the establishment of Civil Service held their positions indefinitely. Therefore, education, like agency administration, remained static for a generation. It was not until after 1928 that the boarding schools began to show any tendency to progress from the original methods used at Carlisle. The entire system of Indian education was essentially the same as it had been forty years earlier, when the federal government first began to give serious attention to the schooling of its younger wards.

Day schools were established in the Southwest, especially among the Mission Indians of California, the Pueblo of New Mexico, and the Hopi and Pima of Arizona. Additional schools were founded in other jurisdictions, wherever a sufficient number of Indians resided permanently at one location to make such schools practicable. A few larger day schools had several teachers, but the typical day school had but one teacher and a housekeeper, often the farmer's wife or mother. One of her duties was to prepare, with the aid of three or four of the older girls, a noonday lunch for the children from supplies furnished by the government. The half day of vocational training was also the rule for many years at the day school.[32]

Mission schools for the education of Indian children were also subsidized by the federal government. About 1870 the practice of

30 *Annual Report of Commissioner of Indian Affairs, 1931*, 1–2. Of these, the only one from the states included in the Mexican Cession was Commissioner Denver of California, who served two brief periods prior to the Civil War, one of fourteen and the other of six months. Five of the seven served a total of sixty-two months, or an average of slightly over a year each, and from 1867 to 1913 only Commissioner Price of Iowa came from a state west of the Mississippi River. Of the entire thirty-one commissioners, none except Denver of California and Burke of South Dakota came from a state containing any large number of Indians.

31 The average term of the eighty-one commissioners to 1933 was only slightly over three years, and the twenty-five who held that office up to 1893 served on an average only a little more than two years. *Ibid.*

32 In 1917 there was 3,521 pupils enrolled in government day schools in the five states considered in this study, as compared with 6,949 in the boarding schools. *Ibid., 1917*, 145–51.

187

making formal contracts with such schools was begun, and thereafter they were often referred to as "contract schools." By 1892 funds allotted to such schools throughout the United States as a whole amounted to $611,570.[33] There were a number of these schools in the Southwest as well as other mission schools with which no contract was made. In 1897 Congress declared that it was the settled policy not to make appropriations in the future for education in any sectarian school.[34] They were continued, however, for a few years, being progressively reduced until 1901, when authority for such contracts was omitted. The practice was revived in 1905, using tribal funds, at the request of the Indians. This use of tribal funds was challenged in the courts but the Supreme Court of the United States decided that they could be so used.[35] The greater portion of the Indian children enrolled in mission schools in the Southwest were in mission boarding schools, although some were in day schools.[36]

The federal government also sought to advance Indian education by the payment of tuition for those enrolled in local public schools, but with the exception of California, and to a less extent Nevada, few Indian children were enrolled in the public schools of the Southwestern states.[37]

With the mission schools not under contract, the federal government did not concern itself, but the Indian Office did give some attention to contract schools and to those public schools enrolling children for whom the government paid tuition. Even in the noncontract mission boarding schools, however, Congress agreed that children who would have been entitled to government rations at home should receive them.[38] Government day schools were under the control of the agent of the jurisdiction inspecting them. Nonreservation and reservation boarding schools alike were visited and checked periodically by officials of the Indian Bureau. The number of pupils

[33] Schmeckebier, *op. cit.*, 212.

[34] 29 *Stats.*, 345.

[35] *Quick Bear* v. *Leupp* (1908), 210 U. S., 81–82.

[36] The total enrollment of Indian pupils in the mission schools of the Southwest in 1917 was 1,152, which had risen to 2,335 by 1925 and to 2,961 in 1933. See *Annual Report of Commissioner of Indian Affairs*, for these years.

[37] In 1917, California, Arizona, New Mexico, Nevada, and Utah enrolled 2,260 Indian children in their public schools. Of these, all but 176 were in the schools of California and Nevada. In 1925, California enrolled 2,383 Indians in public schools and Nevada 517 out of a total of 3,252 while in 1933 the figures for these two states were 3,100 for California and 513 for Nevada. That year Arizona enrolled 559 Indian children in the public schools as compared with 16 in 1917. The total number in the public schools of these five states in 1933 was 4,379. *Ibid.*

[38] 34 *Stats.*, 326.

in the government boarding schools in the Southwest rose to 8,357 in 1925 but by 1933 had decreased to 7,456.[39]

The Meriam Survey gave particular attention to education. The staff visited every government boarding school in the Southwest, many of the day schools, and all of the important mission schools. Eighty-three pages of its report are devoted to education. It is the most complete analysis of the federal government's Indian schools, educational policies, and methods that has been published.[40]

The survey staff reached the conclusion that the most fundamental need was a change in point of view. In the past the Indian Service had proceeded on the theory that the child should be removed as far as possible from his home environment, while the modern viewpoint in education and social work stresses the importance of upbringing in the natural setting of home and family life.[41] The year prior to the beginning of the survey the Indian Bureau stated that there were in the entire United States 77,577 Indian children of school age and eligible for attendance. Of these 8,542 were in nonreservation boarding schools, 10,615 in reservation boarding schools, and 4,604 in government day schools. Also 2,047 children were in mission contract boarding schools and 3,685 in non-contract boarding schools, and 1,-307 in mission day schools.[42] Although both the federal government and mission organizations depended so largely upon the boarding school for the education of Indian children, 34,452 of these children were in the public schools, and the government was paying tuition for a great number of them.[43]

The Meriam Survey staff found wide variations of conditions in the government boarding schools in the Southwest. In 1927 all were still following the old system of military discipline—one-half day given to classroom work and the other to vocational training—and all were operating on funds quite inadequate to meet their needs.[44] Most of them had only $225 for each child enrolled, while the lowest-cost boarding schools of the United States charged $700 a year, and the Thomas State Indian School maintained on the Cattaraugus Reservation in New York received an appropriation of $610 annually

[39] See *Annual Report of Commissioner of Indian Affairs*, for these years, 40–43 and 145–48.

[40] Meriam *et al.*, *op. cit.*, Chap. IX.   [41] *Ibid.*, 346.

[42] *Annual Report of Commissioner of Indian Affairs, 1925*, 44.

[43] For a brief but comprehensive discussion of Indian education, see Mrs. Evelyn C. Adams, *American Indian Education*.

[44] In 1926 the Indian office announced a policy of three-fourths of the day to be given to schooling and one-fourth to work, but few schools had it in operation in 1927.

per capita. It was plain that from the standpoint of education "the Indian Service was almost literally a 'starved' service."[45]

The first recommendation for immediate action made by the Meriam Report was that an additional appropriation of a million dollars be sought from Congress at the earliest possible moment to improve the quantity, quality, and variety of food in the boarding schools.[46] The need of such improvement was apparent at every boarding school in the Southwest, but it was more pressing at some than at others. Pratt had managed to provide, even on his appropriation of $167.50 a year, a standard army ration for students at Carlisle. It is probable, however, that the purchasing power of $167.50 was greater for many years after the founding of Carlisle than was that of $225 at any time after we entered the first World War.

Apparently no boarding school in the Southwest expended more than twenty-three cents a day per pupil for food and in some instances as little as seventeen cents. This paid not only for food but also for the fuel used in cooking, and the salaries of the cooks and dining room matrons. It was supplemented by the products from the farm and gardens, which alone made it possible to operate on so small an amount without actual starvation. Every school had a farm, but they varied widely in size and productivity. Some had little fertile land or lacked sufficient water for irrigation. Some schools maintained a dairy herd, but it seldom provided an adequate milk supply. Frequently the proper facilities for the storage of food were lacking, and often the antiquated equipment of the kitchen and bakery made the preparation of meals difficult.

Governmental red tape sometimes delayed the shipment of supplies so that some did not arrive until midwinter. This left a surplus which had to be carried over the summer, and such articles as dried fruit or cereals often spoiled or became infested with worms or weevils during the hot summer months. A resourceful school superintendent always sought to can and dry vegetables and fruit grown on the farm, and some schools kept a beef herd as well as pigs and poultry to add to their food supply. A good cook who made the most of the resources available made all the difference between an extremely poor diet and a moderately satisfactory one. With so many factors involved, it is not surprising that conditions varied widely in the food situation of the schools of the Southwest, but in very few instances did the pupils have a suitable diet for growing children.

[45] Meriam *et al., op. cit.,* 348 and 428.
[46] *Annual Report of Commissioner of Indian Affairs, 1925,* 52.

The clothing of the pupils was also poor in quality and frequently ill-fitting and unsightly in appearance. To keep within the budget, shoes were sent to the shop to be repaired again and again and were worn until they literally fell apart. Each student had a neat "Sunday uniform," but the clothing worn during the week was often faded, patched and mended. Members of the survey staff often commented on how difficult it must have been to teach self-respect and proper pride to children so poorly clothed.

Housing was usually as poor as the food and clothing. A number of abandoned military posts had been turned over to the Indian Service to be converted into reservation boarding schools or agencies. Such buildings were frequently not suited for the purposes for which they were used. Dormitories lacked proper facilities for lighting and ventilation and were difficult to keep clean and sanitary. Some of them were veritable fire traps. They were also overcrowded because of the necessity of enrolling as many students as possible in order to secure more funds for the maintenance of the school. The dangers already inherent in such a situation were greatly increased by those in charge of the dormitories, since outside doors were usually locked at night, the windows so arranged that they could be raised only a few inches, and even outlets leading to fire escapes were often locked. Such practices were considered necessary to keep pupils from running away or to prevent boys from entering the girls' dormitories.

The military system under which the pupils lived and worked was not conducive to the development of individual initiative or resourcefulness. The student soon learned to follow blindly the daily routine and do what he was told to do. He had little opportunity to think for himself. The so-called "vocational education," the daily work necessary to maintain the school, had a value, but there was so much of it to be done that not enough time was left for sufficient training in any vocation to enable the Indian boy or girl after graduation to compete with white graduates of the better trade schools.

Students seldom developed correct work habits. For many years after the founding of the earlier boarding schools in the Southwest, the pupils, even in the lower grades, were large, strong boys and girls, fifteen to eighteen years of age, quite capable of working. Later, when children six or seven years old were placed in school, they were too young and small for some of the work that must be done. The child quickly discovered that as soon as he had completed a task, he was immediately assigned another. Accordingly, he developed the defense of taking plenty of time for the first one. The official in charge, faced with the necessity of getting the job done, would sometimes assign three or four pupils to a task that should have been done by one.

It was also apparent to the members of the survey staff that teachers were handicapped by being expected to follow a standard course prepared by officials of the Indian Bureau without regard to the great differences between Indians of various tribes. Teachers and matrons were usually conscientious in their work and dealt kindly and sympathetically with the children, but many of them lacked the training and ability necessary to achieve success. Salaries were too low, living quarters and conditions bad, and the yearly turnover of teachers in some schools was very great. New appointees usually came from Eastern states or the Middle West and had no knowledge or understanding of Indians prior to taking up their duties.[47]

Although the Indian survey staff of the Institute for Government Research found much to condemn in the federal government's administration of Indian education in the Southwest, it also found many things to commend. In no school could conditions be called ideal, and in a few they were little short of deplorable; but even in the poorest ones the teachers and administrative officers were doing the best they could with the funds provided and the outmoded system which had grown up and under which they must operate. The responsibility for these inadequacies lay with Congress, the officials of the Indian Office in Washington, and the indifference of the general public.

One great weakness in the scheme for Indian education, particularly in the Southwest, was the failure to provide an adequate placement and follow-up service for students graduating from the large nonreservation schools. This was especially needed in view of the fact that students in such schools had never been given the opportunity to develop those qualities of initiative and self-reliance so necessary to success.

The lack of such a placement and follow-up system often had tragic results. A girl from a remote part of one of the great reservations sometimes entered a nonreservation boarding school and re-

[47] Most teachers in the Indian schools of the Southwest, especially in earlier years came from the East. In 1885, of the forty teachers at eleven jurisdictions in the Southwest, four were from New England, twelve from New York, Pennsylvania, and New Jersey, two from West Virginia, nine from Ohio, Michigan, and Illinois, and six were born in Europe. Four of the nine teachers in the Mission day schools and one of the three teachers at Fort Yuma were from California. Only one other teacher of the entire forty came from west of the Mississippi. *Annual Report of Commissioner of Indian Affairs, 1885,* cxxx–cxci.

Hopi Day School, Shungopovi

The home economics class serves in the Phoenix school

mained for ten or twelve years. During this time she had almost no contact with her own family, since she either remained in school during the summer months or was sent out to work for a white family under the outing system originated by Pratt at Carlisle. During all of these years she arose at the sound of the bell, went to work by the bell, and quit by the bell. All of her waking hours were rigidly supervised, and she slept behind the locked doors of the dormitory at night. Then she was graduated and left the school to face a future for which she was most inadequately prepared.

She had two alternatives: to return to her family on the reservation or to seek employment in a town or city. Frequently the lure of a large city took her to the nearest important one, where she sought employment. Her training had not fitted her for anything but domestic service. In such a position her mistress seldom understood her shy, sensitive Indian nature, and in some cases was no more sympathetic than she was understanding. The girl knew no one and was terribly lonely. On her afternoons out there was nothing to do except to visit a picture show or walk in the park. She sought companionship where she could find it, and all too often it was not of the right kind. If she got into bad company and found herself in trouble, her mistress very often discharged her without a recommendation. It was not always easy to find another position, and she drifted from bad to worse. And critics declared that it was useless to educate Indians because they always seemed to go to the bad!

If she chose the other alternative and returned to the reservation, her situation was little better. Her own family were strangers to her and she to them. She was appalled by the conditions under which they lived, and they were equally horrified by her appearance, clad as she probably was in a white blouse, short skirt, silk stockings, with her hair bobbed and her nails manicured like any white girl. To wear such clothing in her parents' home was impossible. Her mother was as much shocked by her strange garb as a white mother would be if her son after some years among the Indians should return home clothed in a blanket and leggings, with his hair in two long braids and silver earrings in his ears. The girl would find it necessary to return to her native costume and manner of living if she remained with her parents.

Reservation superintendents have often told of an attractive girl just returned from school who after a few days at her parents' home would come to the agency office with tears streaming down her face and say: "Mr. Superintendent, I cannot endure living with the members of my own family. They are dirty, sleep on sheepskins, and have no understanding of the first principles of cleanliness and sanitation. Won't you please help me to get a job that will enable me to live the way I have been taught to live." Unfortunately the superintendents were remote from any town, had no contact with employment agencies, and could seldom offer any help. In consequence, the despairing young woman returned to her home, put on a blanket, and within a year or so married some uneducated man on the reservation and reared her family in a hogan or tepee. Critics were again ready to say that it was useless to educate Indians because they immediately "go back to the blanket." A study of the case histories of a number of graduates of the larger Indian boarding schools up until recent years will reveal many similar instances.

What the Indian Service needed in 1927, when the Meriam Survey was made, and had needed for many years, was adequate training for competitive life among the whites, and satisfactory placement and follow-up service to find positions for graduates and help them adjust to life in our modern industrial world.[48]

The publication of the Meriam Report undoubtedly had an immediate and far-reaching effect upon Indian education. A year after the appearance of the report, the schools had a million and a quarter dollars more money annually for provision of food in the boarding schools, which made the difference between a bare subsistence diet and well-balanced, substantial meals.

Charles J. Rhoads, who became commissioner of Indian affairs in 1929, earnestly sought to carry out the major recommendations of the Meriam Report. He was ably assisted by Dr. W. Carson Ryan, who was appointed Director of Indian Education. Many old school buildings were replaced by new ones or repaired. The military system was abolished and discipline was relaxed. Pupils were no longer dressed in uniforms but in neat, well-fitting clothing chosen with some regard for the child's personal preference. The "platoon system," by which children devoted one-half day to academic subjects, one-fourth to vocational training, and one-fourth to work about the school was in operation in few schools by 1928. It was now greatly extended. Overcrowding in the boarding schools was eliminated by enrolling no more students than the capacity of the school warranted. Many new community day schools were established to care for the education of pupils formerly in the boarding schools, and the per capita allowance for the latter was eventually increased to about $375 a year.

[48] Meriam *et al., op. cit.,* 434–35.

The teaching was improved by requiring higher qualifications for all new appointees and by changes in teaching methods.

Well-trained supervisors were appointed to advise and assist the teachers. The disciplinarians and matrons were supplanted by advisors and house mothers. An effort was made to develop greater initiative and self-reliance on the part of students by giving them increased responsibility for their own conduct and the successful completion of the tasks to which they were assigned. Some school officials brought up under the old regime wondered pessimistically what would happen when the dormitory doors were left unlocked, and pupils were allowed to open their windows at will and given free access to the fire escapes. But these things were done and nothing happened. Cases calling for discipline were not increased in the slightest. An attempt was also made to find positions for graduates and to keep in touch with them for several years after they had finished school.

Obviously, reforms came slowly. The improvement in the food and clothing of children in the boarding schools was apparent at once, and better housing was provided within a few years. Changes in personnel were more difficult and the results of the new methods of administration could hardly be reflected in the lives and success of students for many years. By 1930, however, it was clear that the traditional system of Indian education which had existed for half a century or more almost without change was gone forever. Under it the federal government had brought great advancement to the Indians of the Southwest, but it had become plain that it was out of date and that radical reforms and changes had long been overdue. Commissioner Collier, who succeeded Rhoads in 1933, continued the educational reform.

XIII

Health and Medical Services

THERE IS A POPULAR BELIEF, apparently shared by some very old Indians, that before they had any contact with whites, all Indians were strong and healthy. The assertion is often made that the whites are responsible for all disease among the Indians, including those frightful epidemics that have at times carried off nearly half the members of a tribe. This is sheer nonsense. The Indian is a human animal and as such has always been subject to most of the physical ailments that afflict the people of other races. Nature, like Justice, is blind, and she punishes any violation of her laws without regard to the color of the offender's skin. There is every reason to believe that the Indian in his native habitat was subject to coughs and colds, stomach and intestinal disorders, pulmonary and skin troubles and most other diseases which afflict his white brothers.[1]

It is true that the health and physical stamina of the Indian race deteriorated greatly after its contact with the whites. There were many reasons for this. Under the hard conditions of primitive Indian life, the process of selection operated to produce strong bodies because only the hardy lived to maturity. Infant mortality must have been terrible among the western Indians of a hundred years or more ago; it is still very high in those tribes that have been least affected by white civilization. Puny or ailing children a century ago seldom lived to be three years old. Those that reached the age of ten were almost invariably excellent physical specimens. Poor diet, exposure, and lack of hygiene and sanitation combined to take a fearful toll of lives among the very young. The diet available for children in the earlier days was hardly a suitable one. There were not enough green vege-

---

[1] See *Tuberculosis Among the North American Indians,* Senate Committee Print, 67 Cong., 4 sess., 4–12 for reports of early travelers about disease among Indians.

tables or fruit, and little milk, although children with no younger brothers or sisters were often nursed by their mothers until six or eight years of age.[2]

Some Southwestern tribes made fermented drinks, or tiswin and tulapai, both with a considerable alcoholic content, long before they had had any contact with European civilization; but the white man brought to the Indian distilled liquors. The fiery whiskey dispensed by traders or bootleggers, often adulterated with red pepper, tobacco, or gunpowder, obviously played havoc with the red man's internal organs. Moreover, once a taste for alcohol had been acquired, the Indian drank anything that contained it, including bitters, flavoring extracts, painkiller, patent medicines of various kinds, and even "canned heat." Liquor has probably killed more Indians than have the guns of the United States soldiers.

In the process of transition from the roving life of his fathers to the more sedentary one of the white man, the Indians also suffered greatly in health and vitality. It was difficult for him to bridge the gap between Indian and white civilization without "being burned up rather than lifted up." So long as his home was a grass tepee or a crude structure built of cactus or palm leaves, he could rid himself of dirty unsanitary surroundings by the simple expedient of removing to a clean, attractive spot a mile or so away. It was far easier to move and build a new home than to clean up the old one. During the period given over by the average wife to spring housecleaning, her husband doubtless sometimes thinks that the old Indian custom had something to commend it!

Officials of the federal government, eager to see the Indian adopt the outward forms of white civilization, sometimes built him a house or encouraged him to build one for himself before he had learned how to occupy it in healthful fashion. He lived in a permanent house but was still "tepee minded." His dwelling became dirty, unsanitary, and infested with vermin, but he could not well abandon it. Ventilation was poor because he found it easier to close all windows than to chop more wood, especially when the latter was scarce, as it often was on the plains and deserts of the Southwest. Crowded conditions usually prevailed. An entire family of five or six lived, cooked, and ate in a single room and slept on sheepskins or on piles of hay on the floor. If one person contracted a communicable disease, it was nearly certain to sweep through the entire family, whether it was tuberculosis, trachoma, measles, smallpox, influenza, or common colds. Filthy sur-

2 *Annual Report of Commissioner of Indian Affairs, 1851*, 506.

roundings or clothing and lack of washing and bathing brought on impetigo or other skin diseases. Itch was prevalent. Venereal diseases were most common among those groups of Indians living near a military post or in close contact with the lower class of whites, all too common on every frontier. As a result of all these factors, the health and physical well-being of the Southwestern Indians declined rapidly after they came into contact with a large number of whites, although they were by no means free of sickness and bodily infirmities previous to that time. It seems possible, too, that Indians had not developed the resistance the Europeans had to some types of disease, for instance, measles and smallpox; these caused a shocking mortality among Indians, caused by overcrowded conditions and the methods of treatment. On the other hand, the Indian had developed a resistance to some other diseases, notably typhoid fever.

The sedentary tribes, as the Pueblo and Hopi, lived in stone or adobe houses, some of them accommodating a number of families. Often they were dark and poorly ventilated, while the village usually lacked cleanliness or proper sanitary facilities. Horses, burros, cows, and sheep were sometimes kept in corrals among the houses; garbage and other refuse was dumped into the streets; and the water supply was brought from springs or a near-by stream. Sometimes the governor and caciques enforced regulations for keeping the village reasonably clean and many of the people took considerable pride in neat housekeeping. Moreover, the pure, dry desert air and the hot sun were great purifiers. Disease germs found it difficult to survive and multiply due to the dry air and the rays of the blazing desert sun. The health of the people was better than might be expected and doubtless far better than it would have been had they lived in a humid climate.

Few Indians of the Southwest had received medical care from white physicians prior to 1848. The mission fathers in southern California, and to some extent in the region south of Gila in Arizona, had undoubtedly ministered to the sick and cared for those who had been injured, but their efforts were confined to a few tribes. All other Indians of the Southwest looked exclusively to the medicine man for treatment in times of illness, as well as for dressing wounds and setting broken bones. Among the Indians, as with all other primitive peoples, disease was frequently regarded as the result of supernatural causes and the practice of medicine was closely associated with the priesthood. Illness was regarded as due to evil spirits that must be exorcised, or to the displeasure of the gods who must be propitiated, or to witchcraft, through the efforts of some evil-disposed person endowed with power to cause sickness and death. Witches were executed among the Pueblo in 1853 and probably much later.[3] Some other tribes also punished witchcraft with death even after 1848.

The Pueblo fully realized that illness might be caused by exposure to cold or the eating of unripe fruit and sickness of this nature was not attributed to evil spirits or supernatural causes. Among these Indians one who wished to become a medicine man must join a healing society or "medical guild." Any attempt to appease the Great Spirit or drive away demons, however, was not to be made by an individual but by the entire group. Trances, dreams, and orgies had no place in the Pueblo art of healing or in Pueblo life.[4]

Among most other tribes, the medicine man was an individual practitioner. Charms and amulets were regarded as having a peculiar efficacy, as were also the beating of drums, shaking of rattles, and the chanting of some particular song. Many medicine men, however, had a very good knowledge of the curative properties of various plants, and absorbed a fair degree of skill in surgery. The sweat bath was freely used in the Southwest and among most other tribes of North America, but mingled with the actual work of healing was much curious mummery and a "bedside manner" calculated to impress the patient and his relatives and friends.

The young Indian (outside of the Pueblo tribes) who desired to become a medicine man usually studied with some older man who had been a practitioner for many years and who taught him the secrets of the craft. In addition, however, he must sometimes fast and pray that "power" be granted him, appealing sometimes to the animal or bird alleged to be the father of his clan, as the bear, eagle, antelope, or snake. Once admitted to the charmed circle, his popularity and prosperity depended largely upon the measure of success attained in healing. Contrary to popular conception, the medicine man in more recent years has not always been an aged grandfather steeped in the lore of ancient days but a comparatively young man, educated in the boarding school, who has sought to capitalize upon his learning and at the same time to maintain a position of influence in his tribe.

A charm or tailsman was commonly worn or kept by healthy individuals to ward off disease. This might be a medicine bag, shirt, or maternity belt, or sometimes, a necklace or other article of jewelry regarded as a "good luck piece." Among almost all tribes, it was cus-

[3] *Ibid., 1854,* 173.
[4] William Thomas Corlett, *The Medicine Man of the American Indian and His Cultural Background,* 150–52.

tomary to burn the house or tepee in which death occurred, together with the effects of the dead person, a custom which probably grew out of their earlier experience with contagious and infectious diseases. Few Indians, even today, will live in a house in which someone has died, or even enter it willingly, and this is true of many educated Indians.

The first federal officials who came among the tribes of the Southwest had to combat these time-honored beliefs, customs, and superstitions when they sought to provide medical service. Most Indians viewed with suspicion, not unmixed with hostility, the activities of any agency physician. They had far greater faith in the medicine man; and the latter, seeing his prestige and even his livelihood threatened by the Indian Service doctor, did his best to foster the Indians' distrust. If a physician was reluctantly summoned after the efforts of the medicine man had proved unavailing, it was frequently too late to save the patient, and the doctor received the blame for his death. When a hospital was erected, this white man's "medicine house" was viewed with grave misgivings, and as soon as a patient had died in it, most Indians flatly refused to enter the "death house" in which the ghost of the deceased still lingered or where the evil spirits that had caused his death yet lay in wait for another victim. Under such conditions, medical work progressed slowly in the Southwest.

It is difficult to place with any degree of certainty the first medical services rendered to the Indians of the Southwest by the federal government. No doubt army doctors dressed wounds, set broken bones, and treated sick Indians at times during the first few years after the United States had acquired that region and established military posts there. The Indian Appropriation Act approved August 18, 1856, carried an item for the pay of doctors, smiths, and laborers on the California reservations,[5] and mentioned the employment of a physician and the establishment of a hospital in northern California in 1857. But few Indian Service doctors were employed in the Southwestern region for twenty years or more after the acquisition of that territory, and not many until the reservation system had been fairly well established.[6] In fact, it seems that the first physicians appointed were more for the benefit of the agent and his family and the other employees of the agency than for the Indians. On days when rations were issued, or other occasions when considerable numbers of Indians were assembled near the agency, the doctor sometimes had

5 11 Stats., 79.
6 Tuberculosis Among the North American Indians, 93.

an opportunity to show his skill and gradually a few Indians began to avail themselves of his services.[7] It seems remarkable, however, how few references to medical work are found in all the reports of agents and other officials in the field prior to 1870. At least three or four physicians were early appointed as agents in the Southwest, and they no doubt gave some attention to medical work, but their administrative duties must have left little time for this.

By 1865 it was generally agreed by persons most familiar with conditions in the Southwest that the Indian population was steadily decreasing, caused largely by the prevalence of disease, and that some sort of health service should be established by the federal government.[8] Accordingly, in 1873 a medical and educational division was established in the Indian Bureau. In 1874, however, only about one-half of the agencies in the United States had been provided with physicians.[9] In the Southwest, several agencies had no doctor and most other agencies had only one, who was furnished little equipment—sometimes not even a means of travel over the reservation. Lacking a team and wagon, or even a horse and saddle, it was, of course, impossible for the agency doctor to visit any considerable number of patients, and he could treat only those who came to him or dispense a few drugs and medicines when requested to do so.[10] For some years the great Navajo Agency had but one doctor, and obviously he could do little toward giving medical service to fifteen to twenty thousand people spread over a region larger than some of the smaller states of the Union.[11] In 1877 the medical division was abolished, in spite of the great need for additional medical service and the insistent requests of agents for physicians.

The discontinuance of the medical division did not mean that the federal government abandoned its health program. On the contrary, it increased its efforts in both preventive and remedial work. In 1878 the Commissioner of Indian Affairs stated in his annual report that in the future persons employed as physicians on Indian reservations must be "graduates of some medical college and have the necessary diplomas."[12] He added that in the past, persons had been employed who had assumed the responsibilities of physicians but had met with poor success in keeping down sickness and had

7 *Ibid.*
8 *Ibid.,* 93–94.
9 *Ibid.,* 94.
10 *Ibid.,* 94–95.
11 *Ibid.,* 97. Quoting *Annual Report of Commissioner of Indian Affairs, 1902.*
12 *Tuberculosis Among the North American Indians,* 94.

caused the Indians "to lose faith in the superiority of the white man's medicine and return to their former methods of curing the sick."[13]

Apparently the first permanent hospital was established in 1882, and by 1888 there were four in the entire Indian Service, but the number was increased to five before 1900.[14] In 1895 there were seventy-four physicians, eight nurses, and three field matrons, but by 1900 the numbers had increased to eighty-six physicians, twenty-five nurses, and twenty-one field matrons; these had been further increased to ninety-six, thirty-three, and forty, respectively, five years later.[15]

The first decade of the twentieth century was to see a tardy recognition of the importance of health and medical service to be rendered to the Indians by the federal government. In 1907 Dr. Ales Hrdlicka made a rapid survey of a number of Indian tribes to collect data on the prevalence of tuberculosis to be presented to the International Congress on Tuberculosis which met the following year. This survey was sponsored jointly by the Indian Office and the Smithsonian Institution, and the results published as *Bulletin 32* of the Bureau of American Ethnology. In 1909 the Medical Division, which had been discontinued in 1877, was revived by Commissioner Valentine and a medical supervisor for the entire health service appointed.[16] That same year Congress made a special appropriation of $12,000 to investigate, treat, and prevent the spread of trachoma.[17]

It might be said that the systematic organization of health work among the Indians, not only in the Southwest but throughout the entire country, had its beginning in 1909. For the fiscal year 1911, $40,-000 was appropriated to relieve distress and to provide for "the prevention and treatment of tuberculosis, trachoma, smallpox, and other contagious and infectious diseases."[18] This was only the first of a series of appropriations of the same character, with the amounts increased in later years.

On August 10, 1912, President Taft submitted to Congress a special message calling attention to the need of increased medical work among the Indians by the federal government and requesting the appropriation of $253,000 for the Indian Medical Service, which was the amount the Indian Bureau had asked. The President referred

13 *Ibid.*
14 *Ibid.,* 101.
15 *Ibid.* Of these the Indians of the Southwest had their proportional share.
16 Schmeckebier, *op. cit.,* 229.
17 35 *Stats.,* 642.
18 36 *Stats.,* 271.

to the prevalence of tuberculosis on the Colorado River Reservation in Arizona and the Mescalero Reservation in New Mexico, and to trachoma at Phoenix School, urging the necessity for efficient physicians, nurses, and field matrons.[19]

By the Indian Appropriation Act approved August 24, 1912, the Public Health Service was given an appropriation of $10,000 to enable it to make a survey of the prevalence of contagious and infectious diseases among the Indians.[20] The area to be covered was so large that fourteen officers were assigned to the work, each being given a specific district. All of these were men with special training in inspection work and the diagnosis of trachoma. They spent three months in field work, during which twenty-five states were visited and the medical records of agencies and boarding schools were examined, in addition to the examination of 39,231 Indians. Portions of the Southwest were included in four districts. Nevada, together with Oregon and northern California, were assigned to Passed Assistant Surgeon W. C. Billings; Arizona, to Passed Assistant Surgeon L. D. Fricks; Utah and southern California, to Passed Assistant Surgeon R. D. Herring; and New Mexico and Colorado were surveyed by Passed Assistant Surgeon F. C. Smith.[21]

It had been apparent for many years that a large percentage of the Indians of the Southwest were afflicted with either trachoma or tuberculosis and some with both. Up to this time, however, despite a number of minor surveys conducted by some states or individuals or organizations, there had been little conception of how widespread these diseases were among the tribes of this region. Trachoma, a disease of the eyes which frequently causes blindness, is commonly regarded as a disease of Oriental origin. It is quite prevalent in parts of Europe and is also found among whites in various parts of the United States, particularly in the mountainous areas of Kentucky and West Virginia. The Indians had long been afflicted with it but just when and where it first appeared among them is doubtful.[22]

Highly contagious, the disease spread rapidly among the Indians due to careless personal habits. Crowded living conditions, the use of common towels and washbasins, and prevalence of flies all favor the spread of the disease. It seems that while trachoma had existed for generations among the Indians, few physicians recognized it as

19 Congressional Record, August 10, 1912, 10,643–44.
20 37 Stats., 519.
21 Contagious and Infectious Diseases Among the Indians, Report to U. S. Senate by Public Health Service, 62 Cong., 3 sess., 11.
22 Ibid., 16–17.

such prior to 1900. Reservation records prior to that time, however, reveal mention of many cases of eye afflictions often referred to as "sore eyes," "conjunctivitis," "granulated lids," "bad eyes," or "scrofulous eyes."[23]

The nearly forty thousand Indians examined by the physicians of this survey included both sexes and all ages from most reservations and the various schools of the United States. Of that number nearly nine thousand or 22.7 per cent were found to be in a trachomatous condition.[24]

Tuberculosis was also found to be prevalent among the Southwestern Indians. No accurate data could be obtained about how long the disease had existed among the Indians, but it was clear that it had steadily increased since their first contact with whites. In Arizona 22.7 per cent of all deaths were due to tuberculosis, which was higher than among the Indians of any other state except Iowa.[25]

This survey revealed some significant figures as to birth and death rates in the various states. These indicated that in 1912 the Indian population of Arizona as a whole was stationary, there being 57 births and 57 deaths per thousand of population. In Nevada there was a decrease of 17 persons, in Utah a slight increase, and in New Mexico an increase of 271, or slightly less than three per cent.[26] Taken as a whole, the Indians of the Southwest were slowly increasing by 1912.

With respect to other contagious and infectious diseases, the survey revealed that the work of the federal government in providing general vaccination for the Indians had greatly reduced smallpox. In the Southwest most of the younger Indians had received the protection of vaccination, although many older ones had refused to accept it; and a few tribes or pueblos as a whole, notably Ácoma, Zuñi, and Cochiti, had persistently resisted the preventive. There had been no widespread epidemic, however, for many years and little indication that one need be feared in the future.[27] Epidemics of measles had

23 *Ibid.*, 19.
24 *Ibid.*, 20–31. Of the five states surveyed, Utah had 39 per cent of Indians with trachoma; California, 15.64 per cent; Arizona, 24.9; New Mexico, 22.38; and Nevada, 26.9. On the whole, the percentage was less on the reservations than in the schools, particularly the boarding schools, in one of which, Chin Lee, 50 per cent of the pupils were trachomatous.
25 *Ibid.*, 49. In the states surveyed, the percentage of tubercular Indians was higher on the reservations than in the schools. It ranged from 32.67 per cent of the Indians on the Pyramid Lake Reservation to 4.39 per cent of all Utah Indians.
26 *Ibid.*, 49.
27 *Ibid.*, 53–54.

been common in the Southwest at various times prior to 1912 and had taken a heavy toll of lives at some jurisdictions, especially Zuñi, where in that year 577 cases had resulted in 123 deaths. Such heavy mortality seems to have been due primarily to the malpractice of the medicine men, for in the boarding schools measles proved no more serious than among white children and almost never resulted in death.[28]

This survey showed that typhoid fever, scarlet fever, and diphtheria were very uncommon among Indians either in the Southwest or elsewhere, while whooping cough, chickenpox, mumps, and contagious skin diseases as scabies, impetigo, and eczema were common. None of these were mortal, except whooping cough, which was often fatal to infants.[29] Venereal disease, contrary to the general impression, was also found to be comparatively rare and it was suggested by the physicians making the survey that probably impetigo had often been mistaken by laymen for syphilis.[30]

The report of the survey staff pointed out the serious consequences of the widespread prevalence of trachoma and tuberculosis among Indians, not only to them but to whites, since contact between the two races was constantly growing closer. It recommended a close co-operation between the Indian Service and state health agencies, improvement of the economic status of the Indian, as well as education in personal and domestic hygiene by means of home instruction, lectures, demonstrations, and the use of moving pictures. It urged that reservations be divided into sanitary districts, each with a medical officer under direction and control of the chief medical officers of the various reservations. Other recommendations were that reservation medical officers be placed under the supervision and control of a medical bureau, that an accurate census be made of each sanitary district, and that careful records be kept by agency physicians. Only competent doctors should be appointed. Medical officers should in a large measure be independent of agency or school superintendents in all matters relating to health and sanitation, and their compensation should be made sufficient to attract well-trained men.

For the treatment of trachoma the report recommended the establishment of hospitals on each reservation for the serious cases. A dispensary, either permanent or portable, was recommended for infected districts, and a sufficient number of field nurses to administer home treatments under the supervision of a physician and to teach

28 *Ibid.*, 57.
29 *Ibid.*, 57–58.
30 *Ibid.*, 59.

Indians to treat themselves were required. It was urged[31] that children suffering from trachoma not be admitted to uninfected schools but that special schools be provided for them if possible. When this could not be done, it was urged that separate dormitories, class rooms, dining rooms, and playgrounds be assigned for their exclusive use. All boarding schools to which trachomatous pupils were admitted should be provided with a special nurse and ample facilities for the treatment of the disease. The regulation providing for systematic medical examination of all children in the boarding schools should be rigidly enforced.

The recommendations concerning tuberculosis were for regular inspection of each sanitary district or reservation for the detection of cases of tuberculosis, and specific regulations devised for the guidance of those suffering from the disease. All persons who could not, under such regulations, live in their homes without menacing others should be removed to a suitable site and there housed and given proper care. Hospital facilities should be provided on reservations, although such hospitals need not be large or expensive. Greater efforts should be made to educate Indians to protect themselves against tuberculosis. As in the case of trachomatous children, no pupil with active tuberculosis should be admitted to boarding schools, and children who developed the disease subsequent to their enrollment should be excluded. It was suggested that open air boarding schools located in a suitable climate be established for tubercular children of school age.[32] The recommendations concerning smallpox merely urged the strict enforcement of the already existing regulations for vaccination of school children and Indians on the reservations.[33]

Detailed discussion has been given to this survey because it was the most comprehensive one made up to that time by a group of well-trained scientists and constitutes a landmark in the government's medical service for Indians. Its recommendations undoubtedly were given serious attention by officials of the Indian Bureau, and an earnest effort made to carry them out so far as possible with the resources available. Unfortunately, here as in other work of the Indian Service, appropriations were not sufficient to enable the Indian Bureau to make adequate provision for a first-class medical service. The salaries of doctors, while increased slightly, still remained far lower than salaries in the army and navy, or in the Public Health Service.

31 *Ibid.,* 81–85.
32 *Ibid.*
33 *Ibid.,* 85.

Progress was made, however, in the creation of additional hospitals, the employment of more physicians, and in educating the Indians to accept hospitalization and treatment by agency doctors instead of relying upon the services of the medicine man. The general appropriation for medical work was increased from $60,000 in 1912 to $90,000 in 1913; it was $200,000 in 1914, $300,000 in 1915, and $350,000 in 1917. No great addition was made until 1925, when it rose from $370,000 to $500,000 and to $700,000 in 1926.[34] Obviously a great amount of funds from general appropriations must have been spent for medical work prior to 1912, since the number of hospitals, only five in 1900, had risen to fifty-three in 1912, including rooms in dormitories used for ill pupils. By 1916 the total number of Indian hospitals in the entire United States was eighty-one,[35] Arizona having fourteen, California six, Nevada four, New Mexico ten, and Utah one. The total capacity of all was 886 and the number of persons admitted to all during the fiscal year of 1916 was 4,739.[36]

By 1920 the number of hospitals in these five states had increased from thirty-five to thirty-six, one having been established in both Arizona and New Mexico and the number in Nevada reduced from four to three. The capacity remained practically the same, but the number of Indians admitted was 5,877, an increase of eleven hundred over the fiscal year ending June 30, 1916.[37] The Indians of the Southwest were apparently taking advantage of the government's medical services to a far greater extent than formerly; it is possible that the shocking flu epidemic in the preceding years may have alerted them to the wisdom of using the hospitals in increasing numbers.

Undoubtedly 1919 was the most disastrous year in the entire recorded medical history of the Indians of the Southwest. The vigorous health measures begun by Commissioner Valentine in 1909, and continued more aggressively after the survey in 1912, were showing commendable results when interrupted by the outbreak of the first World War. Medical attention became exceedingly difficult to secure. Many Indian Service doctors entered the armed forces, and it was impossible to secure replacements. The same situation prevailed with respect to nurses. In the meantime, the calamitous flu epidemic of 1919 swept over the United States, bringing death to thousands of people. Nowhere did it strike in more virulent form or cause greater

---

34 Schmeckebier, *op. cit.*, 352.
35 *Ibid.*
36 *Annual Report of Commissioner of Indian Affairs, 1916*, 1934–36.
37 *Ibid., 1920*, 136–38.

mortality in proportion to the total population than among the Indians of the Southwest. Every one of the five states showed a sharp increase in the number of deaths over the preceding year. In Arizona the mortality rose from 743 in 1918 to 2,254 in 1919, approximately threefold. The number of deaths in California doubled, in Nevada rose fifty per cent, in New Mexico more than tripled, while in Utah the increased mortality was almost 90 per cent. In the entire five states the number of deaths was 4,699, most of them caused by influenza. This number out of a total population of 88,968 was startling.[38]

The Navajo suffered terribly—more, perhaps, than any other tribe. It was impossible to provide them with adequate medical attention, and the cold, bleak nature of much of their reservation, together with its great size and the primitive nature of the people were all factors that contributed to the heavy mortality. The disease swept through the tribe as a real pestilence. Whole families, huddled in their hogans to escape the bitter cold, were stricken, and almost every household lost one or more members. In entire communities there were hardly enough well persons to care for the sick. Not since General Carleton's war and the tragedy of Bosque Redondo had the Navajo faced such dark days or endured so much suffering.

By 1921 the medical service was about back to its normal situation, with 1 chief medical supervisor, 6 special physicians for diseases of the eye, ear, nose, and throat, 7 traveling field dentists, and about 175 doctors. In addition there were about 100 stationed nurses, 6 traveling nurses, and 87 field matrons.[39] It was still necessary to fill some positions with practical nurses, but the policy was announced of replacing all of these with graduate nurses as soon as they could be obtained. In 1921 there was a minor outbreak of typhus among the northern Navajo at San Juan jurisdiction, but by earnest work and with the aid of the Public Health Service, it was kept in one locality. Of the fifty-two cases among the Indians, there were twenty-one deaths.[40]

Late in 1921 the National Tuberculosis Association appointed a committee of six members, with Dr. George M. Kober chairman, to make a study of tuberculosis among the American Indians. The Indian Office had expressed a desire for any assistance that this association could render and gave all possible co-operation to the committee

38 *Tuberculosis Among the North American Indians*, 65–69.
39 *Annual Report of Commissioner of Indian Affairs, 1921*. Perhaps one-third of the 175 doctors were contract physicians, giving only part time to Indian patients.
40 *Ibid.*

Fort Defiance, Arizona Territory

Hopi family, Second Mesa

in its efforts to secure information. Its report, made in 1922, gave a comprehensive account of medical work of the United States Indian Service during the ten-year period from 1911 to 1921. It also gave a large amount of historical data concerning tuberculosis among the Indians from the time it was first observed by French explorers in 1633. Admitting that vital statistics submitted by the Indian Office prior to 1911 were unreliable, the committee reached the conclusion that the annual death rate per thousand among the entire Indian population had steadily risen from 23.6 in 1880 to 32.24 in 1913. That year apparently marked the peak of excessive mortality, and the following years showed a steady decline (except in 1919). In 1920 it had dropped to 22.33 per thousand.[41] In 1911 the percentage of all deaths due to tuberculosis was 32; in 1915 it was 35; and from that year it declined to 27 per cent in 1920.[42]

The committee recommended two or three sanitaria for adult Indians, including one for terminal cases. The employment of additional field nurses was also recommended, as well as increased compensation for all full-time salaried medical officers, and the vigorous continuance of all health activities that had been inaugurated combining education and the health program. The keynote of the former should be proper living and of the latter "an ounce of prevention is worth a pound of cure." Finally it was urged that the Indian Bureau be provided with sufficient funds to help the Indians achieve a better standard of living and to provide them with food in emergencies.[43]

During the 1920's the medical work was greatly strengthened. The medicine men were still powerful, but it is possible that many young Indians were more willing to accept hospitalization or treatment by agency physicians because of their war experiences than they had previously been. These veterans were probably able to influence some of their fellow tribesmen to accept the services of the agency doctors and hospitals, but the conservative old men and women still clung to the medicine man.[44]

In 1925 southern California, Arizona, New Mexico, and Utah had a total of thirty-two hospitals of all types: eleven agency hospitals, two agency and school combined, thirteen school hospitals, and six sanitaria. Of these, Arizona had fifteen, southern California three,

41 *Tuberculosis Among the North American Indians*, 40.
42 *Ibid.*
43 *Ibid.*, 45–46.
44 Among most Indian tribes the older women have a great influence, becoming in some cases virtual matriarchs. These were as a rule extremely conservative.

Nevada four, New Mexico nine, and Utah one. Their total capacity was 1,068, and in 1925 they cared for 11,486 patients for a total 190,242 hospital days of treatment.[45]

Obviously the school hospitals treated a far larger number of individuals each year than the agency hospitals did, despite the fact that the number of pupils enrolled in the boarding schools was only a fraction of the total population. The per cent of possible utilization of Indian hospitals was low, but this did not mean that there were too many hospitals or that their capacity was too great; it was simply that the Indians failed to make full use of the facilities provided for them.

Many agency hospitals in 1925 were not well designed, properly equipped, or sufficiently staffed. The Indian Service had taken over, in certain places, the buildings of abandoned military posts, and had converted some of them into hospitals. Most other hospitals in the Southwest were small and cheaply constructed. Some were frame, others adobe, brick, or stone. Lack of funds had made it impossible to provide adequate equipment, and while there were many competent physicians in the Indian Service in 1925, salaries had previously been so low that the qualifications of a very great number of doctors had been exceedingly poor.

In 1924 the Indian Bureau organized the Southwestern Trachoma Campaign for work in a district including all of Arizona, New Mexico, Nevada, southern California, and a part of Utah. Over thirty-eight thousand Indians were examined and 19 per cent found to be trachomatous. Operations were performed upon 4,285 of these and 2,951 were treated without an operation. Demonstration clinics were held at Fort Defiance, Albuquerque, Phoenix, and Riverside.[46]

The medical work of the Indian Service was reorganized in 1926. A surgeon from the Public Health Service was detailed to be in general charge, and the entire country was divided into four districts, each under a medical director. With the exception of Utah, the Southwestern states were included in district three, with headquarters established at Albuquerque. Three of the four medical directors were detailed from the Public Health Service, which also co-operated with the Indian Bureau by doing some inspection work from its branch offices and making surveys of water supplies through its corps of sanitary engineers. The Indian Office also provided for a supervisor of field nurses and field matrons. The special physicians dealing

[45] Schmeckebier, *op. cit.*, 234–35.
[46] *Annual Report of Commissioner of Indian Affairs, 1925*, 3–4.

with diseases of the eye, ear, nose, and throat continued to travel throughout the districts, each accompanied by a nurse, holding consultations with local Indian Service physicians and nurses. They also performed operations and acted as advisors to the district medical director in professional and administrative matters. Dental service, which was begun in 1910, was by this time well developed. Dentists traveled in each district and conducted a general dental practice on the various reservations and in the schools. The contract physicians were local practitioners employed to care for the health of reservations or schools when a full-time physician was not employed. The tendency was to reduce the number of contract physicians, however, and employ full-time doctors when they could be obtained.[47]

The report of the Meriam Survey, published in 1928, included a detailed discussion of the federal government's health work for the Indians. Its conclusions were that while the variation between the best and the worst was very wide, the health work of the Indian Service fell far below the standards maintained by the Public Health Service, the Veteran's Bureau, and the army and navy. This was caused largely by lack of sufficient appropriations, especially for salaries.[48]

Most Indian hospitals and sanitaria were below minimum standards in plant, equipment, and personnel.[49] The birth rate for all the Indians of the United States was around 50 per cent higher than for the whole population, but the death rate in Nevada was 39.2 per thousand, Arizona 38.9, and Utah 35.8.[50] The Indian death rate from tuberculosis in Arizona was 15.1, which was more than seventeen times as high as the average of all states in the Union within the birth registration area. Infant mortality was especially high among Indians.[51]

The survey found the number of tubercular children in the boarding schools alarming, apparently caused by the failure to make complete health examinations of the children admitted and also to a poorly balanced diet, overcrowding, and the industrial system of operating these schools. The government was found to have been waging an active campaign against trachoma for several years. Trachoma schools had been established; at Fort Defiance one began in 1927 with 450 trachomatous children.[52]

47 Schmeckebier, op. cit., 232, 274, and 344–46.
48 Meriam et al., op. cit., 189–90.
49 Ibid., 190.   50 Ibid., 201.
51 Ibid., 199.   52 Ibid., 211.

The Indian Service had in 1927 announced a policy of employing no more practical nurses, but the number of graduate nurses was not sufficient to render much service outside the hospitals. The reservation Indians, therefore, were receiving little public health nursing. The survey revealed that most hospitals were much understaffed, often lacked necessary equipment, and had insufficient maintenance funds. The average cost per diem in the Indian hospitals was about $1.80, while in the Public Health Service hospitals in 1926 it was $3.71.[53] Indian Service sanitaria were also forced to operate at a far lower per diem cost than were others throughout the country.[54]

The health expert for this survey visited nearly every hospital and reservation in the Southwest, and found much to commend in the medical service in spite of the existing handicaps. Recommendations boiled down to the need for greatly increased appropriations, in order to provide better personnel; more nearly adequate funds for hospital maintenance; a greater emphasis upon prevention of disease; a more vigorous attack upon tuberculosis; and educating the Indians to utilize the services of agency physicians and hospitals. An earnest recommendation was also made for a better diet for pupils in the boarding schools and for relieving the crowded conditions found in many of them. Special emphasis was placed upon the need for higher salaries and better working conditions for all medical officials, and for more hospital equipment. More careful examinations of children admitted to the boarding schools and frequent re-examinations were recommended, and the importance of keeping complete and accurate data was stressed. The need for regular health surveys and the collection of vital statistics was also urged.

The findings and recommendations of this survey undoubtedly had an important influence upon the later policies and work of the Indian Bureau where the Health and Medical Service were concerned. During the administration of Commissioner Rhoads, much larger appropriations were secured from Congress, the hospitals were vastly improved, and several new ones were established. The number of physicians and nurses was largely increased, and better salaries and working conditions provided. By 1933 the Medical and Health Service for the Indians was much better than it had been five years earlier. The system set up in 1926 was continued, except that the number of medical districts was increased, and, eventually, the detailing of physicians from the Public Health Service was discontinued, and all doctors were employed by the Indian Bureau.

53 *Ibid.*, 285.   54 *Ibid.*, 295.

There were many devoted men and women among the medical officers of the Indian Service in the Southwest who could not have rendered more or better service regardless of compensation. In heat and cold they drove the cheap, open cars supplied by the government over the wretched trails called roads to reach and minister to the suffering even on the most remote parts of the great reservations. Often their living quarters were poor and many of them lacked nearly everything necessary to the successful practice of their profession except a strong heart, a willing spirit, and an intense devotion to duty. They had to help many Indians who were unwilling to receive help at their hands. They had to combat prejudice, superstition, and often the hostility of the medicine men. However, some of the wiser physicians were able to enlist the medicine men's co-operation and help by pointing out to them that they were both seeking the same objectives by different methods. Clever agency doctors would sometimes summon the local medicine man for a conference, and the two would give treatment to the patient.

By such means the prejudices and hostility of the Indians were gradually broken down. "Nothing succeeds like success." Once an Indian had been cured or relieved by the agency physician, he not only had faith himself but was able to influence his relatives and friends. Each year, Indians accepted hospitalization in increasing numbers. More and more Indian babies were born in hospitals instead of in hogans and tepees with only the aid of an Indian midwife. In 1928 there were only 595 live births in Indian Service hospitals while in 1933 there were 2,277.[55] Moreover, infant mortality steadily declined. By 1933 the health and medical service rendered to the Indians of the Southwest had become one of the major activities of the Indian Bureau in that region. There was still much to be done. The liquor problem as it affected the health and physical welfare of the Indians was still acute. The use of peyote was probably on the increase in some areas, and in some localities in Nevada a considerable number of Indians were addicted to the use of narcotics. Trachoma was still the scourge of the Indian race, and tuberculosis was a constant menace. After 1933 renewed efforts were made to solve these and other health problems.

[55] *Annual Report of Commissioner of Indian Affairs, 1933*, 81.

XIV

A New Regime and Some Current Problems

IN 1933 JOHN COLLIER, who for ten years had been executive secretary of the Indian Defense Association, and for seven years editor of the *American Indian Life Magazine,* succeeded Charles Rhoads as commissioner of Indian affairs. He had, therefore, for a long time been deeply interested in the American Indians, especially those of the Southwest. He was an experienced social worker and brought to his task an able and aggressive personality. He had been one of the most outstanding critics of the Indian Bureau, and he now had the opportunity to put into effect the reforms which he had so long advocated. He served as commissioner for more than twelve years, which was a far longer tenure than that of any of his predecessors, and during all of that time had the full confidence and support of both the President and the Secretary of the Interior.

It is impossible at present to evaluate the work of Commissioner Collier during his long term of office or to appraise the final results of the sweeping changes and radical reforms which he inaugurated. The most that can be done is to state very briefly what his ideas and policies were and leave it to time to write the final verdict.

The new commissioner viewed with much concern the rapid alienation of Indian lands which had resulted in reducing the area of lands they owned from nearly 130,000,000 acres at the time of the passage of the Allotment Act in 1887 to around 49,000,000 acres in 1933. He felt that this alienation of Indian lands must be stopped, that allotted lands must be consolidated into tribal or corporate ownership with individual tenure, and that new lands must be acquired for the ninety thousand Indians who had none. Training in the modern techniques of land use must be given to the Indians, a modern system of financial credit established to enable them to utilize their own natural resources, and soil erosion must be checked.[1]

[1] *Annual Report of the Secretary of the Interior, 1933,* 68.

Concerning education, Commissioner Collier felt that far too much emphasis had been placed on the boarding schools. He proposed to substitute for many of them community day schools which would be educational centers for children and adults alike. The remaining boarding schools would have their enrollments reduced to their normal capacity and would specialize in occupational training for older children or supply the needs of children requiring institutional care. More Indians would be employed in the Indian Service and all Indians were to have a greater tribal and local participation in the management of their own properties and in the administration of their own affairs.[2] He believed that the Indian Service should be decentralized and its special functions be more closely integrated with one another and with local areas and local groups of Indians. An enlarged responsibility must be vested in the reservation superintendents and other officials, or concurrently in the Indians themselves. Any such reorganization would in part depend upon the revision of the land allotment system and in part upon the development of co-operative relations between the Federal Indian Service and the states, counties, school districts, and other local units of government.[3]

Certain features of the Commissioner's proposed reforms applied with peculiar force to the Indians of the Southwest. A large part of the Indians of California and Nevada were landless. Because of the rapid increase in the population of the Navajo, that tribe no longer had sufficient pasturage, especially since erosion had greatly reduced the fertility of large areas of range. No large portion of the lands in the Southwest had been lost to the Indians by the sale of allotments, since allotments had been made on few reservations, and for these, few fee patents had been issued. The need of decentralization of administration, giving a larger measure of authority and responsibility to local officials, had been particularly apparent in the Southwest, because of the disparity in the living habits of the tribes there.

The new administration came into power in the midst of the nationwide depression. Certain groups of Indians, living in permanent villages or settlements and depending largely upon subsistence farming for a livelihood, felt the depression less than did the average agricultural community among the whites. The Indians of southern California and some jurisdictions in Arizona, however, had depended on earnings from seasonal labor, and they felt the depression keenly.

2 *Ibid.*, 68–69.
3 *Ibid.*, 69.

Low prices of such products as lambs, wool, piñon nuts, and articles produced by handcrafts naturally left the Navajo and a few other groups in a poor economic condition. Indian relief had to be greatly increased, and Congress, by the second deficiency act of the fiscal year of 1932, granted an additional $50,000 to the Indian Office for relief. More than forty carloads of clothing were secured from the surplus stocks of the War Department for issue to Indians, and through the American Red Cross about five million pounds of flour, many thousands of yards of cloth, and a large quantity of clothing and blankets were secured for distribution among the various tribes. Congress also made available $1,400,000 for the construction of roads, $1,000,000 by the Emergency Relief Act and $400,000 in the regular annual appropriation act.[4] This was for the Indian Service as a whole, but the Southwest had its share of these funds.

The launching of the emergency conservation program, early in 1933, marked the beginning of a more adequate system for relieving distress among the Indians, by providing funds to pay for their employment in much needed work. The Civilian Conservation Corps, created by the act of Congress approved March 31, 1933, provided for the establishment of some fourteen hundred conservation camps, each with two hundred men enrolled for six months' service. A separate branch of the C.C.C. was set up for the Indians. $15,875,200 was allotted to the Indian Office, which was authorized to appoint its own erosion experts, foresters, and engineers, and to disburse funds. Smaller groups and shorter enlistments were authorized for the Indian Emergency Conservation work, and age limits were modified to include any able-bodied man over eighteen years of age, free from communicable disease. The work included projects in road building, forestry, fencing, erosion and flood control, improvement of public camping grounds, water development, and many other activities.[5]

An order was sent out to all superintendents on August 14, 1933, prohibiting the offer for sale of any more trust or restricted Indian lands, allotted or inherited, except in case of grave emergency. Another order was issued that no more certificates of competency, patents in fee, or removals of restrictions be submitted to the Indian Office for approval until further notice.[6] Large additions were made to the Navajo Reservation in 1933, and additional lands were purchased for some of the Indians of southern California. Such additions included the Barona Ranch of 5,000 acres in San Diego County, purchased at a cost of $75,000 for the Indians of the Capitan Grande Reservation, and

[4] *Ibid.*, 106–107.　　[5] *Ibid.*, 70–72.　　[6] *Ibid.*, 100.

a small tract added to the Coahuila Reservation. The Pueblo Land Board had awarded some of the Pueblo villages in New Mexico compensation for lands wrongfully taken from them, and by an act of Congress approved May 31, 1933, an appropriation of more than three-quarters of a million dollars was granted to these Indians to be used for the purchase of additional lands and water or other permanent economic aids.[7] The Indian Office continued the cancellation of patents in fee granted prior to 1920 to Indians who had not applied for them. Such cancellation had been authorized by acts of Congress in 1927 and 1931.

By an act of Congress July 1, 1932, the secretary of the interior was authorized to adjust or eliminate reimbursable charges of the government of the United States existing as debts against certain tribes or individual Indians.[8] During 1933, debts aggregating more than $3,000,000 were cancelled. Charges of nearly $900,000 against nineteen separate roads and bridges, of which ten were in the Navajo country, were cancelled. In addition, indebtedness of more than $100,000 advanced for the purchase of tribal herds was eliminated, as was $2,000,000 for irrigation, construction, operation, and maintenance which was reimbursable from individual Indians. A very large part of these loans for irrigation work had been in the Southwest.[9]

To carry out Commissioner Collier's program was impossible without additional legislation by Congress. He therefore sponsored and, with the aid of both the President and the Secretary of the Interior, succeeded in securing the passage and approval of the Indian Reorganization Act, commonly called the Wheeler-Howard Act. This is one of the most important pieces of legislation with respect to the Indians ever enacted by Congress. It marks the definite beginning of a new regime, and its effects upon the Indians and the Indian Service have been enormous.

The act, approved June 18, 1934, has not always been fully understood and has frequently been thought to be quite complex. As a matter of fact, it is very simple. Its provisions, embodied in nineteen sections, were carefully drawn in a fashion which made it possible for the commissioner and the secretary of the interior to put into operation the policies referred to above.[10] It repealed the previous allotment acts and provided that the trust period for Indian lands should

---

7 *Ibid.*, 101.
8 44 *Stats.*, 1247, and 46 *Stats.*, 1205.
9 *Annual Report of the Secretary of the Interior, 1933*, 103.
10 48 *Stats.*, 984–88.

be extended indefinitely. The secretary of the interior was authorized to restore to tribal ownership the remaining surplus lands of any reservation heretofore opened or authorized to be opened to sale or other disposal by presidential proclamation, so long as the valid rights, or claims, of any person to any lands so withdrawn were not affected. This was not to apply to any lands within a reclamation project previously authorized on an Indian reservation. The order withdrawing Papago lands from mineral entry was revoked, but the Papago were to be paid damages that might result from mineral entries on their land and to receive rental upon lands so used.

No sale or transfer of restricted Indian land or shares in the assets of any tribe could be made, but the secretary of the interior was authorized to transfer lands or shares of a tribe to a successor corporation. The secretary was also authorized to secure additional lands and a sum not to exceed $2,000,000 in any one year was authorized for that purpose. Title to the lands purchased was to be held in trust by the United States for the tribe or individual, and such lands were not taxable.

The secretary was given authority to make rules concerning forestry units and to restrict the number of livestock on grazing units. He was also authorized to proclaim new reservations from additional lands that might be acquired or to add such lands to existing reservations. The act did not apply to Indian homesteads or allotments on the public domain outside reservation limits, nor did it apply to Alaska or Oklahoma, although it was later extended to them. A sum not exceeding $250,000 was authorized to set up Indian chartered corporations or other organizations provided for in the act, and a revolving fund of $10,000,000 to make loans to Indian chartered corporations was voted. Educational loans to Indian students to attend vocational or trade schools and high schools and colleges were sanctioned. The secretary was directed to establish standards of health, age, and training for Indians who might be appointed to positions in the Indian Service without regard to Civil Service laws, and Indians were to receive preference in appointments to fill vacancies. It was specifically stated that the act did not prejudice the claim which any tribe might have against the United States.

The most outstanding provisions of the act were those relating to the formation of constitutions and charters. Any tribe, or number of tribes living upon the same reservation, might adopt a constitution and by-laws, which would be legal when approved by a majority vote of the adult members and the secretary of the interior, and which might be repealed or amended in the same manner. In addition to powers already vested in the tribe or tribes, the constitution should also vest in the tribe or council the following rights: (1) to choose legal counsel, the choice and the fees paid to be approved by the secretary of the interior; (2) to prevent the sale, lease, or encumbrance of tribal lands or other assets without the consent of the tribe; and (3) to negotiate with federal, state, and local governments. The secretary of the interior should advise the tribe or its council prior to their submission to the Bureau of the Budget or Congress. The secretary of the interior, upon petition of one-third of the adult members of the tribe, might issue a charter of incorporation which would become operative when approved by a majority vote of the adult Indians living on the reservation.[11] Such charter might give to the incorporated tribe the power to purchase, take by gift or bequest, or otherwise hold, own, and control property, real or personal, and to dispose of it— including the power to purchase restricted Indian lands—and to issue in exchange interests in the corporate property; and such further powers necessary to the conduct of corporate business not inconsistent with law. No power was given, however, to sell or mortgage any land of the reservation or to lease any for over ten years.

The act was not to apply to any reservation where a majority of the adult Indians voted against its application. It was made the duty of the secretary of the interior to call, within one year, an election for that purpose, giving thirty days' notice of the date of such election. The term "Indian" was defined as a member of any tribe under federal jurisdiction and his descendants living on the reservation on June 1, 1934, and others of as much as one-half Indian blood; the term "adult" was defined as anyone twenty-one years of age. The term "tribe" was defined as any tribe or band living on one reservation.

It has seemed necessary to give the provisions of the Indian Reorganization Act in some detail, not only because it has often been misunderstood, but also because of its enormous influence upon federal relations with Indians of the Southwest. Ever since its passage and approval, it has been the subject of much controversy. Its proponents hailed it as the Magna Charta of Indian liberty, while its opponents —which included many members of Congress, as well as numerous Indians and perhaps some members of the Indian Field Service— viewed it with frank skepticism not unmixed with active hostility. Nevertheless, it was the law and it provided the Commissioner with both the authority and the machinery necessary for carrying out his

11 This was later changed to a majority of those voting on the question.

policies and the reforms which he felt were so much needed. With characteristic energy he set to work to put the provisions of the act into operation, proclaiming a "New Deal" for Indians which he was certain must prove of incalculable benefit to them.

Despite his energy and enthusiasm, the Commissioner found himself faced with an arduous task. The dead hand of the past rested with almost as great weight upon the Indian Service as it did upon the Indians themselves. It was hardly less difficult to turn the feet of the Indian from the old trail traveled for so many generations by his forefathers than it was to change the practices and procedures of the Indian Bureau. A few employees who had spent most of their lives in the Indian Service must have found it difficult to accept new viewpoints, or to change the methods which they had pursued so long. No doubt a few of them viewed with grave forebodings the changes in the schools, for instance. It must have seemed almost revolutionary to leave the dormitory doors unlocked at night, to allow children to speak their own language, and to permit and encourage them to ultilize their own Indian designs in drawing, painting, and handcrafts instead of the conventional ones copied from books used in white schools. For generations the Indian Service had sought to eradicate everything which might remind the child of his former life and to substitute the forms of white civilization. Also, the formation of constitutions and charters which gave tribes a large measure of self-government and permitted them to share in the control of their own affairs was thought by some people to be a grave error.

A very great number of Indians, too, were doubtful about the changes. The Indian is naturally conservative, and his experience with new policies and procedures in the past had not been encouraging. He was accustomed to the old methods of administration and had some understanding of them. It is true that he often complained of them and of existing conditions, but these new ideas often left him bewildered and uncertain. He wanted to think about it a long time before accepting changes that he could not readily comprehend. The Indian refuses to be hurried, and any one who seeks to do it finds himself in the same position of the man referred to by Kipling "who tried to hustle the East."

Even with opposition, Commissioner Collier promptly set to work to reorganize the Service. Elections were held to determine what tribes would accept the terms of the act and come under its authority. Great disappointment was felt when the very large Navajo tribe, numbering more than one-half of all the Indians in the Southwest, voted by a narrow margin against the acceptance of the act. The Commissioner asserted that the Navajo had been misinformed concerning the purpose and probable effects of this legislation by certain interests, including some livestock men who feared the loss of the advantages which they possessed if the act were accepted.[12] It must be borne in mind, however, that the Navajo were nearly all full-bloods and were in consequence extremely conservative; it is possible that they might have shown reluctance to make a change even if no outside influence had been brought to bear upon them. The various groups of Mission Indians in southern California did not accept the new regime, nor did most villages of the New Mexico Pueblo. With these exceptions, however, most tribes in the Southwest came under the provisions of the Reorganization Act, and most of them by 1939 had formed constitutions approved by the secretary of the interior; many had drafted and adopted charters. Ten tribes of California had formed constitutions, but all of these were in the northern or central part of the state except the Tule River and the Quechan Tribe of Fort Yuma, neither of which had received a charter. Arizona had ten constitutions set up by June, 1939—San Carlos, Pima, Fort McDowell, Hopi, Papago, Camp Verde, Colorado River, Fort Apache, Hualapai, and Havasupai. Only two of these, Pima and Fort McDowell, had charters at the above date. Nevada tribes had eight constitutions, including Pyramid Lake and Walker River, and all eight had secured charters. New Mexico had three constitutions, Santa Clara Pueblo, Mescalero, and Jicarilla, the last two also having charters. In Utah, Uintah and Ouray had a constitution and charter, as did the Southern Ute tribe of Colorado.[13]

Some tribes in the Southwest promptly took advantage of the opportunity to secure loans from the revolving credit fund. By 1937 the Mescalero Apache had borrowed $163,000; two years later this had been increased to $242,000. The greater part of this money was used for the construction of homes and the remainder reloaned to individuals to purchase teams and farm tools. By 1939 the Indians of this tribe had constructed 183 farm units, each consisting of a four-room house, barn, poultry house, and other improvements.[14] Repayments, made regularly, were largely derived from the sale of lumber. The Pyramid Lake Indians had also borrowed $15,000 from this fund by the close of 1937, and additional loans that year included $85,000

---

12 *Annual Report of the Secretary of the Interior, 1935,* 116.
13 See *Indians at Work,* June, 1939, following page 45.
14 *Ibid.,* 1937, 202–209. See also *Indians at Work,* June, 1939, 44.

to the Indians of the Jicarilla Reservation, $22,000 to those of Walker River, and $6,000 to the group at Yerrington, Nevada.[15]

Officials encouraged the tribes of the Southwest to establish co-operative organizations of various types. Community gardens were developed in Nevada and some other states and a co-operative trading post was opened at Carson Agency.[16] The Jicarilla Apache established a tribal store, while the San Carlos Apache incorporated ten cattle associations.[17] Various other tribal enterprises suited to the resources of the reservations were planned throughout the Southwest with the collaboration of the Indian Service. These included co-operative sawmills, stores, cattle and sheep associations, community canneries, farm chapters, and individual stores.[18]

The revolving credit fund seemed to be meeting such a great need that Congress authorized an addition to it of two million dollars, making a total of twelve million dollars authorized, but only a little less than four and a half million dollars of this had actually been made available by 1945.[19] A revolving cattle pool was created in 1934 to overcome drought conditions. To relieve stricken stockmen, the federal government purchased large numbers of cattle, and as Indians in some areas had range and needed animals to consume the grass, arrangements were made with the Federal Surplus Relief Corporation and the Department of Agriculture by which high grade cattle were assigned to the Indian Service. These were loaned to Indians on contracts providing for repayment in kind, and when cattle were repaid they were loaned to Indians on reservations not originally included in the program. In 1934 the pool was begun with 40,000 head. By the end of 1944 over 60,000 head had been repaid and recontracted and 12,000 head had been transferred to reservations where the Indians had not been able to participate in the original program. It was estimated that this cattle pool enabled 10,000 Indians, including a large number in the Southwest, to engage in the cattle business.[20]

A great amount of income was derived from the sale of silver jewelry, rugs and blankets, baskets, and pottery. The Indian Service, eager to promote work in Indian arts and crafts, secured the creation of an Arts and Crafts Board, which was authorized by Congress August 27, 1935.[21] An appropriation of $45,000 was granted for its work,

15 *Indians at Work*, December 1, 1937, 25–26.
16 *Ibid.*, April 1, 1937, 26–33.
17 *Ibid.*, June, 1939, 44.   18 *Ibid.*
19 *Annual Report of the Secretary of the Interior, 1945*, 242.
20 *Ibid.*, 241.
21 49 *Stats.*, 891.

and it was given wide powers to establish and administer suitable trademarks, explore marketing possibilities, grade qualities, and serve as a management corporation for traders and groups of craftsmen.[22] The Board, consisting of five members, was appointed the following year and by January, 1937, was able to define its policies and initiate its first projects.[23]

In the Southwest it initiated a silver project for the Navajo, Hopi, and Pueblo, and established and made public standards of genuineness and quality for the silver work of the Indians of these tribes. A government stamp was devised to be applied only to pieces which met the required standards. Efforts were also made to teach better workmanship and to arrange to supply raw materials to craftsmen. In addition a Navajo textile project was established and certificates of genuineness and quality were issued to be attached only to such fabrics as were made of wool and woven in the traditional Navajo manner.[24] Copyrights of the marks to be attached to Indian work of standard quality were later secured.

The Indian Office made every effort to utilize the authority given by the Reorganization Act to acquire additional lands for the Indians of the Southwest. In several instances the need was great. The population of almost every tribe was increasing, but the area of some reservations, such as Uintah and Ouray, had been radically reduced. Only the Navajo lands had been greatly increased, but the pastoral economy of these people and their growing numbers had left them in a critical condition.

The act of Congress approved June 14, 1934, created a new boundary for the Navajo, authorized exchanges of lands for consolidation purposes, and appropriated money for the purchase of other lands.[25] Withdrawals of land from the public domain for the use of the Indians, special purchases, and the exchange of white-owned lands inside the reservation boundaries for others outside had, by January, 1937, increased Indian-held lands in Arizona 697,695 acres. In a similar fashion the holdings of the Indians of New Mexico had been increased 681,969 acres, a large part having been purchased for them by the Resettlement Administration. The increase in Nevada amounted, in 1937, to 177,200 acres, and some small additions had

22 *Indians at Work,* July 15, 1936.
23 The first board consisted of Commissioner Collier, W. W. Beatty, E. K. Burlew, A. V. Kidder, and Lorenzo Hubbell. It appointed as manager L. C. West of Cleveland.
24 *Annual Report of the Secretary of the Interior, 1937,* 224–25.
25 48 *Stats.,* 960.

been made to the Indian lands of California and Utah. The land holdings of all Indians in the United States had been increased by 2,-100,000 acres in the three-year period from 1934 to 1937.[26]

Other purchases were pending, but those made, or that might be made in the future, were far from solving the problem on some reservations, where overgrazing had resulted in so much erosion that great areas were left little better than barren deserts. Large parts of some reservations had been leased to white ranchmen, and on others there had been much trespassing of animals owned by white livestock men. In both cases these men, realizing the temporary and uncertain nature of their tenure, had exploited the range in shameful fashion. Large numbers of worthless ponies consumed pasturage that should have been utilized for cattle or sheep.

The most critical situation existed in the Navajo country, where the range was most inequitably distributed. It was asserted that one family monopolized 331,000 acres and another 228,000 acres. Four families were said to utilize 10 per cent of all Navajo range resources. It was estimated that the 25,000 square miles of the reservation could be made to yield an income of $317 annually for every family if the range were equally divided and restored to its former carrying capacity. To do this, however, would necessitate a great reduction in the total number of sheep on the reservation temporarily, and most of such reduction would have to be made by the large owners.[27] Eventually, but only by strong measures, this was pretty well accomplished. A laboratory was established in 1935 at Fort Wingate to try to produce sheep with wool suitable for hand weaving.[28] In addition a project was established at Mexican Springs, New Mexico, to experiment in range restoration and the rebuilding of eroded areas. Its success attracted widespread interest.[29]

In the field of education, equally extensive and far-reaching changes were wrought. Commissioner Rhoads had initiated important reforms in the boarding schools by reducing overcrowded conditions, improving the quantity and quality of food, and relaxing the rigid military discipline which had characterized these institutions. Commissioner Collier went much further than had his predecessor. He abolished a number of boarding schools, greatly reduced the enrollment in others, and placed the children in community day schools.

[26] *Indians at Work,* December 1, 1936, 17–19.

[27] *Ibid.,* June 15, 1936, 19.

[28] *Annual Report of the Secretary of the Interior, 1935,* 126. Congress appropriated $75,000 for its work.

[29] *Indians at Work,* September 15, 1936, 33–34.

Courtesy Milton Snow, Navajo Service

Hopi trading post, Second Mesa

Hopi home, Second Mesa

Ten boarding schools in the country as a whole were either abolished or transformed into day schools during 1934. Two of these were in the Southwest; the Navajo school at Tohatchi, New Mexico, and the Mescalero Apache school in the same state became day schools. The number of students in the large nonreservation boarding schools was radically reduced. Sherman Institute, which formerly had 1,000 students, had in 1934 only 650, Phoenix had its enrollment cut from 725 to 500, and Albuquerque from 850 to 650. The total enrollment in all boarding schools in 1932 was 22,000, but it was planned that there should be not over 13,000 in the school year 1934–35.[30]

This obviously meant that educational facilities must be provided for Indian children in the day schools or in white public schools. The Johnson-O'Malley Act, authorizing contracts with states to educate Indian children by aid of government funds, was passed by Congress in April, 1934. Such a contract was made with the state of California, and the day schools which had been operated for so many years for the Mission Indians were closed. The Indian Office continued to operate Sherman Institute as a nonreservation boarding school. The contract with California provided that the state would fit the school program to the special needs of the Indians of the community.[31] In Arizona and New Mexico very few Indian children attended white public schools, but a number of new Indian day schools were established. Thirty-seven new day schools had been opened on the Navajo Reservation by 1937, and the number of pupils had increased in two years from 882 to 2,147.[32] By this time a large part of the Indian children in Utah and Nevada were in public schools. In Utah approximately three-fourths of the Indian children were educated in either public or day schools, most of the remainder being enrolled in the boarding school on the Uintah and Ouray Reservation.[33]

The community day schools served Indian adults as well as children. Many were provided with shops, workrooms, kitchens, or laundries available to the community. Approximately one hundred young Indian men and women were employed in the Navajo day schools.[34] School gardens and poultry clubs were established; a traveling library and visual education service was begun in southern Arizona with books, magazines, visual education material, and music records cir-

30 *Annual Report of Commissioner of Indian Affairs, 1934*, 84–85.
31 *Ibid.*, 88.
32 *Ibid., 1937*, 228.
33 *Ibid., 1936*, 220–23.
34 *Ibid., 1935*, 133.

culated to pupils and adults alike; motion pictures were provided for many Indian communities.[35] The new educational program was designed to reach out into the Indian homes and affect old and young.

The agencies set up by the federal government to provide work for the unemployed not only aided the Indians of the Southwest very much economically but also did a great deal to promote the development of the day school program. New buildings were constructed and old ones repaired by P.W.A. or W.P.A., and the Indian Division of the Civilian Conservation Corps built roads and bridges, both sorely needed on most reservations, especially where children must be transported to schools by bus.

These depression-born federal agencies seemed peculiarly designed to promote the advancement of Indian welfare in the Southwest. Here was a great, undeveloped area, where much work of a permanent nature was vitally needed, and here were large numbers of perennially unemployed Indians whose low standard of living could be achieved by the modest wages paid. The need was urgent that they be taught to work regularly under suitable supervision. The labor which the Indians performed had an educational value greater than the amount of the wages they received. In the work of water development, such as drilling wells, building dams, constructing ponds, canals, and ditches, they learned how to use machinery. The same was true in road and bridge construction, and even the building of fences, telephone lines, and fire watchers' towers, or checking erosion and eliminating rodents and insect pests often had a real educational value. On the Fort Apache Reservation some work was done in excavating the ruins of a prehistoric town, but the greater part of the Indian C.C.C. work was of a highly practical nature. By 1936 it was asserted that the average number of Indians on the C.C.C. payroll had been 8,991 for the past three years.[36] The Indians were permitted to work in camps, with the federal government providing food and lodging just as it did in white C.C.C. encampments, or to work from their own homes. Those Indians who lived at home were paid $15.00 a month for food and lodging, and the family camp was encouraged.

The Health Division of the Indian Service, too, was able to expand its work among the Indians of the Southwest during the decade 1933–43. The appropriation given the Indian Office for health and medical work was increased from $3,486,085 in 1935 to $4,011,620 in 1936. In the latter year there were in the Indian Service as a whole

[35] *Ibid., 1936,* 168–69.
[36] *Ibid.,* 189.

160 full-time and 78 part-time physicians, 378 staff nurses, 105 field nurses, 15 nurses at large, 13 full-time dentists, and 13 part-time dentists.[37] In the same year there were 9 field nurses in the Navajo area and three to five new positions to be established. A new hospital built by P.W.A. at Zuñi was opened in 1936, and others were under construction at Western Shoshone, Fort Yuma, and Fort Duchesne, Utah, as well as the large Navajo Hospital at Fort Defiance. The last named opened June 20, 1938,[38] with 136 beds; it eventually had 150 beds. When a sanatorium of 100 beds was established at the same place, Fort Defiance became the great medical center for the Navajo jurisdiction.

The fight against trachoma and tuberculosis was pushed vigorously. In 1937 a special advisory committee for work on trachoma was appointed by the Secretary of the Interior.[39] Trachoma hospitals were established at Leupp and Toadlena. The Theodore Roosevelt Boarding School on the Fort Apache Reservation was operated as a trachoma school for five or six years beginning in 1933. In 1939 the Indian Service began the use of sulfa drugs in the treatment of the disease, with the result that the trachoma cases among all Indians dropped from 30 to 5 per cent by 1943, and it was possible to close Leupp and Toadlena hospitals.[40]

The Indian Office sought as a part of the new regime to decentralize administration, give the Indians a larger share in dealing with their own affairs and to promote greater democracy in the work of the Field Service. Among the co-operative organizations was the Navajo Arts and Crafts Guild, a tribal enterprise employing some three hundred weavers on the reservation.[41] Superintendents of each jurisdiction were directed to hold regular staff meetings to discuss local problems. The tribal courts were reorganized. Heretofore, tribal judges had been appointed by the reservation superintendent, who must also approve their decisions and might modify them if he so desired. Provision was made for the election of these judges. The accused was allowed to give bail, to receive a jury trial, and to be represented by counsel.[42] Two outstanding women were appointed superin-

---

37 *Ibid.*, 174.
38 *Indians at Work*, June 1938, 14.
39 *Ibid.*, December 1, 1937, 32.
40 *Annual Report of the Secretary of the Interior, 1943*, 281.
41 *Indians at Work*, May-June, 1945, 35.
42 *Ibid.*, February 1, 1936, 34–35. For many years the United States courts had had jurisdiction in cases involving eight major crimes. The number was later extended to ten.

tendents of jurisdictions in the Southwest. One, Miss Alida C. Bowles, was the first woman superintendent of an agency in the history of the Indian Service; she served for five years as head of the Carson Agency in Nevada. The second, Dr. Sophie D. Aberle, was appointed superintendent of the Consolidated Pueblo jurisdiction in 1935, when the northern and southern Pueblo agencies were joined. She served until April 12, 1944, when she was succeeded by Superintendent John Evans.[43]

It must not be supposed that these pronounced changes in Indian administration were always met by unqualified approval and support. Some members of Congress made a determined effort to modify or repeal the Indian Reorganization Act. The Commissioner was an aggressive fighter, however, and he was supported by the Secretary of the Interior and President Roosevelt. Collier was a firm believer in the efficacy of printer's ink and was himself a gifted and forceful writer. Early in his administration he began to issue the illustrated magazine, *Indians at Work,* described as "a news sheet for the Indians and Indian Service," although its circulation was by no means limited to these two groups. Published for a time semi-monthly, later once a month and still later—because of paper shortage—issued every two months, it continued throughout his administration to be a powerful agency for advertising the accomplishments of the Indian Service and the work and activities of the Indians themselves. Though perhaps a trifle critical of all that had gone before, and depicting in too glowing colors the activities and accomplishments of the new service, the files of this magazine furnish a wealth of information about Indian administration during this period.

Some Indians, too, showed active hostility toward the new program. Almost every tribe is divided into two or more factions, and anything favored by one of these is nearly certain to be opposed by the other. The Navajo voted against putting themselves under the terms of the Reorganization Act, and at first many members of this tribe objected to the new administration, particularly to the reduction of their sheep, a step which overgrazing had made absolutely necessary. The Taos Indians also offered, through a white attorney, violent objections to certain aspects of the work of the Indian Service. They complained that children were permitted to speak their own language in school, that they were required to work in the school garden, and that the relaxing of discipline at the Santa Fé Boarding School had resulted in immorality. They also reported that the government had

[43] *Ibid.,* May-June, 1944, 29.

not kept the machinery it furnished them in repair, and had not properly equipped the new school built by P.W.A., or supplied it with a full corps of teachers. Finally, they complained that the Indian Office had interfered in a local controversy which had developed between members of the Native American, or "Peyote Church," and the opposing faction.[44]

One piece of constructive work done by the federal government in California was the resettlement of the Indians of Owens Valley. Many of them had little or no land and derived a scanty living by labor for whites. When Los Angeles acquired the water resources of this area and dried up the larger part of it, the Indians who were under the jurisdiction of the Carson Agency in Nevada were left in a precarious condition. Through the influence of Dr. John R. Haynes, president of the Water and Power Board of Los Angeles, Superintendent Alida C. Bowles of Carson Agency, and James M. Stewart, Director of Lands, the City of Los Angeles agreed to exchange the arid land of the Indians for contiguous bodies of fertile, irrigated lands. President Roosevelt made a rehabilitation grant of funds for the resettlement.[45]

Another and much more important resettlement project for Indians of the Southwest was well under way on the Colorado River Reservation in the early part of 1947. The act establishing this reservation in 1865 stated that it was created "for the Indians of said river and its tributaries." No colonization of Indians from tributary areas was attempted, however, for three-quarters of a century because of the lack of water for irrigation. About 1940, the Indian Service made plans for building a diversion dam and irrigation system which it hoped would provide water for some 100,000 acres within the boundaries of the reservation along the east bank of the river. Since this would be far more land than the Indians on the reservation could use, it was planned that Indians from other tribes within the Colorado watershed should be colonized there.[46]

At the outbreak of the second World War, however, the War Department took over a portion of this land, south of where the inhabitants of the reservation lived, for the establishment of a large Japanese relocation center. Three communities, one for 10,000 and two for 5,000 each, were laid out and constructed by the War Department and their administration was turned over to the Indian Service.

44 *Ibid.*, September 15, 1936, 1–6.
45 *Ibid.*, March, 1939, 1–2.
46 *Annual Report of the Secretary of the Interior, 1942*, 233–34.

The superintendent of the Papago jurisdiction was made director of the project, with the superintendent of Hualapai as his associate. A number of other employees of the Indian Field Service had to be assigned to this work; for it was necessary to give education and medical services to some twenty thousand people. With the close of the war and the dispersal of the Japanese to their former homes, Indian colonization became feasible. Accordingly in February, 1945, the Council of the Colorado River Tribes adopted an ordinance opening the southern three-fourths of the reservation to colonization by Indians from within the limits of the Colorado basin. In May, 1945, the War Relocation Authority returned to the control of the Indian Service 2,000 acres of irrigated land in the southern area. Some twenty families of Hopi applied for permits to occupy forty-acre units and the greater part of them moved to these lands. It is believed that additional Hopi families, as well as a considerable number of Indians from the Navajo, Papago, and other tribes, may be resettled on these lands by 1950 or soon thereafter.[47]

The war obviously had important far-reaching effects upon the Indians of the Southwest, although only the briefest possible statement of these can be given. Since all Indians had been made citizens in 1924, they were subject to draft in the second World War. This had not been true of restricted Indians in the first world conflict, but many thousands had volunteered for service. Approximately 65,000 Indians left their homes to fight or work during the second World War. Of these, 25,000 were in the armed forces, usually in the army, while nearly one-half of the remaining 40,000 were engaged in war work.[48] It would be difficult to estimate just what percentage of these came from the Southwest, but it was large. A large number of Indians from this area, however, were deeply disappointed when they were rejected for military service because they could not read or write. In spite of the absence of so many Indians from their reservations, their production of livestock and crops was greater during the war years than ever before.[49] It was estimated that by 1944 Indians had invested $50,000,000 in war bonds and the Papago had exceeded their quota for the fourth war loan by nearly 600 per cent.[50]

[47] *Ibid., 1945*, 238. Two other War Relocation Centers, the Gila River Center and the Leupp Detention Camp were established on Indian lands, but only the one on the Colorado River Reservation was administered by the Indian Service.

[48] These figures include only men. In addition, 10,000 women and children left the reservations during the war. *Ibid., 1944*, 237, and *1945*, 233.

[49] *Ibid., 1944*, 237.

[50] *Ibid.*, 238.

The government's work among the Indians was greatly handicapped by the war. Replacements could not be had for physicians and nurses who entered the armed services or retired, and medical work had to be reduced. Bus service for school children was curtailed, because of the lack of gasoline. Most of the older boys in the boarding schools enlisted, as did many teachers. Some schools were forced to close for lack of teachers and the enrollment in others was considerably reduced.

War restrictions and scarcities, and the mounting cost of living affected the Indians, although perhaps not as much as it affected city dwellers with higher standards of living. Compensation for high prices was found in greatly increased earnings. The earnings of the Navajo, for example, which amounted to $198,200 in 1940, had risen in 1945 to $6,700,000.[51]

In December, 1944, a long-delayed measure of justice was accorded the Indians of California when the United States Court of Claims awarded them $5,024,842.34 in partial satisfaction of the Senate's failure to ratify eighteen treaties made with them in 1852. By these treaties, as stated early in this study, the Indians had ceded some 75,000,000 acres, for which they were promised reservations aggregating 8,619,000 acres and certain benefits and services by the government of the United States. They received only 624,000 acres, much of which was poor and unproductive land. The sum awarded them represented the difference between the estimated value of the lands, goods, and services promised them by these treaties and the value of the land actually received, plus the cost of the services since rendered them by the federal government. The amount was placed in the Department of the Treasury to the credit of the Indians, to draw interest at the rate of four per cent annually, and the appropriations from it for the benefit of the Indians will be authorized by Congress.[52] Thus, more than ninety years after the completion of the task assigned to McKee, Barbour, and Wozencraft, the work of these three commissioners at last brought tangible results for the great great grandchildren of those Indians with whom they had made treaties. Truly, the mills of democratic government, as well as those of the gods, grind slowly!

Even the bitterest opponents of Commissioner Collier's theories must agree that the Indian Service made great strides in the Southwest from 1933 to 1945. The large additions to Indian land holdings,

---

51 Superintendent J. M. Stewart to E. E. Dale, October 11, 1946.
52 *Annual Report of the Secretary of the Interior, 1945*, 243–44.

the checking of erosion, the new roads, trails, bridges, irrigation works, homes, hospitals, and schools built are tangible accomplishments which speak for themselves. Other important accomplishments are the greatly increased herds of Indian cattle on many reservations, the improved quality of livestock, the larger areas of cultivated lands, and the greater value of crops produced. The improved medical service, the great reduction in trachoma, the formation of the Arts and Crafts Board and its work, the development of close co-operation with such agencies as the Grazing Service, Public Health Service, Department of Agriculture, and others are all noteworthy achievements.

Important as were the accomplishments of the New Regime, there still remained in 1947 many ancient problems whose complete solution lies far in the future. They are human problems to be found to a greater or less degree among the peoples of every race and country in the world. The standard of living for many thousand Indians of the Southwest was still distressingly low. The health situation on numerous reservations left much to be desired. Tuberculosis, the scourge of the Indian race, was far too prevalent. Among some tribes the liquor problem had grown worse rather than better, and the use of peyote, marijuana, and narcotics of various types was found in some areas. More than three-fourths of the Navajo could not read or write or speak English with any degree of fluency, and there were undoubtedly fewer Indian children in school than at the time of the outbreak of the war. Such problems cannot be immediately solved by new methods of administration or new viewpoints. Their solution demands earnest and patient effort extended over a long period of years. Time and yet more time will be required to aid the Indians of this region to advance to a point where they can be merged on equal terms with the whites.

XV

Southwestern Indians and the Government in 1947

In March, 1945, Commissioner Collier resigned and was succeeded by William A. Brophy. The new commissioner had been closely associated with the Indian Service for ten years and had married Dr. Sophie Aberle, formerly superintendent of the United Pueblos jurisdiction. It was expected that he would continue the policies inaugurated by his predecessor.

A reorganization of the Field Service was made in 1946. The country was divided into five districts, each to be administered by an executive staff composed of a district director, a district counsel, and a small group of supervisors. The director was made responsible for the execution and control of all activities in his district and the supervisors provided technical and professional assistance to the field jurisdictions. It was the duty of the director to carry out the plans and policies established by the office of the commissioner, and the district office might also conduct programs beyond the capacity of any single jurisdiction.

The Secretary of the Interior, in September, 1946, delegated additional authority to the Commissioner of Indian Affairs, who was authorized to delegate powers to the assistant commissioners, district directors, or agency superintendents. Brophy did delegate many of his powers, resulting in a greater flexibility of the Field Service. Much more initiative and responsibility was granted to officials in direct contact with the Indians, something which had been earnestly recommended by the Meriam Report in 1928.

Because of crowded conditions in Washington, most of the work of the Indian Bureau was transferred to Chicago during World War II, where the headquarters organization, commonly called the Office of Commissioner was set up, leaving in Washington only a liaison office to maintain the necessary relations with Congress and the other departments and agencies of the federal government. The headquarters organization was made up of the commissioner, who divided his time between Chicago and Washington, an assistant commissioner in each of these cities, two staff offices, and five technical branches.

Soon after the close of the war the Chicago division of the Indian Office was returned to Washington, but the administrative organization remained essentially the same. The only unit of the Indian Office remaining in Chicago is the Chicago Property and Supply Office, successor to the old Chicago warehouse. The staff offices are the Office of the Chief Counsel, under the general supervision of the solicitor of the Department and the Office of Information. The technical branches, each controlling and directing the work of the Indian Office in its own field, are administration, education, engineering, health, and resources. These together with the Indian Arts and Crafts Board make up the Headquarters Staff. In the field, district directors had general supervision of the jurisdictions within their respective districts. These jurisdictions are of four types: the agencies, nonreservation boarding schools, the detached hospitals and sanitaria, and the detached irrigation projects.

This reorganization of the Field Service was a long step in the right direction. It broke down the old inflexible system under which officials of the Field Service had been forced to operate, and gave far greater responsibility to the men who were familiar with local conditions and with the Indians and their problems. Each director was an outstanding man who had already worked for many years among the Indians. With this change the outlook for the future of the Indian Service seemed very bright.[1]

The Indians of the Southwest were placed in two districts. Those of California and Nevada were in District Three, which also included the states of Oregon, Washington, and Idaho, and maintained its office at Portland, Oregon. Arizona, New Mexico, Utah and Colorado comprised District Four, with its office at Phoenix, Arizona.[2] The responsibility of the director of District Four was great since he had general supervision of some thirteen important jurisdictions with a total population of nearly a hundred thousand Indians, in addition to the nonreservation schools and detached sanataria of his district. The district system set up by the Indian Office seemed promising but

---

[1] Appeals from a decision of any field official to whom authority has been delegated might be taken to the commissioner, and from him to the secretary of the interior.

[2] Department of the Interior, *Information Service Release,* June 17, 1946.

was largely abolished in 1948 by a failure on the part of Congress to appropriate sufficient funds for its continuance. Of the five field offices or regional offices (headquarters) the offices at Minneapolis, Phoenix, and Oklahoma City were done away with. Only two such offices remain, one at Portland, Oregon, and one at Billings, Montana. A few field employees remain at the locations where the offices were abolished, but the "headquarters" angle has vanished.

While it is impossible to provide in a single chapter any detailed description of existing conditions at every Southwestern jurisdiction, it seems well to give at least a brief sketch of each agency in 1947, and of its more important problems. No attempt will be made to discuss each and every small reservation, colony, or settlement of Indians but only to present in broad general terms the conditions prevailing in the more important ones. The operations of the Indian Service, like everything in the world today, are subject to change. Some schools and hospitals may be closed, new ones established, and minor reservations or Indian groups be transferred from the jurisdiction of one agency to that of another. Such adjustments are not important, however, and it seems probable that the Indian situation in the Southwest existing in 1947 will remain essentially the same for years.

With the exception of Sherman Institute near Riverside, the only jurisdiction in Southern California in 1947 was the Mission Agency with headquarters at Riverside. It included thirty-two reservations with a combined area of 263,636 acres including 210 acres of government-owned land set aside chiefly for agency and school sites. Of this 14,952 acres were held in trust allotments while the remainder was tribally owned. The reservations vary in size from Morongo and Palm Springs, with 31,724 and 31,128 acres respectively, to the little Santa Ynez Reservation of only 99 acres or Twenty-Nine Palms of 161 acres.[3] The number of Indians enrolled on the reservations is 3,018. There are no government schools for the Mission Indians, but by contract with the State of California the children attend some forty-three public schools.[4]

The agency maintains a hospital of thirty-four beds and three full-time physicians and five contract physicians. There is also one full-time field nurse and three nurses employed part time. Relief in the form of pensions for old or blind people and widows with de-

[3] *Statistical Supplement to the Annual Report of the Commissioner of Indian Affairs, 1944,* 22.
[4] Statement of Superintendent John W. Dady, December 26, 1946. The average school attendance in 1945–46 was 699.

pendent children is given by the federal government to slightly over two hundred persons.

The Mission Indians derive a livelihood largely from agriculture, stock raising, and ranch labor. Over 10 per cent of them served in the armed forces during the recent war, while some 15 per cent left the reservations to work in defense plants, and an additional 5 per cent were employed permanently on the larger ranches. There has been very little unemployment since 1939. Prior to the war nearly a million dollars was spent by the federal government under E.C.W. and C.C.C. for building roads and fences, bridges, cattle guards and other improvements on the reservations in addition to constructing about fifty-seven storage reservoirs. Also during the period from 1933 to 1940 approximately one hundred and twenty-five new homes were erected for these Indians under the gratuity plan of Indian Rehabilitation and Resettlement. A great number of these were constructed by W.P.A., the Indian furnishing 35 per cent of the cost, either in labor or money, 65 per cent being provided by the government.[5]

Nearly all of these Indians can read and write English and the most of them also speak Spanish. Many of the able-bodied·men are skilled workmen, and drew high wages in the defense plants during the last war. A large number are still poorly housed and there are the usual problems of liquor, disease, and immorality. The more than five million dollars awarded to the Indians of California by the Court of Claims should go far toward elevating these people, and the outlook is far more promising than ever before.

Sherman Institute, notwithstanding the fact that the enrollment was so greatly reduced under the new regime in Indian education, remains a very important institution, exercising a wide influence on Indian education in California and adjoining states. Many tribes are represented in its student body, including Papago, Pima, Apache, Hopi, Pueblo, and a large number of Navajo. The school gives work through the twelfth grade but specializes in vocational and industrial training. It has extensive orchards, gardens, and fields, excellent shop equipment, and many beautiful buildings of the Spanish type of architecture. Many of the older boys entered the armed services during the war, but by 1946 a large number of these were back in school, as were other young men and women who had been working in war plants.

In 1947 there were eleven jurisdictions in Arizona: eight agen-

[5] *Ibid.*

cies, two detached sanitaria, and one nonreservation boarding school. These were Colorado River, Truxton Canyon, Fort Apache, Hopi, Navajo, Papago, Pima, and San Carlos agencies, Phoenix Sanitarium, San Xavier Sanitarium, and Phoenix School.

The Colorado River Agency at Parker, Arizona, had jurisdiction in 1947 over five reservations and some six or seven tribes. The Fort Mohave Reservation under this jurisdiction was in Mohave County, Arizona, San Bernardino County, California, and Clark County, Nevada. It had an area of some twenty-seven thousand acres but very few Indians resided on it in 1947. Most of them had been living for many years in and around Needles, California, and with the completion of the Parker Dam, which resulted in the flooding of nearly all of the agricultural lands of the reservation, most of the remainder had removed to Needles or some other point off the reservation. The census lists a population of 340 belonging to the reservation but only a very small number remain there, living by pasturing cattle on the high, arid lands unfit for cultivation. The Fort Mohave Boarding School, formerly an important institution, was closed in 1932.[6]

The Colorado River Reservation in Yuma County, Arizona, has an area of 242,709 acres and the population was given in 1946 as 873, in addition to about one hundred Hopi who came soon after the close of the war under the resettlement program referred to in the preceding chapter. There still remains the task of clearing and leveling the remainder of the 100,000 acres, which is to be irrigated by a diversion dam, and making it ready for irrigation, a work of several years. It is contemplated that Indians from various reservations will be brought in and colonized until eventually some two thousand families of Hopi, Navajo, Papago, and other tribes are so settled. Probably some of the Indians from Needles will be located there. This resettlement program is one of the major activities of the Indian Service in the Southwest.[7]

The Colorado River Agency also exercises jurisdiction over the Yuma tribe of slightly over nine hundred Indians. Their reservation consists of 7,153 acres partly in Imperial County, California, and partly in Yuma County, Arizona. The lands have all been allotted, but approximately one-third of the Indians live off the reservation where they eke out a poor living by labor for the whites. Those on the reservation live partly by agriculture, but the Yuma are none too eager to farm, and the lands which they do not cultivate are leased to

6 Statement of Superintendent C. H. Gensler, October 29, 1946.
7 *Ibid.*

whites, since it is necessary to pay operation and maintenance costs for water regardless of whether or not the land is farmed. Leases are also made on the Colorado River Reservation but to a less extent since the Indians there are more inclined to agriculture than the Yuma. It will be remembered that the Yuma Reservation was at one time attached to the Mission Agency but had been a separate jurisdiction for several years before it was attached to the Colorado River Agency in 1934.[8]

Another small tribe under the supervision of the Colorado River agent is the Cocopa, which owns two small reservations with a total area of some nine hundred acres in Yuma County. They have an enrolled population of only forty-three, but there are at least two or three hundred more not enrolled, some of whom live on the reservation, although the majority reside in or around Somerton, Arizona, and work for the whites. Few of the Cocopa seem to have much interest in farming.

This agency maintains two hospitals, one of forty-two beds on the Colorado River Reservation and one of twenty-eight beds on the Yuma reserve. There is a full-time physician at each hospital, a part-time contract physician at Needles, and one social worker for the entire agency. Health conditions are fairly good, but there is some venereal disease and tuberculosis. With the exception of the Cocopa, who make little use of the hospitals, the other Indians utilize them quite regularly; probably four-fifths of their babies are born in these hospitals.[9]

In 1947, 550 children of school age were listed for this jurisdiction. The children of the Indians at Needles attend public schools, while those of the Colorado River Reservation go to the day school there or the public school at Parker. On the Yuma Reservation a public school is operated in the buildings of the old Fort Yuma Boarding School, abandoned as such soon after 1930. A California public school has been established on this reservation with an all-Indian school board. The high-school pupils attend the Yuma Union High School in Arizona under the terms of a contract made by Imperial County, California, with the Yuma, Arizona, school board. Some children from this agency attend Sherman Institute, Phoenix, and Carson Boarding School, and various public schools in California, Arizona, and Nevada.

The Truxton Canyon Agency at Valentine, Arizona, in 1944,

8 *Ibid.*
9 *Ibid.*

had jurisdiction over about twelve hundred and fifty Indians of the Hualapai, Camp Verde, Havasupai, and Yavapai reservations, but before 1947 the little Moapa River Reserve in southeastern Nevada, formerly under Carson Agency, had been transferred to the Truxton Canyon jurisdiction. Except Hualapai, of 991,510 acres, all these reservations are very small. Yavapai was listed as having seventy-one acres with a population of forty-seven in 1944, Moapa River had 1,128 acres and 169 Indians, and Havasupai, located in the Rainbow Canyon, only 519 acres on which lived a population of 243 Indians. Camp Verde was reported as having an area of 498 acres and a population of 453, but obviously a great number of these did not actually live on the reservation.[10]

There were slightly over 500 Hualapai living on their reservation of nearly a million acres. They owned nearly 6,000 head of cattle in 1944 and most of them depended upon livestock raising and a little farming, although some worked for the railroad or for white ranchers. They have for many years maintained a tribal herd of cattle but about two-thirds of the reservation has usually been leased to white cattlemen. The Havasupai depend almost exclusively upon agriculture, and the other tribes either farm or work at seasonal jobs. There was a small hospital at the agency listed in 1944 as having ten beds. The children of school age belonging to this jurisdiction number about 325. They are educated in day schools, of which there is one for Camp Verde, one for the Havasupai, and one at Peach Springs for the Hualapai. Also a number of children attend public schools. The fact that a large part of the Hualapai Reservation had been granted to the Santa Fé Railway in alternate sections caused these Indians much concern for many years, but the controversy was finally ended by extinguishing the title of the railway, thus guaranteeing all lands within the reservation boundaries to the Indians.

Another dispute as to the ownership of Peach Springs had not been settled at the beginning of 1947. Some of the Indians of this jurisdiction derive a large amount of income from the manufacture and sale of baskets, but these tribes are quite poor except for the large acreage owned by the Hualapai. The health situation is not good, since there are many cases of tuberculosis and trachoma, and the liquor problem is a serious one.[11] On the whole, the situation at Truxton Canyon was not encouraging at the beginning of 1947, primarily because of the lack of energy and ambition on the part of

[10] *Statistical Supplement, 1944.* Hualapai (or Walapai).
[11] For figures above see *ibid.*, tables on population, school census, etc.

the Indians themselves. Yet, the range resources of the Hualapai are great and it is possible that the picture may become more attractive.

The Pima Agency at Sacaton, Arizona, had jurisdiction in 1947 over four reservations with a total area of 465,169 acres and an Indian population of 7,052. The most important is the Gila River Reservation with an area of 372,022 acres and a population of 5,738. The Salt River Reservation, occupied by 1,328 members of the Pima and Maricopa tribes, embraces 46,627 acres. The Maricopa, or Ak Chin, Reservation has an area of 21,680 acres and the Fort McDowell Reservation 24,480 acres; on the former live 137 Papago, and on the latter 209 Mojave-Apache.[12]

In 1944 approximately 120,000 acres, or one-third of the lands in the entire jurisdiction, had been allotted, the remainder were tribally owned. Most of the allotments were on the Gila River and Salt River reservations. One-third of the former and half of the latter had been allotted in severalty. The lands of Maricopa and Fort McDowell were all held in tribal ownership.[13]

The economy of most of the Indians of this jurisdiction is based upon agriculture, as it has been for centuries. There is some livestock raising, but it is far less important than farming under irrigation, because of the aridity of the land and long periods of drought which makes the pasturage extremely scanty. The federal government maintains an extension service here to teach the Indians scientific methods and to substitute commercial agriculture for their age-old system of subsistence farming. It also maintains an experiment station under the joint control of the Indian Service and the Department of Agriculture which has done excellent work in the development of the long staple "Pima cotton" and other activities in plant breeding.[14] Crops grown are cotton, corn, alfalfa, and various kinds of fruits and vegetables. The chief problem is lack of water. In 1946 there were but 14,600 acre feet of water for 100,000 acres of land to be irrigated. Most of the water comes from the San Carlos Project, or the reservoir created by the construction of the Coolidge Dam on the Gila River, and is shared by Indian and white landowners. There is some prospect of constructing a dam on the San Pedro to provide additional water.[15]

Education for the more than one thousand children of school

12 Statement of Superintendent A. E. Robinson, December 2, 1946.
13 *Statistical Supplement, 1944*, 48.
14 Statement of Superintendent A. E. Robinson.
15 *Ibid.*

Navajo family and hogan

The Papago Agency, Sells, Arizona, from the air

age is provided by eight day schools, with a total of some thirty-five teachers.[16] The course of study emphasizes agriculture and rural living, although some attention is given to Indian arts and crafts. The Medical Service maintains a forty-two-bed hospital at Sacaton, and hospital care is supplemented by the work of field nurses. When complete, the medical staff will consist of four physicians, four field nurses, six hospital nurses, and one dentist, but during the war it was impossible to maintain a complete staff. Throughout most of 1946 there was but one doctor and three field nurses for the entire jurisdiction. The health of the Indians has been greatly improved during recent years, however, and the percentage of infant mortality has been greatly reduced.[17] In addition to a lack of water, the chief problems are those common human problems of liquor, inadequate housing, lack of hygiene and sanitation, and a low standard of living.

South of the Pima Agency is the great Papago jurisdiction which has supervision over some seven thousand Indians of the Papago tribe occupying three reservations. These are the Papago Reservation of 2,636,615 acres, the San Xavier Reservation of 70,080 acres, and the little Gila Bend Reserve of 10,253 acres. The only allotted lands are on San Xavier where 41,602 acres were allotted in severalty in 1891 and 1915.[18]

The Papago live primarily by cattle raising and subsistence farming. There are a few sheep on the reservations, but these Indians are not shepherds as are the Navajo. They owned in 1947, however, about twelve thousand head of cattle. Agriculture is largely "flood farming," in which a small area is flooded by building a low earthen wall about a tract of land at the base of a hill and wheat, corn, and vegetables are planted as soon as the water, thus impounded, has been absorbed by the ground. A considerable number of Papago work off the reservation, either as laborers or in domestic service. Theirs is a strange land of desert, mountains, and hills with open forests of giant cactus and thickets of thorny shrubs, but in some areas pasturage is fairly good. The people live in small communities, often in rude habitations built of cactus plastered with mud. Many of them

---

[16] George C. Wells, *Roster of Education Staff*, Dist. Four, 19–20.

[17] There are certain special activities carried on in the Southwest by officials of the federal government that deserve mention. One of these is the work of Miss Oleta Merry, a home economics teacher, who devotes full time to work among the adults of the Pima Agency. She has organized and directs the work of a large number of clubs and holds an important fiesta every year in May. George C. Wells, Supervisor of Education, Dist. Four, to E. E. Dale, December 6, 1946.

[18] Statement of Superintendent Morris Burge, December 6, 1946.

have a veneer of Spanish culture and speak Spanish, and their customs are not greatly unlike those of the Mexicans who live across the international boundary forming the south line of the Papago Reservation.

Their children are educated in eight government day schools, with a total of about a dozen teachers, and seven mission schools, six Catholic and one Presbyterian. The enrollment in the government schools was 450 in 1946–47 and 425 in the Mission schools. In addition about 135 children attend Phoenix Boarding School and approximately two hundred are in public schools of the towns in which their parents are employed, near the reservation. Educating the Papago children is perhaps the most serious problem confronting the government officials of this jurisdiction. The great size of the reservation, the widely scattered population, and the inadequacy of educational facilities in the past have combined to prevent at least one-third of the Papago children from receiving any schooling. School attendance is seriously interfered with because many Papagos leave the reservation for several months each year to pick cotton, usually taking their children with them. Transporting children to school by bus is difficult. While many miles of road were built by various government work agencies prior to the war, proper facilities for maintenance have not been available during the war years and since.

Health conditions are fairly good. There is a forty-bed hospital at Sells, the site of the agency, but less than sixty babies were born in it in 1944, most births being in the homes. A considerable number of Papago tuberculosis patients are cared for at the forty-six-bed San Xavier Sanatorium, an independent institution which had in 1944 a total of 135 patients and gave treatment to approximately a hundred more outside the institution. The Papago have never had adequate medical attention, due to their isolation. Until the opening of C.C.C., few of them had ever earned money except at cotton picking or other seasonal labor, but under its operation they were able to increase their income very much and also to build many *charcas* or reservoirs enabling them to use their pasturage.

East of the Pima Reservation is the San Carlos Agency, having jurisdiction over the San Carlos Apache Reservation of 1,650,000 acres. Except along the Gila and San Carlos rivers the entire reservation is mountainous. The census made in 1944 showed a population of 3,366 Indians of whom all but about 150 were full bloods.

The tribe has been organized with an elected tribal council

which appoints the judges of the tribal court and enforces the tribal code of laws, while Indian police are used in the maintenance of law except for one Indian Service special officer who deals mainly with liquor cases off the reservation. These Indians derive most of their living from cattle raising which in 1947 was carried on by eleven cattle associations on the reservation. There were two tribal herds, a "social security herd" of 4,450 head, and a registered breeding herd of 1800 animals. The total number of cattle owned by the San Carlos Apache at the above date was around 37,500 head and the two seasonal sales of cattle in 1946 plus the sale for store and home use yielded more than $1,250,000. This gave a substantial sum to the 727 families of the reservation, almost all of whom own cattle. Much of the reservation was formerly leased to white ranchmen but by 1947 it was all utilized by the Indians themselves.[19] Much of the cattle raising program is doubtless due to the efforts of the late James B. Kitch, who was superintendent of this agency from 1923 to 1938. In addition to the income derived from cattle, many Indians work off the reservation, especially during the cotton picking season, and there is some crop growing on the level lands along the San Carlos and Gila rivers.

The agency maintains two day schools, one at San Carlos with an average daily attendance in 1946 of 341, and the other at Bylas with a daily attendance of 131 pupils. In addition there are two Lutheran Mission Schools on the reservation, the one at Peridot having an enrollment of about 120, and one at Bylas with about sixty. Some students attend Phoenix Boarding School, and a large number are enrolled in the public schools of the towns near the reservation.

The health situation is, on the whole, discouraging. The agency maintains a forty-five-bed hospital with dispensary care for out patients, and the medical staff consisted, in 1947, of one doctor, six nurses, and one field nurse. Seventy-five per cent of the babies are born at the hospital, but there is much trachoma, venereal disease, and tuberculosis. The situation with respect to trachoma is much improved, but the medical personnel is not sufficient to carry out an aggressive health program and to bring in and give treatment to all of those persons needing it, especially the older people. School children all receive a physical examination twice a year and an annual innoculation against communicable diseases, but a large part of the adults brought to the hospital show a positive blood test for either tuberculosis or venereal disease. The problem at this agency, as at most others, involves reducing the use of liquor, raising the standard

19 Statement of Superintendent A. E. Stover, January 17, 1947.

of living, and teaching the importance of sanitation and hygiene. The San Carlos Apache have come far, however, since the days of Agent Clum.

Adjoining the San Carlos Reservation on the north is the Fort Apache Agency at White River which has jurisdiction over a single reservation of slightly over 1,600,000 acres, on which live a little more than 3,200 Apache. The reservation is very mountainous and none of the lands have been allotted. Like their neighbors to the south, the White Mountain Apache depend largely upon cattle raising and the wages earned by labor for whites. The range has a carrying capacity of perhaps 24,000 head of cattle, but it is not fully stocked. Most of the Indian families own some cattle, the number varying from a few head to more than a hundred, but cattle raising has not been developed to anything like the same extent that it has at San Carlos. Many Indians operate small subsistence farms.[20]

Education is provided by the Theodore Roosevelt Boarding School, which also receives some day pupils. It had a total enrollment of 695 in 1946. Like all Indian boarding schools, it gives much attention to vocational education, but it also provides academic training through the tenth grade. In addition there are three day schools known as the Cedar Creek, Cibecue, and White River day schools. These have a total of about twenty employees, about one-half of whom are teachers; while the boarding school has approximately twenty-eight employees, about one-third teachers.[21] Probably a few students from this reservation attend Phoenix Boarding School, though not many, and some children attend public schools in nearby towns during the periods when their parents are working off the reservation.

The agency maintained, in 1947, a fifty-bed hospital at White River with one doctor and a small staff of nurses. The hospital also dispensed medicine to Indians on the reservation. The health program seeks to encourage better home conditions and child care but like most agencies, is unable to provide all the medical services needed during the war years. Health conditions are fairly good, although there is some tuberculosis and probably some trachoma; there is comparatively little venereal disease. There is the usual liquor problem and the difficulty of educating the people to maintain proper standards of cleanliness and sanitation.

Phoenix Indian School, an independent jurisdiction, is located

[20] Statement of Superintendent R. D. Holtz, January 13, 1947.
[21] George C. Wells, *Roster of Education Staff*, Dist. Four, October, 1946, 5.

just north of Phoenix, Arizona. It had at one time approximately a thousand students, but the enrollment was greatly reduced after the inauguration of the day school program, until, in 1946, it had only about six hundred in grades from the first through the twelfth. This is the full capacity of the school and is a larger enrollment than at any time since before the war. At least twenty tribes are represented in the student body, the greater part of them coming from agencies in Arizona. The school has about one hundred buildings of all types and utilizes 186 acres of land in addition to farming 55 acres belonging to the near-by Phoenix Indian Sanitarium. This institution was formerly a part of the school but is now an independent jurisdiction. This sanatarium also administers the medical work of the Phoenix School Hospital. Phoenix School specializes in vocational training and gives much attention to Indian arts and crafts. It is a beautiful place with attractive flower gardens, orchards, and well kept fields. The number of employees in 1946–47 was fifty-eight, with about twenty teachers.[22] Phoenix Sanitarium, with 30 beds, received 1,203 patients during 1944, while Phoenix School Hospital, with 64 beds, had 1,559 patients during the same year.[23] There is one other jurisdiction wholly in Arizona. This is the Hopi, but since it lies in the midst of the great Navajo country, the two are discussed together.

Of the three agencies of New Mexico, Mescalero, Jicarilla, and United Pueblos, the last is by far the most important. United Pueblos has jurisdiction over some twenty-two reservations with a total area of 1,987,117 acres and a population listed in 1944 of 14,640 Indians. These are all Pueblo except a few hundred Navajo who occupy three comparatively small reservations known as Ramah, Canoncito, and Puertocito, the three having a total area of 155,691 acres. The Pueblo reservations vary much in size. Laguna and Zuñi each have more than 400,000 acres while San Juan, Picuris, and Pojoaque each has less than 15,000 acres. There is a correspondingly wide variation in population. Laguna had 2,712 and Zuñi 2,406 people in 1944, Pojoaque had but 26; Nambe, Picuris, Sandia, and Tesuque each had less than a hundred and fifty; and San Ildefonso had only a little more than that number.[24]

The Pueblo grow fruit, vegetables, corn, and other products for their own use, and also make pottery and silver jewelry which

22 *Ibid.*, 18. Also statement of Superintendent Charles E. Morelock, November 20, 1946.

23 *Statistical Supplement, 1944*, 18.

24 *Statistical Supplement, 1944*, 9 and 26.

yield a reasonably large income. They work as laborers or in domestic service and in recent years have earned relatively high wages. For a long time there has been a tendency for families to leave the village and erect their adobe homes adjacent to the fields which they cultivate. Each little tribe has a governor and council, which exercise governmental functions.

United Pueblos Agency has jurisdiction over the two large boarding schools, Albuquerque and Santa Fé, formerly nonreservation schools. Albuquerque formerly had an enrollment of 850 or more and Santa Fé around 550. These numbers were reduced to around 700 and 500, respectively, by 1934 and have since remained at about that figure. Both specialize in vocational work and give much attention to Indian arts and crafts. Albuquerque had a staff of sixty-eight employees in 1946–47 and Santa Fé had a total of forty-eight employees.[25] The agency also maintains twenty-six day schools, one or more for every Pueblo. These vary in size, small schools having but one teacher, while Zuñi has a total of seventeen employees.[26]

The health of the Indians under this agency is fairly good, although there is some tuberculosis and trachoma. Albuquerque has a sanitarium of one hundred beds and a hospital with sixty beds, while Santa Fé Sanitarium has seventy-six beds. In addition, there is a hospital of ten beds at Taos and one of forty-two beds at Zuñi. The agency maintains a staff of physicians, and hospital and field nurses, but the difficulty of finding sufficient personnel during the war years and immediately after has been so great that no exact figures can be given.[27]

The Pueblo are kindly, hospitable, industrious people who live much the same today as they have for a century or more. Most of them speak Spanish and still retain some Spanish culture. The people of those villages most visited by tourists have been somewhat spoiled by too much attention, but this is not true of the more remote settlements; the visitor who first calls upon the governor and explains his desire to visit the little community will usually be courteously received.

Mescalero Agency, located at Mescalero, New Mexico, has control of a reservation of approximately 460,000 acres, mostly of forest and open grazing land, of which about 4,000 acres are arable. The chief resources of the 875 Indians of the jurisdiction are therefore

---

[25] George C. Wells, *Roster of Education Staff*, 1946, 23 and 26.
[26] *Ibid.*
[27] *Statistical Supplement, 1944*, 19.

pasturage and timber. None of the land has been allotted but the farming land is assigned to individuals by the governing council of the tribe.

Education through the eighth grade is provided in four community day schools, Mescalero, Carrizo, Whitetail, and Elk-Silver. These schools have a total of seven classrooms and an enrollment of approximately 175 pupils. High school education is provided for in white public schools or in one of the nonreservation boarding schools. The agency maintains a forty-bed hospital at Mescalero, and weekly clinics are held in each of the three outlying districts. There is one full-time physician, who divides his time between the hospital and the field clinics, and one public health nurse.[28] The Mescalero Apache have had a rugged and colorful history ever since they ran away from Bosque Redondo, but conditions greatly improved between 1938 and 1948. By 1944 they had received an advance of $328,000 from the revolving credit fund, a larger amount than had been received by any other tribe in the United States at that time. The use of this in rehousing and the purchases of livestock and equipment have made an enormous change in living conditions and economic advancement. It almost seems that the Indian Service sought to use this little agency as a "proving ground," or experiment station, to show what it was possible to accomplish under the New Regime.

The Jicarilla Agency, located at Dulce near the northern border of New Mexico, exercises jurisdiction over a reservation of approximately 744,000 acres on which live about 830 Apache. The reservation is divided into two distinct parts known as the North Half and the South Half. The former is a high, mountainous area, used as a summer range, while the lower and warmer South Half is the winter range. More than 200,000 acres were allotted many years ago, but a reorganization program was under way in 1946–47 to restore inherited allotted lands to tribal ownership and to concentrate all individual holdings within a single area, whereas they have been widely scattered over the reservation.

These Indians derive most of their living from raising sheep and cattle, but they do a little farming. The timber resources were formerly large, especially in the northern part of the reservation. From 1912 to 1936 timber to the value of more than half a million dollars was sold and the proceeds put into tribal funds. There was some timber sold in 1946–47, but little future activity in timber sales is anticipated, at least for many years. The Extension Division of the agency has

28 Statement of Superintendent John O. Crow, December 23, 1946.

charge of range management and prevents overgrazing. Water development has given the northern portion of the reservation a fairly adequate water supply, and similar work is going on in the southern area.[29]

Children are educated in the boarding school located at the agency, which has an enrollment of about two hundred pupils and gives academic work through the tenth grade. Students desiring further schooling are sent to nonreservation schools. There is a hospital of twenty-eight beds at the agency, which also dispenses medicines and gives treatment to outpatients. The tribe organized under the Indian Reorganization Act and by 1944 had received an advance of $75,000 from the revolving credit fund.[30] There are three small irrigation projects but little irrigable land. The future prosperity of these Indians apparently lies in sheep and cattle raising. There is the usual liquor problem, but it is not so acute here as it is at some other agencies.

The Indian situation in Nevada at the beginning of 1947 was confusing, and any comprehensive description of it and of each of the numerous small reservations, colonies, and communities would require far more space than can be given here. Of the two jurisdictions of Nevada, by far the more important is Carson Agency, since its authority extends over not only Carson Boarding School and the old Pyramid Lake and Walker-River reservations, but also over other small reservations, colonies, and Indian communities scattered over approximately two-thirds of the state and to a small extent over Alpine, Mono, and Inyo counties, California. Altogether there were thirteen reservations and eight colonies or communities within the jurisdiction in 1947.[31] The total number of Indians under the jurisdiction was about six thousand, and they owned 926,641 acres, of which 89,785 acres had been allotted in severalty. The Indians had by 1946 established range rights over about 1,000,000 acres of public lands under the administration of the National Forest Service and Bureau of Land Management. There were, in 1947, five Indian livestock associations incorporated under the laws of Nevada and one tribal farming enterprise. Seven tribal groups had organized under

29 Statement of Acting Superintendent James H. Hyde, December 17, 1946.
30 *Ibid.*, and *Statistical Supplement, 1944*, 18 and 86.
31 Statement of Superintendent Ralph M. Gelvin, December 20, 1946. See *Statistical Supplement, 1944*, 7–8. Some of the more important reservations were Duckwater, Fallon, Yomba, Washoe, Fort McDermitt, and Fort Independence, the last named in California. A few of the colonies were Dresslerville, Las Vegas, Lovelock, Reno-Sparks, Winnemucca, and Yerrington.

the terms of the Indian Reorganization Act.[32] Most of the Indians derive a living from livestock raising, farming, and wages. They owned approximately 9,500 head of beef cattle and some sheep and poultry in 1947.

In addition to Carson Boarding School, which had an enrollment of 545 students in 1946–47, there were four day schools located at Nixon, Yomba, Duckwater, and McDermitt. Some eight hundred children attended the public schools, tuition being paid for those in Nevada, while those in California were educated under the contract drawn with that state. A general hospital of forty-four beds is located on the Walker River Reservation, while Carson School has an infirmary which cares not only for the health of students but for some outside patients.

This agency has the problems of most others in the Southwest, but they are aggravated because the population is so widely scattered. Health conditions are not good, and there is the usual difficulty of securing and retaining the necessary medical staff. There are the problems of liquor and narcotics and of gambling in some communities. Housing is often poor and the standard of living low. The allotted lands create a serious problem since with the death of the original allottee his heirs each have an undivided interest in his landed estate. With the number of heirs constantly increasing, the situation steadily grows more complicated. The officials charged with the administration of the Revolving Credit Fund have advanced considerable sums of money to almost every tribal group accepting the terms of the Indian Reorganization Act, sometimes revealing a degree of faith which the average observer will feel unjustified.

The Western Shoshone Agency at Owyhee, Nevada, has jurisdiction over ten reservations and colonies in Nevada and Utah in addition to a few Indians in Elko County. The only important reservations are Duck Valley, partly in Idaho, with an area of 312,000 acres and a population of 900; Goshute with 147,000 acres and 180 Indians; and Skull Valley which has 18,000 acres but only 48 permanent residents. The two last named are in Utah. The other colonies and reservations are very small, with populations ranging from less than fifty to about three hundred. The total area of Indian lands under this jurisdiction is 482,440 acres and the number of Indians 2,258.[33] All of the land is held in tribal ownership except 160 acres. The only government school for this agency is a day school at Goshute

[32] Superintendent Ralph M. Gelvin, *op. cit.*
[33] Statement of Superintendent E. J. Diehl, January 8, 1947.

which had an enrollment of 38 pupils in 1946–47. All other Indian children attend the white public schools in the vicinity of their homes.

The Indians on the larger reservations derive most of their income from cattle raising; they increased their herds from 3,000 in 1932 to 10,000 in 1947. In addition to caring for their livestock, they grow some crops. The average family income from livestock and farming in 1946 was about sixteen hundred dollars. This applies only to the reservation Indians, for the Indians in colonies depend almost exclusively upon wages. The trend in agriculture is toward tractor farming, and there is a definite desire for better housing and living conditions. On the whole, most of these Indians, in dress and appearance, are much like the whites of the area in which they live.[34]

The only agency in Utah in 1947 was Uintah and Ouray, at Fort Duchesne in the Uintah Basin, a huge, circular, mountain-rimmed valley in which lived, in addition to the Indians, about 12,000 whites. The chief reservation under this agency is Uintah and Ouray, but it also has usually maintained jurisdiction over the Indians of such smaller reservations as Kaibab, Shivwits, Kanosh, Koosharem, Indian Creek, and Cedar City, the land of the last named being church property. These reservations are small, however, with a total population of not much over 200 Indians.

As previously shown, the Ute of the Uintah Basin, consisting of the Uintah, White River, and Uncompahgre tribes, have had a long and troubled history in their relations with the federal government. In 1947 they numbered 1,472 people, owning 53,334 acres of trust-allotted irrigable lands upon which they had first water rights, together with 511,160 acres of tribal grazing lands.[35] The tribe is organized under the Indian Reorganization Act. They have a constitution and charter, and their affairs are conducted by a tribal business committee of six members, two elected from each of the three tribes. Most of the irrigable land is leased to whites, although in 1946 the Indians farmed about 4,000 acres. They owned at that time about 5,000 cattle and 7,000 sheep. They had organized three livestock associations, and in addition there were three more such associations on other reservations, at Kaibab, Shivwits, and Kanosh.[36] The allotments given, mostly early in the present century, were 80 acres to every head of a family and 40 acres to all others. The tribe had by

34 *Ibid.*
35 Statement of Superintendent Forrest R. Stone, January 10, 1947. At this time the population was 523 Uncompahgre, 708 Uintah, and 241 Whiterivers.
36 *Ibid.*

1944 received a loan of $100,000 from the Revolving Credit Fund and had embarked upon a project to expend $275,000 for the purchase of lands in what had been the old Uncompahgre Reservation. The tribe is also seeking to purchase the rights to the irrigable lands in order to return such lands to tribal ownership.[37]

The federal government maintains for these Indians a modern thirty-bed hospital at Fort Duchesne and a field nurse who works under a Public Health program. The children are educated in a combined boarding and day school at Whiterocks which had an enrollment of 213 children in 1946–47, and a staff of 17 employees.[38] Many Indian children are enrolled in the public schools of this area and seem to be making excellent progress. The Indians of this jurisdiction have many claims against the United States for lands which they assert have been taken from them wrongfully and without their consent. They have employed an attorney who has filed more than a dozen suits to recover lands, or compensation for large areas formerly held by these Indians in Utah or in Colorado.[39]

The only remaining jurisdictions in the Southwest are the Hopi and Navajo, the agencies for both being located in Arizona. The Hopi Reservation consists of over 600,000 acres in Arizona, lying in the midst of the great Navajo country. The Hopi claim nearly 2,000,000 more acres used by the Navajo, but they have never succeeded in ousting these Indians. The Hopi tribe numbers about four thousand, most of whom live on or near their three mesas, although there is one community known as Moencopi far to the west near Tuba City. In 1942 the Hopi derived 34 per cent of their income from livestock, 22 per cent from agriculture, and 36 per cent from wages. The remainder came from private business, labor, arts and crafts, the sale of native products, and unearned income. The average income for each of the 645 families that year was listed as $439.82, which probably did not include the value of all of the vegetables, fruit, and field products grown for consumption. It is clear, therefore, that the Hopi are very poor and must practice thrift and rigid economy in order to live at all. Unquestionably, their income from wages increased after 1942.

The government maintains for them two boarding schools and five day schools. The boarding school at Keams Canyon, the location

---

[37] *Ibid.*

[38] *Ibid.*, and George C. Wells, *op. cit.*, 22.

[39] Statement on briefs of Ernest L. Wilkinson of Washington, D. C., attorney for the Ute Indians.

of the agency, however, had only about 40 Hopi and 145 Navajo pupils in 1947. The Oraibi Boarding School had 190 students enrolled but only 25 of these were housed in the dormitory, the remainder being day pupils, some of them brought in by bus from Hotevilla and Second Mesa. It has both grade and high school students. The day schools are Polacca, Toreva, Shungopavy, Hotevilla, and Moencopi. A few Hopi children attend mission, nonreservation schools, or college. These Indians have apparently overcome their former prejudice against schooling, however, because 983 Hopi children were reported to be in school, and not over 30 of those eligible for schooling were not attending in 1946–47.

The health conditions in 1947 were not good; there was much malnutrition. The Hopi General Hospital, rated in 1944 as a 38-bed institution, served a large area containing a population of some 3,500 Hopi and 6,500 Navajo. There were three field nurse positions, but only one was filled at the beginning of 1947. The doctor and nurse hold a clinic at every village one-half day each week. These Indians willingly accept vaccination for smallpox and other communicable diseases, since many of the older ones remember the frightful epidemics of earlier years. The annual birth rate is high, averaging 40 per thousand population as compared with 25.3 among all Indians of the country and 19.5 in the United States as a whole. More than one-third of the births are in the hospital. On the other hand, the death rate is also high, averaging 25 per thousand population as compared with 13.3 among all Indians and 10.5 in the entire United States. Infant mortality is especially high, as it is 180 per thousand compared with 110 for the Indians as a whole and 44 for the United States. Even so, the population increase is 1.5 per cent, higher than that of the Indian population of the country and much more than that of the entire United States.[40]

The Hopi are peaceful and present no problems with respect to liquor, crimes, or the wasting of food or other resources. The chief problem which they have is how to sustain themselves on a reservation which has not sufficient resources to provide them a decent living. Although they accepted the Indian Reorganization Act, much to the surprise of many persons who know them well, they have great difficulty in working together, since each village has always operated independently, and the people seem to have little conception of a unified tribal government. Some villages cling closely to their old

[40] Hopi Hospital Records, 1942–43. Also Superintendent Burton A. Ladd to E. E. Dale, November 5, 1946.

religious customs of deferring to their high priests, who inherit their positions for life, while others are seeking to break away from this system.

The Hopi occupy a reservation entirely surrounded by the great territory of the Navajo, who are their traditional enemies. The Navajo is by far the largest and in many respects the most important tribe of Indians in the United States. They numbered some 56,000 people in 1947, which was more than the population of all other tribes in the Southwest combined, and their land holdings are far greater than is the total area of all other Indian reservations in the Southwest. The Navajo Reservation lies in the four states of Arizona, New Mexico, Utah, and Colorado, most of it lying in the two states first named. It has an area of slightly over 15,000,000 acres, including the 2,500,000 acre reservation given to the Hopi, of which all but about 600,000 acres is utilized by the Navajo. In addition the Navajo own, or occupy approximately 1,645,000 acres outside the limits of their reservation or a total of nearly 17,000,000 acres.[41] Approximately 42,000 Navajo live on the reservation proper and the remaining 14,000 on these other lands which are largely in New Mexico.

The Navajo are today, as they have been for generations, essentially a pastoral people. In 1945 they owned in round numbers, on and off the reservation and including those owned by the Hopi, 388,000 sheep, 59,000 goats, 9,600 cattle, and 35,000 horses. While the number of every type of livestock owned was far greater ten years earlier, the income in terms of pounds of meat, wool, and hides was much larger in 1945 than in earlier years.[42] The reservation was formerly overgrazed, and the range resources unequally distributed. The maximum allowable ownership of sheep over the reservation in 1947 was 350 head. But this limit did not apply to the Navajo living off the reservation, many of whom had far larger flocks than were allowed to graze on the reservation. The work done by the federal government in drilling or digging more than eight hundred wells, developing nearly seven hundred springs, and constructing over a thousand reservoirs has greatly increased the range resources of the Navajo.

Although depending largely upon sheep, the Navajo operated some 5,000 farms in 1945, cultivating thirty-one thousand acres. In

[41] Statement of Superintendent J. M. Stewart, October 11, 1946. By 1946 certain acreages of land outside the boundaries of the reservation were used by the Navajo: allotments, 636,520; homesteads, 4,480; leased by the tribe, 90,518; leased by individuals, 6,237; public domain used for grazing, 905,366. *Ibid.*

[42] *Ibid.*

1946 there were seventy-eight irrigation projects on the reservation, and over twenty-three thousand acres of irrigable land. Crops grown are corn, beans, squash, fruits, and melons, as well as other garden products. In 1945 the value of crops was estimated at nearly a million dollars.

Other sources of income are handcrafts, native products—especially piñon nuts—and wages. During the war years, Navajo craftsmen produced much less than normally, because so many men were away in the armed forces or working in war plants. It is estimated, however, that in 1945 silver to the value of $150,000 and rugs valued at $210,000 were produced by the Navajo and that they received $390,000 from the sale of piñon nuts. The piñon crop is subject to wide fluctuations. In some years the yield is heavy in many areas and very light in others, while there have been some years when the crop was a total failure. The amount received by the Navajo from wages increased enormously in the years following the outbreak of the war. Doubtless the future years will see considerable decline of income from this source. The total income of these Indians in 1945 was around $13,500,000, an average of about $1,200 for each of the 10,977 families. Since over 1,300 families had an income in excess of $2,000, however, a great many received far less than $1,200. In fact, one-half of them had an income of less than $1,000 and more than one-fourth less than $750. Such an income must have meant a very low scale of living, since the average Navajo family is from five to six persons.[43]

With the exception of wages, the income of most Navajo is received twice a year—when wool is sold in the spring and when lambs are sold in the autumn. Upon these occasions they pay any indebtedness which they may owe, and after the remaining funds are exhausted, they establish credit for necessities by pawning their silver jewelry at the trading posts. There were one hundred licensed trading posts on the reservation in 1947 and about ten more, on patented lands inside its boundaries, which were not licensed. In addition, a considerable number of trading posts have been established outside the reservation limits near its border.[44]

Navajo children are educated in both government boarding schools and community day schools. Many children were not in school in 1946–47, and the number out of school was probably much larger at that date than before the outbreak of the war. It was estimated that there were 20,000 Navajo children of school age in 1946,

43 *Ibid.*
44 *Ibid.*

with the government providing teaching facilities for only 5,500.[45] There were ten Navajo boarding schools operating in 1946–47, in addition to the school at Keams Canyon on the Hopi Reservation which had both Navajo and Hopi pupils. These were Chinle, Crownpoint, Fort Defiance, Shiprock, Toadlena, Tohatchi, Tuba City, Fort Wingate, Dinehotso (Kayenta), and Navajo Mountain. Two or three boarding schools were closed during the war, and eleven of the forty-four community day schools were closed prior to 1946–47, leaving only thirty-three in operation during that year. With room for 3,500 pupils, there was an average attendance of only 1,750.[46] Their closing was made necessary by lack of gasoline during the war years, the wearing out, or breaking down of busses, and the deterioration of the roads which had been built by C.C.C. but could not be maintained. Additional factors were the difficulty of securing and retaining teachers, and of keeping a proper enrollment of pupils under the disturbed conditions of war years. There is also some reason to believe that the day school program may have been pushed too rapidly in the Navajo country, and the sites of some of these schools had not been wisely chosen. In any case the operation of a day school program for a pastoral people like the Navajo is very difficult, and education remains a great problem. It is doubtful if, in 1947, one-fifth of the Navajo could read and write or speak English with much degree of fluency.[47] Some Navajo children enroll in non-reservation schools such as public and mission schools. The total number of children thus enrolled was about one thousand in 1945–46.

Health conditions among the Navajo are far below the standard to be found in the average white community, even though much use is made of available medical facilities in areas not too remote from hospitals and where transportation is available. There are some isolated localities, however, where medical service, except such as may be rendered by the medicine man, is virtually nonexistent. A program of vaccination and immunization is carried out in all schools and most Navajo people readily accept such service. The most prevalent diseases are tuberculosis, pneumonia, influenza, and the usual child diseases. Infant mortality is high. Tuberculosis and venereal disease both present a serious problem and there is much trachoma, although far less than formerly. The medicine man is still common.

The federal government maintained, in 1947, six hospitals and sanataria for the Navajo, considering the great medical center at Fort

---

45 *Annual Report of Secretary of Interior, 1946*, 357.   46 *Ibid.*
47 Superintendent James M. Stewart, *op. cit.*

Defiance as one. This had a hospital of 150 beds and a sanitarium of 100 beds. There was another sanitarium at Winslow with 50 beds, and four additional hospitals at Chinle, Tuba City, Shiprock, and Crownpoint with a total of 172 beds available for patients. The number of full-time physicians employed by the federal government for the Navajo in 1947 was thirteen, and in addition there was one part-time contract physician. Forty-three full-time registered nurses were employed and a cadet nurse program carried on at Fort Defiance where an average of forty student nurses trained for a six months' period.[48]

While the internal affairs of the Navajo are to a certain extent administered by a tribal council, consisting of members elected from the various districts, it is obvious that the federal agent, or superintendent, of this great jurisdiction has very heavy responsibilities. He must direct most of the governmental activities and seek to promote the welfare of some 56,000 people thinly spread over a vast area. On April 1, 1946, the Navajo jurisdiction had 1,205 full-time governmental employees. Of these 653 were in the schools and 237 in the Medical Service, leaving only 315 for all other administrative work. Of the total number of employees, 869 were of Indian blood, indicating the extent to which the federal government uses Indians to administer the affairs of their own people. Probably about the same ratio of Indian to white employees prevails at most other jurisdictions in the Southwest.

If the total number of employees appears large, it is necessary only to compare it with the personnel required to render similar services in the average white community of 56,000 people. This would include not only all persons on the public payroll, as school teachers, county and city officials and their clerical assistants, those engaged in maintaining roads, streets, law enforcement, public health, and poor relief, but in addition many others for whose services the individual must pay. Among the latter would be all doctors, dentists, and their office assistants, as well as all hospital attendants, and dispensers of drugs and medicines. Such a comparison will show that the Navajo jurisdiction, in common with most others in the Southwest, is really much understaffed.

Order is preserved by Indian police and a court of Indian offenses. The tribal council has by formal ordinance prohibited the introduction of peyote, but its use is still prevalent and many Indians assert that its suppression constitutes a violation of the rights of a

[48] *Ibid.*

citizen. The liquor problem has grown much more acute in recent years because of the war, the returned veterans, and the great increase of income. There is a strong and increasing demand by the Navajo for the repeal, or modification, of the laws prohibiting the sale of liquor to an Indian. They assert logically that however necessary such laws may have been in the past they are now archaic, and if liquor can be sold to a Mexican, Chinese, Italian, or Negro, there seems no reason why it should not be sold to an Indian.

A more serious problem is how the Navajo are to live in the future. Because of the rapid increase in population, the lands available for their use will soon be insufficient to sustain all their people. Increased production of crops, the reduction of the number of sheep owned by any individual, a better quality of livestock, and range restriction will help; but there are limitations beyond which these cannot go, and while additional lands may be, and should be, acquired, this too has its limitations. The only solution of their problem seems to be in a program of education, in the broadest possible sense of the term, through which young Navajo may be led to leave the reservation and live and work among the whites on equal terms with them and with an equal prospect of success. By such a process of draining away the able and well-educated younger members of the tribe, the population of the reservation may be rendered static or even made to decline. Finally, when those remaining on the reservation have been sufficiently educated to enable them to enter into competition with their white neighbors, it may be possible to abolish the boundaries and largely terminate the services now rendered by the federal government to the Navajo people. The attainment of any such goal obviously lies far in the future, and to attempt to reach it too quickly could hardly fail to prove disastrous.

While the Indians of Colorado lie outside the limits of this book, it may be well to state briefly the situation of the Southern Ute, who are located just east of the Navajo and are the only tribe in that state. They numbered 930 in 1944 and occupied lands largely in Colorado but extending into New Mexico and Utah, aggregating about 850,-000 acres. Of these less than 50,000 acres had been allotted, and the remainder were held in tribal ownership. The agency is at Ignacio, Colorado, where the Ute Vocational School, which had twenty-six employees in 1946–47 is maintained.[49] Most of the Ute children who do not attend this school are educated in public schools. The federal government maintains a 36-bed hospital for this jursidiction.

[49] George C. Wells, *op. cit.*, 4.

The student of federal relations with the Indians of the Southwest since 1848 can take little pride in the methods employed by the government or their results during the first half of that period. There were many instances of shameful neglect and inadequate protection, of inefficiency, maladministration, and broken pledges, bringing bloody warfare in which innocent and guilty alike suffered. There was unseemly bickering between the Department of War and the Department of the Interior which seriously hampered efficient administration. The army never quite forgave those who replaced its officers with agents nominated by church groups, and the churches undoubtedly failed to take full advantage of the opportunities granted them.

Even during the nineteenth century, however, there were many honest and able agents and other officials of the Indian Service in the Southwest who, in spite of bureaucratic bungling and inadequate funds, were able to accomplish a great deal. In the period from 1848 to 1900, an adequate knowledge of all of these widely scattered tribes was secured, and the hostile tribes were subdued. Reservations were set aside for their use, and the Indians on them were afforded at least some measure of protection. Schools and hospitals were established, the wants of the needy relieved, and some understanding given of the meaning of white civilization.

After the beginning of the twentieth century, conditions began to improve, but progress was slow during its first quarter. By the beginning of its second quarter, however, an awakened public conscience was insistently demanding that the federal government assume greater responsibility for the welfare of its Indian wards. Greatly increased appropriations made possible many improvements in the educational and medical services, and higher salaries brought to the Field Service a larger number of competent officials. Appropriations have always been inadequate, however, and looking backward, it seems plain that it would have been cheaper in the long run if Congress, more than half a century ago, had provided sufficient funds to give to the Indians school and medical facilities comparable to the best to be found in progressive white communities.

During the second quarter of the present century, a comprehensive study of the entire Indian problem was made, a definite program evolved, and scientific methods devised for carrying it to completion. Unfortunately, normal conditions have been so complicated by the years of depression and war as to obscure the picture and make it difficult to analyze recent achievements. It is in no sense passing judgment on the New Regime, however, to state that some phases of it have undoubtedly accomplished a great deal but that only the future can reveal how far others may prove successful.

Numerous critics have bitterly assailed the policies and procedures of the Indian Service in the Southwest and elsewhere. Granting that there is ample reason for criticism in some instances, it nevertheless seems doubtful that these persons have fully considered the magnitude of the problem confronting the federal government when it assumed responsibility for the Indians of this region in 1848. It was no small task to seek out the numerous small tribes scattered over an unknown region larger than all of western Europe, to conquer the hostile, protect the peaceful, and grant them lands. Yet this was but the beginning. In addition, it had to create schools to educate the youth, establish hospitals to heal the sick, to feed the hungry, clothe the naked, and teach the Indian how to sustain himself in the midst of a white civilization. All this and more the federal government has done for the Indians of the Southwest. That some of it has been badly done is not strange, considering the obstacles to be overcome, and if the task is still unfinished, it is due to the fact that the time required to civilize and educate a whole people must be measured in generations rather than in years. No reasonable person could have expected in 1848 that it would be completed in a century.

For the achievements of the Indian Service in the Southwest, most of the credit must be given to the agents and other officials in the field. Granting that many of these in the past were incompetent and a few corrupt, the great majority were neither one nor the other. Throughout the entire period, most of them have been capable, conscientious men and women who turned their backs upon the comforts and conveniences of civilization and repaired to some remote post in the deserts and mountains of the Southwest to give their best to the service of the people committed to their care. Here they remained, often for years, enduring without complaint the inconveniences and hardships imposed by their environment, the low salaries, and the poor living quarters, asking little except the opportunity to serve. Undoubtedly the services of the able and efficient Indian agent and his helpers have played a far larger part in the conquest and development of the Southwest than is commonly realized, and they deserve much more recognition than they have ever received.

The danger now is that the American people may grow impatient and demand that the federal government discontinue its services to the Indians, refusing to accept further responsibility for their welfare. While this seems most improbable, it has been seriously proposed by many persons, including some members of Congress. Such action, if taken at any time in the immediate future, could hardly fail to prove tragic both for the Indians and for the entire people of those states with a large Indian population. It is difficult to escape the conclusion that any person who favors such action must either be motivated by the hope of personal gain or else have ignored the inevitable consequences. A civilized people must assume responsibility for its own incompetent, sick, poor, and helpless. If the responsibility for those Indians who fall within these classes is surrendered by the federal government, it must fall upon the state and local governments, which could not possibly give to the Indians the same services now rendered by the federal government.

The solution of the problem of the Indian of the Southwest lies in a program of education that will fit him to become a part of the white civilization which envelopes him, still retaining all that is best of his own culture. That this is possible is evidenced by what has happened in the state of Oklahoma, where more than three-fourths of the population of some 120,000 Indians is now completely merged with that of the whites. Here people of Indian blood hold high state and local offices, and join with their white neighbors on equal terms in the social and economic life of the community in which they live. Their young men and women attend the colleges and universities, where they become members of the fraternities and sororities and are frequently leaders in campus life. In Oklahoma persons of Indian blood are regarded not as members of another race but of another nation and are accepted on the same basis as are those whose ancestors were Scandinavian, German, Scotch, Irish, or French.

Such a situation can eventually be brought about in the Southwest, but it will require a comprehensive program of education carried on patiently and persistently for a long period of years. Moreover, it will be necessary to do something for the education of the whites as well. There is still racial prejudice and intolerance on the part of many people, and the Indian is sometimes regarded as a "museum piece" rather than as a man or woman with the same characteristics and capabilities as other persons.

Bibliography

The volume of material on this subject is so great that it is impracticable if not impossible to list everything which has been consulted. The following includes only those manuscripts, documents, books, pamphlets, and articles that have been found most useful.

I. MANUSCRIPTS

Andrews, Ferdinand. "The Indians of New Mexico and Arizona." Two volumes written about 1867 or 1868. In Manuscript Collections of the Henry E. Huntington Library.

Dale, E. E. Field Notes and Diary, 1926–1927. About 150 pages of field notes made while visiting Southwestern reservations as a member of the Indian Survey Staff of the Institute for Government Research. The diary covers the months from January to April, 1927. Tribes visited include the Apache, Ute, Papago, Pima, Mission, Walapai, Pueblo, Hopi, and Navajo.

Diary Kept During Kit Carson's Expedition Against the Navajo, 1863, August 4–24. Author does not give his name but was in command of Co. B, New Mexico Volunteers. Huntington Library.

Jackson, Helen Hunt. Letters. In Fields Collection, Huntington Library.

Kern, Richard H. Diary of a Trip with the Sitgreaves Expedition of 1851. Huntington Library.

Letters of Indian Children. About one hundred letters written in 1927 to E. E. Dale by Indian children in various boarding schools. They describe home life and conditions. Tribes include Apache, Pima, Papago, Ute, Pueblo, Hopi, and Navajo. In Phillips Collection, University of Oklahoma.

Ritch, William G. List of Superintendents of Indian Reservations About 1871. Also List of Horses and Other Property Owned by Indians of New Mexico. Huntington Library.

Rust, Horatio N. Papers, Letters, and Scrapbooks. A large collection but comparatively little on Indians. Huntington Library.

Schuyler Letters and Papers, 1871–90. These consist of fifty-six folders and two envelopes. They include some twenty-nine letters of General George Crook written to Lieutenant Walter S. Schuyler. Huntington Library.

Wilson, B. Papers and Letters. Ten folders giving correspondence between E. F. Beale and B. Wilson. Huntington Library.

II. FEDERAL AND STATE DOCUMENTS AND PUBLICATIONS

Annual Reports of the Board of Indian Commissioners, 1869–1932.

Annual Reports of the Commissioner of Indian Affairs, 1848–1946.

Annual Reports of the Secretary of War. Those from 1870 to 1885 especially useful.

Board of Indian Commissioners. *The Indian Bureau from 1824 to 1924*. Washington, 1925.

California, Legislature, Senate, Special Committee on Indian Affairs. *Majority and Minority Reports*. English report lacks minority report. Minority report (separate) in Spanish, only. Sacramento, 1852. Two pamphlets. Minority report by Jonathan J. Warner.

California, Legislature, Senate, Special Committee. *Ynforme de la Minoria del Comite Especial, 1852*.

Contagious and Infectious Diseases Among the Indians, Report to U. S. Senate by Public Health Service, 62 Cong., 3 sess. Washington, 1913.

Department of the Interior. *Constitution and By-Laws of the Ute Indian Tribe of the Uintah and Ouray Reservation, Utah*. Washington, 1937.

Department of the Interior. *Corporate Charter of the Ute Indian Tribe of the Uintah and Ouray Reservation*. Washington, 1938.

Department of the Interior. *Information Service Release*, June 17, 1946.

Donaldson, Thomas. *Moqui Pueblo Indians of Arizona and Pueblo Indians of New Mexico*. (Extra Census Bulletin, 11th Census.) Washington, 1893.

Eighteenth Annual Report of the Bureau of American Ethnology, Part II. Washington, 1899.

Executive Orders Relating to Indian Reservations from May 14, 1855, to July 1, 1912.

Fletcher, Alice C. *Indian Education and Civilization.* Washington, 1888.

Ives, Joseph C. *Report Upon the Colorado River of the West.* 36 Cong., 1 sess., *Sen. Exec. Doc.* Washington, 1871.

Kappler, Charles J. *Indian Affairs, Laws, and Treaties.* 3 vols. Washington, 1904.

Powers, Stephen. *Tribes of California.* Vol. III of Contributions to North American Ethnology. Washington, 1877.

Reel, Estelle. *Course of Study for the Indian Schools of the United States.* Washington, 1901.

Statistical Supplement to Annual Report of the Commissioner of Indian Affairs, 1944.

Survey of Conditions of the Indians of the United States, Hearings Before a SubCommittee of the Committee on Indian Affairs. 27 vols. Washington, 1927–32.

Tuberculosis Among the North American Indians. Senate Committee Print, 67 Cong., 4 sess. Washington, 1923.

U. S. Congress. *Report of the Joint Special Committee on the Condition of the Indian Tribes.* Washington, 1867.

U. S. 31 Cong., 1 sess., *House Exec. Doc. 17.* Vol. V.

U. S. 37 Cong., 2 sess., *House Exec. Doc. 29.* Accounts of Brigham Young as superintendent of Indian affairs in Utah, 1862.

U. S. 40 Cong., 2 sess., *House Exec. Doc. 97.* Report of Peace Commissioners.

U. S. 41 Cong., 2 sess., *House Exec. Doc. 240.*

U. S. 43 Cong., 1 sess., *House Exec. Doc. 91.*

U. S. 45 Cong., 3 sess., *House Report 93,* 1879.

U. S. 32 Cong., 1 sess., *Senate Exec. Doc. 61.*

U. S. 33 Cong., 1 sess., *Senate Exec. Doc. 34.* 1854.

U. S. 33 Cong., special sess., *Senate Exec. Doc. 4.* A comprehensive account of early Indian affairs in California.

U. S. 36 Cong., 1 sess., *Senate Exec. Doc. 46.*

U. S. 48 Cong., 1 sess., *Senate Exec. Doc. 54,* Vol. IV.

U. S. 52 Cong., 1 sess., *Senate Exec. Doc. 31.* Record of Indian Students returned from Hampton Institute.

U. S. 54 Cong., 1 sess., *Senate Exec. Doc. 272.*

U. S. 39 Cong., 2 sess., *Senate Report No. 56,* 1862.

U. S. Statutes at Large.

Wells, George C. *Roster of Education Staff, District 4.* Phoenix, Arizona, 1946.

III. REPORTS OF SOCIETIES AND ASSOCIATIONS

Indian Rights Association. *Annual Reports of the Board of Directors of the Indian Rights Association,* 1884–1933. Philadelphia, 1884–1933.

————. *The Case of the Mission Indians.* Philadelphia, 1886.

————. *Miscellaneous Publications.* A collection of pamphlets relating to Indians. (Frank Phillips Collection, University of Oklahoma).

Ladies Union Mission School Association. *Among the Pimas.* Albany, New York, 1893.

Meserve, Charles F. *A Tour of Observation Among Indians and Indian Schools in Arizona, New Mexico, Oklahoma, and Kansas.* Philadelphia, 1894.

Proceedings of the Lake Mohonk Conference.

IV. CASES CITED

Botiller v. *Dominguez* (1889), 130 U. S., 238.

Byrne v. *Alas* (1888), 17 Calif., 628; 16 Pacific, 523.

Ex Parte Crow Dog (1883), 109 U. S., 556.

Quick Bear v. *Leupp* (1908), 210 U. S., 8182.

Worcester v. *Georgia* (1832), 6 Peters, 557.

V. BOOKS AND PAMPHLETS

Abel, Annie H. (ed.). *The Official Correspondence of James S. Calhoun.* Washington, 1915.

Adams, Evelyn C. *American Indian Education.* New York, 1946.

Ames, John G. *Report on the Mission Indians of California.* (Published as 43 Cong., 1 sess., *House Exec. Doc. 91.*) Washington, 1874.

Arizona Committee on Apache Indians. *Memorials and Affidavits as to Outrages.* n. p., 1871.

Armstrong, S. C. *Report of a Trip Made in Behalf of the Indian Rights Association to some Indian Reservations of the Southwest.* Philadelphia, 1884.

Austin, Mary. *A Land of Journeys' Ending.* New York, 1924.

Bancroft, Hubert H. *Works* (39 vols.). San Francisco, 1890.

Barrows, William. *The Indian's Side of the Indian Question.* Boston, 1887.

Bolton, H. E. (ed.). *Historical Memoirs of Pimeria Alta.* 2 vols. Cleveland, 1919.

————. *Los Misiones de Sonora y Arizona.* Mexico, 1922.

Bourke, John G. *On the Border with Crook*, New York, 1892.

———. *The Snake Dance of the Moquis of Arizona*. London, 1884.

Browne, J. Ross. *Adventures in the Apache Country: A Tour Through Arizona and Sonora*. New York, 1869.

Bryant, Edwin. *What I Saw in California: Journal of a Tour in 1846–47*. New York, 1848.

Carter, Charles F. *The Missions of Nueva, California*. San Francisco, 1900.

Catholic Grievances in Relation to the Administration of Indian Affairs. Richmond, Va., 1882.

Chipman, Norton P. *Investigation into Indian Affairs*. Washington, 1871.

Cleland, Robert G. *A History of California*. New York, 1922.

———. *The Cattle on a Thousand Hills*. San Marino, 1941.

Clum, Woodworth. *Apache Agent: The Story of John P. Clum*. Boston, 1936.

Connelley, William E. *Doniphan's Expedition*. Topeka, 1907.

Coolidge, Dane and Mary R. *The Navajo Indians*. Boston, 1930.

Corlett, William Thomas. *The Medicine Man of the American Indian and His Cultural Background*. Springfield, Ill., 1935.

Crane, Leo. *Indians of the Enchanted Desert*. Boston, 1926.

———. *Desert Drums*. Boston, 1928.

Cremony, John C. *Life Among the Apaches*. San Francisco, 1868.

Crook, General George. *His Autobiography*. Edited by Martin F. Schmitt. Norman, 1946.

Cruse, Thomas, *Apache Days and After*. Caldwell, Idaho, 1941.

Cushing, Frank H. *My Adventures in Zuñi*. Santa Fé, 1941.

Davis, Britton. *The Truth About Geronimo*. New Haven, 1929.

Davis, W. W. H. *El Gringo, or New Mexico and Her People*. Davisville, Pa., 1856. (Reprinted at Santa Fé, 1938.)

Dictionary of American Biography. 20 vols. plus Supplements. New York, 1943.

Dunn, Jacob P. *Massacres of the Mountains*. New York, 1886.

Eastman, Elaine G. *Pratt, The Red Man's Moses*. Norman, 1935.

Eldredge, Zoeth S. *History of California*. New York, 1915.

Farnham, J. T. *Life, Adventures, and Travels in California*. New York, 1857.

Fergusson, Erna. *Dancing Gods*. New York, 1931.

Frazer, Robert. *Report on the Apaches of White Mountain Reservation*. Philadelphia, 1884.

Haines, Helen. *History of New Mexico*. New York, 1891.

Hamilton, Patrick. *The Resources of Arizona*. San Francisco, 1883.

Harmon, George Dewey. *Sixty Years of Indian Affairs, Political, Economic, and Diplomatic, 1789–1850*. Chapel Hill, 1941.

Harrison, Jonathan B. *Latest Studies on Indian Reservations*. Philadelphia, 1887.

Hebard, Grace R. *Washakie*. Cleveland, 1930.

Hill, Joseph J. *History of Warner's Ranch*. Los Angeles, 1927.

Hittell, Theodore H. *History of California*. 4 vols. San Francisco, 1885–97.

Hodge, Frederick Webb (ed.). *Handbook of American Indians North of Mexico*. 2 vols., Washington, 1907 and 1910. (Published as *Bulletin 30* of the Bureau of American Ethnology.)

Hoopes, Alban W. *Indian Affairs and Their Administration with Special Reference to the Far West, 1849–1860*. Philadelphia, 1932.

Hopkins, Sarah W. *Life Among the Piutes*. Boston, 1883.

Hough, Walter. *The Hopi Indians*. Cedar Rapids, 1915.

Howard, Oliver O. *Account of General Howard's Mission to the Apache and Navajo*. Washington, 1872.

———. *My Life and Experiences Among Hostile Indians*. Hartford, 1907.

Hrdlicka, Ales. *Physiological and Medical Observations Among the Indians of Southwestern United States and Northern Mexico*. (Published as *Bulletin 34* of the Bureau of American Ethnology.)

Hunter, Milton R. *Brigham Young the Colonizer*. Salt Lake City, 1940.

Ickes, Anna Wilmarth. *Mesa Land*. Boston, 1933.

Jackson, Helen H., and Abbot Kinney. *Report on the Mission Indians of California, 1883*. Boston, 1887.

James, George W. *In and Out of the Old Missions of California*. Boston, 1905.

———. *Indian Basketry*. New York, 1901.

———. *Indian Blankets and Their Makers*. Chicago, 1914.

———. *The Indians of the Painted Desert Region*. Boston, 1904.

Kane, Francis F., and Riter, Frank M. *A Further Report to the Indian Rights Association on the Proposed Removal of the Southern Utes*. Philadelphia, 1892.

Kelsey, C. E. *Report of Special Agent to the California Indians*. Carlisle, 1906.

Knight, Richard P. *An Analytical Inquiry*. London, 1808.

Kroeber, Alfred L. *Handbook of the Indians of California*. (Published as *Bulletin 78* of the Bureau of American Ethnology. Washington, 1925.)

Leupp, Francis E. *In Red Man's Land*. New York, 1914.

———. *The Indian and His Problem*. New York, 1910.

———. *The Latest Phase of the Southern Ute Question*. Philadelphia, 1895.

———. *Notes of a Summer Tour Among the Indians of the Southwest*. Philadelphia, 1897.

Lindquist, G. E. E. *The Red Man in the United States*. New York, 1923.

Lipps, Oscar H. *The Case of the California Indians*. Chemawa, Oregon, 1933.

———. *A Little History of the Navajo*. Cedar Rapids, 1909.

Lockwood, Frank C. *The Apache Indians*. New York, 1938.

———. *Pioneer Days in Arizona*. New York, 1932.

Long, Haniel. *Piñon Country*. New York, 1941.

Lummis, Charles F. *Mesa, Canyon and Pueblo*. New York, 1925.

Malin, James C. *Indian Policy and Westward Expansion*. Lawrence, Kansas, 1921.

Manypenny, George W. *Our Indian Wards*. Cincinnati, 1880.

Mazzanovich, Anton. *Trailing Geronimo*. Edited by E. A. Brininstool. Los Angeles, 1926.

Meriam, Lewis, and Others. *The Problem of Indian Administration*. Baltimore, 1928.

Miles, Nelson A. *Personal Recollections of General Nelson A. Miles*. Chicago, 1897.

Miller, Joseph. *Arizona Indians, The People of the Sun*. New York, 1941.

Ogle, Ralph H. *Federal Control of the Western Apaches, 1848–86*. New Mexico Historical Society *Publications*, Vol. IX. Albuquerque, 1940.

Otis, Elwell S. *The Indian Question*. New York, 1878.

Painter, Cornelius C. *A Visit to the Mission Indians*. Philadelphia, 1886.

———. *Condition of Indian Affairs in Indian Territory and California*. Philadelphia, 1888.

———. *The Present Condition of the Mission Indians of California*. Philadelphia, 1887.

Peters, DeWitt C. *Kit Carson's Life and Adventures*. Hartford, 1874.

Petrullo, Vincenzo. *The Diabolic Root: A Study of Peyotism.* Philadelphia, 1934.

Poston, Charles D. *Apache Land.* San Francisco, 1878.

Priest, Loring B. *Uncle Sam's Stepchildren: The Reformation of the United States Indian Policy, 1865–1887.* New Brunswick, 1942.

Reichard, Gladys A. *Navajo Medicine Man.* Sand paintings and legends of Miguelito. New York, 1939.

———. *Navajo Shepherd and Weaver.* New York, 1936.

Reid, Hugo. *Hugo Reid's Account of the Indians of Los Angeles.* Salem, Mass., 1885.

———. *The Indians of Los Angeles County.* Los Angeles, 1926. (Reprint of Early Edition Published at Salem, Mass., 1885.)

Repplier, Agnes. *Junipero Serra.* Garden City, New York, 1933.

Richardson, James D. (comp.). *A Compilation of the Messages and Papers of the Presidents, 1789–1908.* 11 vols. Washington, 1908.

Richman, Irving B. *California under Spain and Mexico, 1535–1847.* Boston, 1911.

Sabin, Edwin L. *Kit Carson Days, 1809–1868.* New York, 1935.

Schmeckebier, Laurence F. *The Office of Indian Affairs.* Baltimore, 1927.

Schoolcraft, H. R. *Information Respecting the History, Condition, and Prospects of the Indian Tribes of the United States.* 6 vols. Philadelphia, 1853.

Seymour, Flora Warren. *Indian Agents of the Old Frontier.* New York, 1941.

Shinn, G. Hazen. *Shoshonean Days.* Glendale, 1941.

Sloan, Richard E. and Adams, Ward R. *History of Arizona.* 4 vols. Phoenix, 1930.

Smith, Dama M. *Indian Tribes of the Southwest.* Stanford University, 1933.

Sniffen, M. K. *Meaning of the Ute War.* Philadelphia, 1915.

Stevenson, Matilda C. *The Zuñi Indians.* Washington, 1905.

Sturgis, Thomas. *The Ute War of 1879.* Cheyenne, Wyoming, 1879.

Sullivan, Bill S. *The Vanishing Navajoes.* Philadelphia, 1938.

Summerhayes, Martha. *Vanished Arizona.* Chicago, 1939.

Tatum, Lawrie. *Our Red Brothers.* Philadelphia, 1899.

Twitchell, Ralph E. *Leading Facts of New Mexico History.* 2 vols. Cedar Rapids, Iowa, 1911.

Vestal, Stanley. *Kit Carson: A Happy Warrior of the Old West. A Biography.* Boston, 1928.

Wellman, Paul I. *Death in the Desert.* New York, 1935.

Welsh, Herbert. *The Apache Prisoners in Fort Marion, St. Augustine, Florida.* Philadelphia, 1887.

———. *Peyote: An Insidious Evil.* Philadelphia, 1918.

———. *Report of a Visit to Navajo, Pueblo and Hualapai Indians of New Mexico and Arizona.* Philadelphia, 1885.

Wetmore, Charles A. *Report on the Mission Indians of California.* Washington, 1875.

White, Eugene E. *Service on the Indian Reservations: Being the Experiences of a Special Indian Agent.* Little Rock, Ark., 1893.

Wissler, Clark. *Indians of the United States: Four Centuries of Their History and Culture.* New York, 1940.

Woodruff, Janette (as told to Dryden, Cecil). *Indian Oasis.* Caldwell, Idaho, 1939.

VI. PERIODICALS AND NEWSPAPERS

Alter, J. Cecil. "Father Escalante and the Utah Indians," *Utah Historical Quarterly,* Vol. II, No. 1 (January, 1929).

Bourke, John G. "General Crook in the Indian Country," *Century Magazine,* Vol. XLI, No. 5 (March, 1891).

Brooks, Juanita Searitt. "Indian Relations on the Mormon Frontier," *Utah Historical Quarterly,* Vol. XII, Nos. 1 and 2 (January and April, 1944).

Cameron, Agnes Deans. "Citizen Lo: Red Tape and Red Indian," *Pacific Monthly,* Vol. XXII, No. 2 (1889–91).

Clum, John P. "Es-Kim-In-Zin," *Arizona Historical Review,* Vol. II, No. 1 (1929).

Curtis, Edward S. "Vanishing Indian Types: The Tribes of the Southwest," *Scribner's Magazine,* Vol. XXXIX, No. 5 (May-June, 1906).

Ellison, William H. "The Federal Indian Policy in California, 1846–1860," *Mississippi Valley Historical Review,* Vol. IX, No. 1 (June, 1922).

The Gallup Independent, August 11 and 12, 1940, and June 26, 1940.

Goodrich, Chauncy S. "Legal Status of the California Indians," *California Law Review,* January and March, 1926.

Hubbell, John Lorenzo. "Fifty Years an Indian Trader," *Touring Topics,* Vol. XXII, No. 12 (December, 1930).

Indian Education Fortnightly. Phoenix, Arizona. *Pamphlet 48* (September 15 to December 1, 1940).

Indians at Work, U. S. Department of the Interior. Washington, 1933 to 1945.

Reeve, Frank D. "Federal Indian Policy in New Mexico," *New Mexico Historical Review*, Vol. XII, No. 3 (July, 1937) and Vol. XIII, No. 2 (April, 1938).

———. "The Government and the Navajo, 1846–1858," *New Mexico Historical Review*, Vol. XIV, No. 1 (January, 1939).

———. "The Government and the Navajo, 1878–1883," *New Mexico Historical Review*, Vol. XVI, No. 3. (July, 1941).

Snow, William J. "Utah Indians and Spanish Slave Trade," *Utah Historical Quarterly*, Vol. II, No. 3 (July, 1929).

Taylor, Eli F. "Indian Reservations in Utah," *Utah Historical Review*, Vol. IV, No. 1 (January, 1931).

Tidwell, Henry M. "Uintah and Ouray Agency," *Utah Historical Quarterly*, Vol. IV, No. 1 (January, 1931).

Washington Daily Morning Chronicle, Nov. 10, 1872. Account of General Howard's mission.

Worcester, Donald E. "Beginnings of the Apache Menace," *New Mexico Historical Review*, Vol. XVI, No. 1 (January, 1941).

VII. MISCELLANEOUS

Albuquerque Progress. United Pueblos Agency Number. Vol. XII, No. 7, Published by Albuquerque National Trust and Savings Bank.

Arizona Highways. Vol. XX, No. 8. Published by Arizona Highway Dept., Phoenix, Arizona.

Clark, Ann. *Little Herder in Spring*. A Publication of the Education Division, U. S. Office of Indian Affairs, Phoenix, Arizona, 1940.

Garische, Alex J. *Letters to Secretary of Interior on Behalf of Coahuila or Mission Indians of California*. 1892.

Indians Yesterday and Today. Information Pamphlet–1. A Publication of the Education Division, U. S. Office of Indian Affairs. Chilocco Agricultural School, Chilocco, Okla., 1941.

Kelsey, C. *Report of Special Agent to Commissioner of Indian Affairs*, 1906.

Letterman, Jonathan. *Sketch of Navajo Tribe of Indians*. Washington, 1856.

Los Angeles Star, July 18, 1868. Photostatic copy in the Huntington Library.

The New Trail. Book of creative writing by Indian students. Phoenix Indian School, Phoenix, Arizona, 1941.

Official Correspondence between the Governors of California and Indian Agents. California Governors, 1852–1856.

Special Statements of Reservation Superintendents: Morris Burge; John O. Crow; John W. Dady; E. J. Diehl; Ralph M. Gelvin; C. H. Gensler; R. D. Holtz; James H. Hyde; Burton A. Ladd; Charles E. Morelock; A. E. Robinson; James M. Stewart; Forrest R. Stone; A. E. Stover.

1940 Statistical Summary, Human Dependency Survey, Navajo Reservation. U. S. Department of Interior, Bureau of Indian Affairs, 1941.

Underhill, Ruth. *Indians of Southern California.* Sherman *Pamphlet No. 2.* Haskell Institute, Lawrence, Kansas, 1941.

————. *The Northern Paiute Indians.* Sherman *Pamphlet No. 1.* Publication of the Education Division, U. S. Office of Indian Affairs. Haskell Institute, Lawrence, Kansas, 1941.

————. *The Papago Indians of Arizona and Their Relatives the Pima.* Sherman *Pamphlet No. 3.* Haskell Institute, Lawrence, Kansas, 1940.

Wheat, Carl I. *Maps of California Gold Region, 1848–1857.* San Francisco, 1942.

Wilkinson, Ernest L. (attorney for the Ute Indians). *Briefs on Cases Filed in the Court of Claims.*

Index

Aberle, Dr. Sophie: 233
Abiquiu Agency (New Mexico): 113–15, 118, 119
Ácoma, Pueblo village: 13, 204
Ácoma Indians, Pueblo tribe: 114 n.
Acts of Congress: *see* United States government—Congress
Agriculture, Indian: 11, 14, 17, 18–19, 20, 21, 22, 38, 57, 64, 72, 78, 87, 121, 124, 127, 143, 163, 164, 165, 167 n., 224, 236, 240, 241, 243, 245, 247, 250, 251, 253
Allen, Russell C.: 93
American Board of Foreign Missions: 82
Ames, John G., special agent: 83–84
Apache Indians: 4, 12, 21, 22, 46 f., 52, 53, 62, 77, 100, 102, 103, 110, 113, 116–17, 127, 128, 161, 166, 167, 236
Apache wars, the: 12
Aqua Caliente Reservation (California): 85, 85 n.
Area of reservations: *see* Indian reservations, area
Arivaipa Indians (Apache): 22, 96
Arizona: 3, 12, 22, 22–23, 46–63, 53, 55, 113–31, 126, 148, 165, 180, 203, 208, 209, 223, 225, 234, 253
Armstrong, F. C.: inspector for Nevada, 145
Arny, W. F.: 54, 56, 122
Arts and Crafts Board, Indian: 223, 232, 234
Ashley, William H.: 64
Atkins, J. D. C.: commissioner, 110
Augur, General C. C.: member of Peace Commission, 44 n.

Bachus, Major Electus: 52
Balcolm, Reverend George: special agent for Pyramid Lake Indians, 135
Bannock Indians: 75–77, 78
Baptist church: 82
Barbour, George W.: 29–36, 231
Barnes, A. J.: agent for Nevada, 142
Basketmakers, Indian: 15, 19, 22, 131, 166
Bateman, C. A.: agent for Nevada, 135, 142
Battle of Cibicu: 108
Beale, Edward F.: 25, 36 f., 43, 79
Bedell, E. A.: 68
Belknap, C. G.: agent at Tule River, 83, 89
Bennett, H.: superintendent of Arizona, 126
Bent, Charles: 46
Bigler, Governor John: 34
Billings, Dr. W. C.: surgeon, 203
Blanket weaving, Indian: Navajo, 21
Bowles, Miss Alida C.: superintendent Carson Agency (Nevada), 228, 229
Black Hawk, Indian chief: 77
Bosque Redondo: 54–56, 58, 58 n., 62, 123, 124, 171, 176, 208
Bridger, James: 64 f.
Brooks, Major: post commander at Fort Defiance, 52
Brophy, William A.: commissioner in 1945, 233
Brown, Ray A.: 152 n.
Browne, James Ross: 40
Brunot, Felix R.: first chairman, Peace Commission, 80
Burke, Charles H.: commissioner of Indian affairs, 155

273

Smith's River Reservation (California): 42 f., 44
Spanish Fork Reservation (Utah): 76
Society of Friends: 82
Southern Apache Agency (New Mexico): 113
Southern Ute Agency (Colorado): 119
Southwestern Indians: geographically defined, 3 f.
Southwestern Trachoma Campaign: 210
Spanish culture, traces of in Indians: 16–17, 18, 19, 30
Spillman, William A.: 152 n.
Stanley, J. Q. A.: special agent for Mission Indians, 81
State legislatures: California, opposed treaties, 34; legal rights of Indians, 90; Nevada, 145; New Mexico, 48, 58; territorial Utah, child labor law, 68
Steck, Michael: superintendent of Indian affairs, New Mexico, 55 f.
Stevens, Robert J.: 26 n., 42
Stewart, James M.: 229
Stottler, Lieutenant V. E.: agent Mescalero Reservation, 129
Stout, J. H.: agent at Gila River, 126
Sumner, Colonel E. V.: led expedition into Navajo country, 50; established Fort Defiance, 50; chief executive of New Mexico, 51
Sutter, John A: 26, 28
Syquan Reservation (California): 85 n., 94

Tabequache Ute Indians: 56, 61, 138
Taft, President William Howard: 202
Taos Indians, Pueblo tribe: 14 n.
Tappan, Senator S. F.: member of Peace Commission, 44 n., 61
Taylor, N. G.: member of Peace Commission, 44 n.; commissioner of Indian affairs, 61
Tejon Reservation (California): 38, 43
Temecula Reservation (California): 82, 94
Terry, General Alfred H.: member of Peace Commission, 44 n.
Tesuque Indians, Pueblo tribe: 14 n.
Tesuque Reservation (New Mexico): 245
Texas: 4, 26

Textile weaving: 223
Tiffany, J. C.: agent at San Carlos, 107
Theodore Roosevelt Boarding School: 244
Thomas, Senator Elmer (Oklahoma): on Senate investigating committee, 156
Thornburgh, Major T. T.: 137
Tonto Indians (Apache): 22
Torres Reservation (California): 85 n., 92, 94
Tourtelotte, Brevet Colonel J. E.: superintendent for Utah, 134
Trachoma: 202, 203, 204 n., 206, 210, 213, 227
Trading house system: 5
Treaty of Guadalupe Hidalgo: 3, 11, 47, 48, 83, 89
Truxton Canyon Agency (Arizona): 237–39
Tuberculosis: 202, 203, 206, 227, 232, 255
Tularosa Reservation (New Mexico): 104
Tule River Agency (California): 83; consolidated Mission Agency, 89, 92
Tule River Reservation (California): 41, 43, 81, 83, 147, 221
Twenty-Nine Palms Reservation (California): 92, 94, 235

Uintah and Ouray Agency (Utah): 148, 250
Uintah and Ouray Reservation: 221, 223, 225
Uintah Reservation: 76–78, 132, 165
Uintah Valley Agency (Utah): 132, 133, 135–36, 139, 181
Uncompaghre Ute Indians: 138, 141, 250
United Pueblos Agency (New Mexico): 113–22, 128, 245
United States Army: 26, 27, 34, 38, 43–44, 46, 50, 52–55, 59, 61, 62, 63, 71, 75, 76, 79, 80–83, 95–112, 118, 122, 134, 137
United States government—Bureau of Indian Affairs: 5, 6, 24, 26, 28 f., 35, 36, 38, 40, 43–45, 48, 51, 57, 59, 63, 64, 67, 78, 79, 80, 90, 93, 94, 97, 103, 105, 107, 125, 127, 134, 135, 144, 145, 146, 147, 148, 151, 152, 153–56, 166, 172, 174, 175, 178, 179, 183, 186, 187, 188, 189, 192, 194, 200, 201, 202, 205,

The Indians of the Southwest

HAS BEEN SET IN

TEN POINT LINOTYPE BASKERVILLE

WITH TWO POINTS LEADING

AND HAS BEEN PRINTED UPON

ANTIQUE BOOK PAPER

UNIVERSITY OF OKLAHOMA PRESS

NORMAN